THAT YOU MAY KNOW

OTHER BOOKS IN THIS SERIES:

Vol. 1 James M. Hamilton Jr. *God's Indwelling Presence: The Holy Spirit in the Old and New Testaments*

Vol. 2 Thomas R. Schreiner and Shawn D. Wright, eds. *Believer's Baptism: Sign of the New Covenant in Christ*

Vol. 3 Barry E. Horner *Future Israel: Why Christian Anti-Judaism Must Be Challenged*

Vol. 4 Timothy M. Pierce, *Enthroned on Our Praise: An Old Testament Theology of Worship*

NAC STUDIES IN BIBLE & THEOLOGY

THAT YOU MAY KNOW

ASSURANCE OF SALVATION IN I JOHN

CHRISTOPHER D. BASS

SERIES EDITOR: E. RAY CLENDENEN

NASHVILLE, TENNESSEE

ISBN: 978-0-8054-4761-3

Published by B & H Publishing Group
Nashville, Tennessee

Dewey Decimal Classification: 234
Subject Heading: SALVATION/BIBLE. N.T. 1 JOHN

Printed in the United States of America

1 2 3 4 5 6 7 8 9 10 11 12 • 15 14 13 12 11 10 09 08
LB

Dedication

To my loving family,
Brandi, Haley, Daniel, Abigail, and Emma
All sources of immeasurable joy in my life

TABLE OF CONTENTS

LIST OF ABBREVIATIONS

ABD	Anchor Bible Dictionary
AsTJ	*Asbury Theological Journal*
AusBR	*Australian Biblical Review*
AUSS	Andrews University Seminary Studies
BDAG	Bauer, W., F. W. Danker, W. F. Arndt, and F. W. Gingrich, *Greek-English Lexicon of the New Testament and Other Early Christian Literature.* 3rd ed.
BECNT	Baker Exegetical Commentary on the New Testament
Bib	*Biblica*
BibSac	*Bibliotheca Sacra*
BK	Biblische Konfrontationen
BNTC	Black's New Testament Commentary
BZ	*Biblische Zeitschrift*
BZNW	Beihefte zur Zeitschrift für die neutestamentliche Wissenschaft und die Kunde der älteren Kirche
CBC	Cambridge Bible Commentary
CBQ	*Catholic Biblical Quarterly*
CBQMS	Catholic Biblical Quarterly Monograph Series
CBR	*Currents in Biblical Research*
CJAS	Christianity and Judaism in Antiquity Series
CJT	*Canadian Journal of Theology*
CR	*Currents in Research*
CTJ	*Calvin Theological Journal*
DSS	Dead Sea Scrolls
DSD	*Dead Sea Discoveries*
ECS	Epworth Commentary Series
EKKNT	Evangelisch-Katholischer Kommentar zum Neuen Testament
EvQ	*Evangelical Quarterly*
EvRTh	*Evangelical Review of Theology*
ExpTim	*Expository Times*
FRLANT	Forschungen zur Religion und Literatur des Alten und Neuen Testaments
GTJ	*Grace Theological Journal*
HKAT	Hanndkommentar zum Alten Testament
HNT	Handbuch zum Neuen Testament
ICC	International Critical Commentary

JBL	*Journal of Biblical Literature*
JBLMS	Journal of Biblical Literature Monograph Series
JETS	*Journal of the Evangelical Theological Society*
JSNT	*Journal for the Study of the New Testament*
JSNTSup	Journal for the Study of the New Testament: Supplement Series
JSPSup	Journal for the Study of the Pseudepigrapha Supplement Series
JTS	*Journal of Theological Studies*
KEK	Kritisch-exegetischer Kommentar über das Neue Testament
KNT	Kommentar zum Neuen Testament
LCL	Loeb Classical Library
LEC	Library of Early Christianity
LSJ	Liddell, H. G., R. Scott, H. S. Jones, *A Greek-English Lexicon*. 9th ed. with revised supplement
MSJ	*Masters Seminary Journal*
MT	Masoretic Text
NA[27]	*Novum Testamentum Graece*, Nestle-Aland, 27th ed.
NAC	New American Commentary
NCS	Newport Commentary Series
Neot	*Neotestamentica*
NIBC	New International Biblical Commentary
NICNT	New International Commentary on the New Testament
NIDNTT	*New International Dictionary of New Testament Theology*
NIGTC	New International Greek Testament Commentary
NIVAC	NIV Application Commentary
NKZ	*Neue kirchliche Zeitschrift*
NovT	*Novum Testamentum*
NovTSup	Novum Testamentum Supplement Series
NSBT	New Studies in Biblical Theology
NTS	*New Testament Studies*
OTP	*Old Testament Pseudepigrapha*
PatS	Patristica Sorbonensia
PBTM	Paternoster Biblical and Theological Monographs
PNTC	The Pillar New Testament Commentary
QR	*Quarterly Review*
RB	*Revue Biblique*
RevExp	*Review and Expositor*
RevScRel	*Revue des sciences religieuses*
RevQ	*Revue de Qumran*

RSPT	*Revue des Sciences Philosophiques et Théologiques*
RTR	*Reformed Theological Review*
SBJT	*The Southern Baptist Journal of Theology*
SBLDS	Society of Biblical Literature Dissertation Series
SBLMS	Society of Biblical Literature Monograph Series
SBT	Studies in Biblical Theology
ScandJTh	*Scandinavian Journal of Theology*
SJT	*Scottish Journal of Theology*
SNTSMS	Society for New Testament Studies Monograph Series
SR	*Studies in Religion/Sciences Religieuses*
SubBi	*Subsidia Biblica*
SUNT	Studien zur Umwelt des Neuen Testaments
TBBB	Theologie Bonner Biblische Beiträge
TDNT	*Theological Dictionary of the New Testament*
THNT	Theologischer Handkommentar zum Neuen Testament
TJ	*Trinity Journal*
TNTC	Tyndale New Testament Commentary
TynBul	*Tyndale Bulletin*
VE	*Vox Evangelica*
VT	*Vetus Testamentum*
WBC	Word Biblical Commentary
WTJ	*Westminster Theological Journal*
WUNT	Wissenschaftliche Untersuchungen zum Neuen Testament
ZAW	*Zeitschrift für die alttestamentliche Wissenschaft*
ZBKNT	Zürcher Bibelkommentare New Testament
ZNW	*Zeitschrift für die neutestamentliche Wissenschaft und die Kunde der älteren Kirche*
ZTK	*Zeitschrift für Theologie und Kirche*

SERIES PREFACE

We live in an exciting era of evangelical scholarship. Many fine educational institutions committed to the inerrancy of Scripture are training men and women to serve Christ in the church and to advance the gospel in the world. Many church leaders and professors are skillfully and fearlessly applying God's Word to critical issues, asking new questions and developing new tools to answer those questions from Scripture. They are producing valuable new resources to thoroughly equip current and future generations of Christ's servants.

The Bible is an amazing source of truth and an amazing tool when wielded by God's Spirit for God's glory and our good. It is a bottomless well of living water, a treasure-house of endless proportions. Like an ancient tell, exciting discoveries can be made on the surface, but even more exciting are those to be found by digging. The books in this series, NAC Studies in Bible and Theology, often take a biblical difficulty as their point of entry, remembering B. F. Westcott's point that "unless all past experience is worthless, the difficulties of the Bible are the most fruitful guides to its divine depths."

This new series is to be a medium through which the work of evangelical scholars can effectively reach the church. It will include detailed exegetical-theological studies of key pericopes such as the Sermon on the Mount and also fresh examinations of topics in biblical theology and systematic theology. It is intended to supplement the New American Commentary, whose exegetical and theological discussions so many have found helpful. These resources are aimed primarily at church leaders and those who are preparing for such leadership. We trust that individual Christians will find them to be an encouragement to greater progress and joy in the faith. More important, our prayer is that they will help the church proclaim Christ more accurately and effectively and that they will bring praise and glory to our great God.

It is a tremendous privilege to be partners in God's grace with the fine scholars writing for this new series as well as with those who will be helped by it. When Christ returns, may He find us "standing firm in one spirit, with one mind, working side by side for the faith of the gospel" (Phil 1:27, HCSB).

E. Ray Clendenen
B&H Publishing Group

AUTHOR PREFACE

The idea for this book flowed from a combination of pastoral ministry in a local church and academic opportunity in a seminary class. While going through my masters program, I served as an associate pastor at a small church in the Greater Houston area. Here I interacted with people all over the spectrum on assurance, from the genuine stay-at-home mom with a weak conscience to the stiff-necked man who lived like the devil but insisted he had prayed a prayer twenty years ago at a youth camp. Then in a class on John's Letters, my then professor and now dear friend, Dr. Rodney Woo, allowed us to choose from a list of paper topics. Desirous to write on something that would help my ministry, I chose "Assurance of Salvation in 1 John," and it was actually in the writing of this paper that I discovered the dearth of literature on assurance in 1 John and realized I might have a dissertation topic on my hands. I then went to The Southern Baptist Theological Seminary for Ph.D. work where I immediately conversed with Tom Schreiner about this topic and received his encouragement to pursue it. So under the wonderful supervision of Drs. William F. Cook, Thomas R. Schreiner, and Bruce A. Ware, I wrote the dissertation, "The Nature of the Believer's Assurance of Eternal Life in 1 John," which was the origin of this book.

Therefore, though I have done so personally, I once again want to thank Rodney Woo, Bill Cook, Tom Schreiner, and Bruce Ware for all they have done for me. Brothers, it has been a wonderful privilege to study with you and learn from you, both in the classroom and in life. Also, I want to thank Ray Clendenen and the staff of B&H Academic for publishing my book in this wonderful new series. David Stabnow and the other editors have read over my manuscript so very carefully and I am most appreciative.

About two-thirds of this book was written while I was living in Vermont and serving at Christ Memorial Church. I cannot even begin to describe the love and encouragement that were lavished upon my family and me by this wonderful congregation throughout my writing process. There are actually too many of you to thank personally, who displayed specific acts of brotherly love and encouragement to me in my writing, but if you are reading this, you are almost certainly one of them. So thank you, my dear brothers and sisters.

I also want to thank my mom and dad for all that they have done for me. You have supported Brandi and me through much encouragement, faithful prayers, and generous finances along the way. This book could not have happened without you. I am also very thankful to Derek Bass, my brother by birth and brother in the Lord. His willingness to be interrupted from his own studies in order to banter back and forth with me on various ideas throughout my research was indispensable. I am ever grateful for the fellowship we have together in Christ.

Words cannot express my gratefulness to my sweet wife Brandi, who in our eight short years of marriage has been willing to live in four states and nine homes as a result of my schooling and ministry. She has embraced the life of a pastor's wife and is a wonderful example of a godly mother who sacrifices her own life daily for the kids and me. My dear Brandi, your love for our Lord's kingdom and desire to see it grow inspires me. And to my dear children—you have helped me more than you will ever know. Much of my writing was done at home, which was challenging because all I wanted to do was quit my research and go outside and play with you. Nevertheless, your little knocks at my door throughout the day always brought a smile to my face and actually served as an impetus to finish this project so I could have more time with you. I love you dearly.

Finally and most importantly, I give thanks, honor, and praise to my God and Father, who has shown us His amazing love by sending His Son as the propitiation for our sins and causing us to pass over from spiritual death to spiritual life. I am ever amazed that wretched sinners like I can be called children of God. John was certainly correct when he marveled: "Behold how great a love the Father has lavished upon us, that we might be called children of God—and this is what we are!" (1 John 3:1).

Chris Bass
August 2008
Boston, Massachusetts, USA

Chapter 1
THE NATURE OF THE BELIEVER'S ASSURANCE OF SALVATION IN 1 JOHN

Introduction

More than 350 years ago Thomas Brooks penned the words, "The being in a state of grace makes a man's condition happy, safe, and sure; but the seeing, the *knowing* of himself to be in such a state, is that which renders his life sweet and comfortable."[1] Such an assertion is as true today as it was then, since the assurance of one's salvation is an issue that individual Christians have wrestled with in virtually every generation since the inception of the church. Surely this is due to the fact that believers, who have taken the Scriptures seriously, have been confronted with passages that offer assurance of eternal life as well as those that bid them to test themselves or even warn them of the perils of falling away. After querying such texts, many ponder whether they can truly be assured that they have been born of God (2:29; 3:1–2,9; 4:4,7; 5:1,4,18)[2] and whether this divine birth will result in final salvation whereby the believer will have eternal life (5:13). In light of this, it is clear that this book grapples with a biblical, theological issue that is of utmost importance for every child of God.

Thesis

No other book of the New Testament speaks of the believer's confidence or assurance of salvation as frequently and explicitly as the first letter of John, for the predominant theme of the entire letter is Christian certainty.[3] This is seen in the way the writer assures his readers that the cross-work of Christ is the effective solution for their sins (1:5–2:2; 4:9–10), the way he reassures them of their present status with God (2:3–6,12–14; 3:1–2; 4:4; 5:18–20), as well as his

[1] T. Brooks, *Heaven on Earth: A Treatise on Christian Assurance* (Carlisle, PA: Banner of Truth, 1654; repr. 1996), 14 (emphasis mine).

[2] All Scripture references are from 1 John unless otherwise noted.

[3] So also J. R. W. Stott, *The Letters of John: An Introduction and Commentary*, TNTC, rev. ed. (Grand Rapids: Eerdmans, 2000), 56.

numerous "tests of life," given to help them "know" that they have come to know God (2:3). This letter, however, also contains warnings regarding false teaching and exhortations to persevere in love, righteousness, and the message heard from the beginning (2:15,24,26–28; 3:7; 4:1; 5:21). Thus, its readers are confronted with the tension between various assurances regarding their present status as children of God and passages that bid them to test themselves, exhort them to live righteously,[4] and warn them of false teaching. To be sure, the very question of assurance of eternal life in 1 John centers on the relationship between such passages. Therefore, this study will seek to answer the question, What is the nature of the believer's assurance of eternal life in the first letter of John?

I will argue that the writer of 1 John grounds his reader's assurance of eternal life on the solid foundation of the person and work of Jesus Christ (1:1–2:2; 4:9–10; 5:18). Jesus is clearly displayed as the believer's παράκλητος ("advocate") with the Father (2:1) and the ἱλασμός ("propitiation") of their sins (2:2; 4:10). Given that sin is inevitable in the life of the believer (1:7–2:2; 5:16–17), nothing other than the work of Christ can be viewed as the foundation of assurance, for it is the only effective remedy for their sins and thus the only ground for confidence of right standing with God. Moreover, it will be argued that assurance is not only grounded in the past work of Jesus on the cross but also on the promise of His ongoing work of protecting those who have been born of God (5:18).

While assurance is fundamentally grounded in the work of Christ, this letter also demonstrates that the lifestyle of the believer serves as a vital corroborating support for such assurance. This is seen in the numerous sets of criteria or "tests" that occur throughout the letter. Here I will argue that John viewed his readers as a new covenant community, expecting God's own Spirit to dwell in them and empower them to walk in the light. The Holy Spirit should produce a change of life in the new covenant believer that is observable in the public arena and therefore able to be tested and validated. John's tests were written with the primary purpose of his readers' introspection and

[4] Phrases such as "persevere in righteous living," "persevere in holy living," and "heeding of biblical warnings" will be used synonymously and varied for stylistic purposes.

subsequent reassurance as they came to understand that it was they who were holding to a right belief in Jesus, striving to live righteously, and loving the brethren. Moreover, I will also argue that these tests have a retrospective aspect in that they enabled John's readers to comprehend that those who departed from the fellowship had done so because they were never genuinely part of the community, as made obvious by their fundamental failure of each of the three tests. Finally, I will argue that the tests at least implicitly have a prospective or exhortative element. In other words, even though the primary purpose of a statement like "no one born of God sins" (3:9) was to distinguish between those who are indifferent to sin and those who strive to live righteously, such a passage would nevertheless serve to motivate a child of God to continue to strive to live without sin.

This prospective element of the tests as well as John's periodic warnings about the false teachers and exhortations to persevere (2:15a,24,26–28; 3:7; 4:1; 5:21) give rise to the discussion on perseverance in 1 John and its relationship to assurance. Here I will argue that those who have truly been born of God will take John's warnings and admonitions seriously and therefore persevere in holy living. Those who fail to do so demonstrate that they have never truly been born of God (2:19). Therefore, this study will argue that John views the believer's assurance of eternal life as compatible with his ongoing need to persevere in righteous living.[5] In fact, it will be argued that these two are inextricably tied together in that the believers'

[5] I will use the terms *assurance* and *perseverance* when synthesizing John's teachings on comfort and exhortation even though neither term is explicitly found in the letter of 1 John. The purpose for substituting these terms for the Johannine terms such as "knowing"/"confidence" (assurance) and "abiding"/"doing"/"keeping" (perseverance) is twofold. First, it would be cumbersome and perhaps confusing to attempt to use such Johannine language when synthesizing his teachings, since such ideas are conveyed throughout this epistle in numerous and variegated ways. Moreover, it is believed that *assurance* is an adequate term to describe John's emphasis on "confidence," "knowing one has eternal life," "knowing one has passed from death to life," "knowing one abides in him and he in them," etc. I also believe that *perseverance* is perhaps the best term to describe John's emphasis on continually "abiding in God," "doing righteousness," "keeping the commandments," "keeping oneself from idols," etc. In addition, the themes of assurance and perseverance are also present conceptually in such things as "God being greater than the believer's heart" (assurance) and the language of interiority and the obligations that follow (perseverance). Thus it seems appropriate to substitute the terms *assurance* and *perseverance* for the Johannine language in some of the synthesis sections for the sake of clarity.

confidence that they are children of God due to the work of Christ is a key impetus to their perseverance (3:3; 4:11) and their perseverance in righteous living actually aids in bolstering their assurance (2:3–5).

Nevertheless, while John emphasizes that his readers' perseverance in righteousness is vital, it cannot be viewed as *the* ground of their assurance. This is clearly found in the work of Christ. Therefore, the thesis of this study is that the letter of 1 John teaches that assurance of eternal life is *fundamentally grounded* in the work of Christ and supported in a *vital* yet *subsidiary* way by the lifestyle of the believer. One's lifestyle is "vital" in that if a person fails to keep the commands, love the brethren, and have a right confession of Jesus, he demonstrates that he was never a child of God and should have any false assurance eradicated. It is "subsidiary" in that the letter also teaches that no one lives perfectly holy (1:6–2:2; 5:16–17), so the believer must continually look back to the work of Christ on the cross for the forgiveness and cleansing of sin.

Such a thesis lands us right in the middle of the historical debate on the nature of the believer's assurance, where one of the central concerns from the Reformation onward has been the outworking of the biblical tension of finding one's assurance in Christ and the relation of that assurance to persevering in godly living.[6] Since the inception of the doctrine of assurance, this tension has been the source of much dispute over such issues as the degree to which the believer's assurance is linked to his perseverance in godly behavior. Of course there is also the question of how much assurance a believer might have without being presumptuous. In other words, can a believer be assured of final salvation, or is he only able to find assurance that he is trusting in Christ today? These and similar questions have been debated since at least the time of the Reformation and continue into the present day. Therefore, in order to move forward properly with this present examination of assurance in 1 John, it is helpful first to look back at some of the history of this debate.

[6] See J. R. Beeke, "Does Assurance Belong to the Essence of Faith?: Calvin and the Calvinists," *MSJ* 5 (1994): 44–45.

Method of Interpretation

Before proceeding to the survey of views, it is important to pause and briefly discuss the method of interpretation that will be used in this work. This book is a biblical theology of assurance in 1 John. No doubt some will take issue with this statement since this study interacts with works that are more dogmatic or systematic in nature (especially in the survey of views below). Moreover, the question of assurance is one that has traditionally been addressed in systematic theology as opposed to biblical theology. Nevertheless, this book is a biblical theology of assurance in that an inductive method of interpretation is used throughout. Every attempt has been made to follow the description of biblical theology described by Carson when he says that a "biblical theology focuses on the inductive study of biblical texts in their final form, seeking progression towards greater and greater faithfulness."[7] I have not started with doctrinal statements on assurance and sought texts in 1 John to support them; rather, I have begun with the text of 1 John and sought to allow it to speak for itself.[8]

Survey of Views

With the importance that was once placed on the doctrine of assurance of salvation, one is a bit perplexed to find that there has been so little written on this issue in the discipline of biblical theology.[9] To be sure, in the areas of historic and systematic theology, there have

[7] D. A. Carson, "Systematic Theology and Biblical Theology," in *New Dictionary of Biblical Theology*, ed. T. D. Alexander and B. S. Rosner (Downers Grove, IL: InterVarsity, 2000), 100.

[8] See also P. Stülmacher, *How to Do Biblical Theology*, trans. J. M. Whitlock, Princeton Theological Monographs 38 (Allison Park, PA: Pickwick, 1995), 1.

[9] To date, I am aware of only two book-length works in the field of biblical studies on assurance of salvation. These are T. R. Schreiner and A. B. Caneday, *The Race Set Before Us: A Biblical Theology of Perseverance and Assurance* (Downers Grove, IL: InterVarsity, 2001); K. M. Gardoski, "New Testament Warning Passages in the Light of the Doctrine of Eternal Security" (Ph.D. diss., Trinity Evangelical Divinity School, 2002). In addition, there are a handful of journal articles including T. R. Schreiner, "Perseverance and Assurance: A Survey and a Proposal," *SBJT* 2 (1998): 32–63; D. A. Carson, "Reflections on Assurance," in *Still Sovereign: Contemporary Perspectives on Election, Foreknowledge, and Grace*, ed. T. R. Schreiner and B. A. Ware (Grand Rapids: Baker, 1995, 2000), 247–76.

been numerous articles[10] as well as monographs and dissertations on assurance in the theology of various noteworthy historical figures or particular periods of time.[11] Nevertheless, in the field of biblical studies, this issue has not drawn the recent attention I believe it deserves.

When we turn to the specific issue of assurance in 1 John, the literature becomes all the more scant. To date, I am unaware of a single monograph and know of only a handful of journal articles written on this subject.[12] While there is one recent dissertation,[13] it is actually in the mold of the previously noted studies that focus on assurance in the theology of a historical figure and would therefore seem to fall into the category of historical rather than biblical theology. Hence, in the survey that follows, I have made every effort to focus on assurance in 1 John when possible, but the lack of materials with which to interact has caused me to venture outside of 1 John in order to summarize each of the various positions on this issue. Such venturing out of 1 John in order to summarize certain views (like medieval Roman Catholic or Arminian) is justified for at least two reasons. First, while this work is a biblical theology of assurance in 1 John, it is my hope that it will aid in furthering the broader theological discussion on assurance.[14] Second, it is important to examine the main historical

[10] A sampling of such articles includes R. M. Hawkes, "The Logic of Assurance in English Puritan Theology," *WTJ* 52 (1990): 247–61; Beeke, "Does Assurance Belong to the Essence of Faith?" 43–71; Z. C. Hodges, "We Believe in: Assurance," *Journal of the Grace Evangelical Society* 3 (1990): 9; A. N. S. Lane, "Calvin's Doctrine of Assurance," *VE* 11 (1979): 32–54; M. Noll, "John Wesley and the Doctrine of Assurance," *BibSac* 132 (1975): 161–77; J. Zens, "The Doctrine of Assurance: A History and an Application," *Baptist Reformation Review* 5 (1976): 34–64.

[11] See J. R. Beeke, *Assurance of Faith: Calvin, English Puritanism, and the Dutch Second Reformation* (New York: Peter Lang, 1991); C. M. Bell, *Calvin and Scottish Theology: The Doctrine of Assurance* (Edinburgh: Handsel, 1985); R. Letham, "Saving Faith and Assurance in Reformed Theology: Zwingli to the Synod of Dort," 2 vols. (Ph.D. diss., University of Aberdeen, 1979); A. S. Yates, *The Doctrine of Assurance with Special Reference to John Wesley* (London: Epworth, 1952).

[12] See D. A. Carson, "Johannine Perspectives on the Doctrine of Assurance," in *Explorations: Justification and Christian Assurance*, ed. R. J. Gibson (Adelaide, South Australia: Openbook Publishers, 1996), 59–97; B. A. du Toit, "The Role and Meaning of Statements of 'Certainty' in the Structural Composition of 1 John," *Neot* 13 (1979): 84–100; J. Lieu, "Authority to Become Children of God: A Study of I John," *NovT* 23 (1981): 210–28.

[13] T. F. Atchison, "Towards a Theology of Christian Assurance from 1 John with Reference to Jonathan Edwards" (Ph.D. diss., Trinity Evangelical Divinity School, 2004).

[14] This is due to my conviction that all theology must begin with the detailed exegetical work of biblical theology. The best way to build a theology of assurance would be to begin with

views of assurance, since such views have no doubt influenced the way many later interpreters have read the text of 1 John.[15]

This survey will begin with four key historical trajectories of assurance of salvation that have been seen in the history of the church. These include (1) Medieval Roman Catholicism, (2) Luther and Calvin, (3) Later Calvinism: *Westminster Confession of Faith*, and (4) Arminianism. This will be followed by a brief overview of some of the current literature on 1 John where we will see that the majority of the contemporary commentators display striking similarities with one of these four historical views.[16]

Medieval Roman Catholicism

While an argument could be made that there was a firm belief in assurance of salvation among some in the Patristic period,[17] it would appear that the predominant view in the medieval period was that there could be no assurance of salvation, except perhaps by some special revelation.[18] Gregory the Great (d. 604), who is considered by Philip Schaff to be the one of the best representatives of Medieval

a biblical theology of each biblical book on this issue. Hence, this study is but one step in an overarching doctrine of assurance.

[15] This insight came through a conversation with T. R. Schreiner on July 25, 2005.

[16] For a more detailed history of research, see C. D. Bass, "The Nature of the Believer's Assurance of Eternal Life in 1 John," Ph.D. Diss., The Southern Baptist Theological Seminary, 6–37.

[17] See especially Yates (*The Doctrine of Assurance*, 149–56), who cites statements of assurance from such church fathers as Clement of Rome, Ignatius, Polycarp, Justin Martyr, Tatian, Irenaeus, Tertullian, Clement of Alexandria, Origen, Hilary, Basil, Gregory of Nyssa, Ambrose, and Augustine. See also J. Zens, who argues that though a doctrine of assurance was "not written propositionally during the first three centuries of the Church, it was observed by the world that Christians had a certainty about God their Father and His destiny in their lives" as a result of their willingness to die the most heinous of deaths for the Christian faith ("The Doctrine of Assurance: A History and Application," 36). Moreover, Robert Letham is probably correct in his assessment that "the emphasis in the early centuries was on the controverted areas of Christology and Trinitarianism. Questions concerning the application of redemption did not become a really major concern until the Reformation. Additionally, the lack of discussion of such matters was explained by the absence of controversy leaving no pressing need for close definitions to be made" ("The Relationship Between Saving Faith and Assurance of Salvation" [Th.M. thesis, Westminster Theological Seminary, 1976], 5–6).

[18] R. Seeberg notes that Duns Scotus "asserted the possibility of being sure of possession of grace on the basis of works," but this does not appear to be a common view during this period (*Text-Book of the History of Doctrines* [Grand Rapids: Baker, 1966], 2:202).

Catholicism,[19] clearly denied that there could be any assurance of salvation for the believer. McGiffert, in his *History of Christian Thought*, says that Gregory believed and taught that "constant anxiety is the only safe attitude until life is over and temptation past. Assurance of salvation and the feeling of safety engendered by it are dangerous for anybody and would not be desirable even if possible."[20] Gregory believed that the church helped her faithful ones by mixing both hope and fear.[21] This can be seen in his response to a woman who inquired about assurance at the imperial court: "Thou shouldst not become easy in mind about thy sins."[22] This is because he believed that "assurance was the mother of all negligence."[23] Likewise, Thomas Aquinas (1225–1274) taught that actual certainty of salvation is unattainable, "since the grace of God lies beyond the sphere of human perception, and hence the possession of grace can only be inferred *conjecturaliter* from good works."[24] Thus, according to Aquinas, most Christians do not have personal assurance of their salvation unless by chance God reveals it to them through some special privilege.[25]

Though the Council of Trent was not until 1547, it is worth mentioning at this point since its teachings fundamentally sum up the Medieval Catholic view of assurance. Here the writers went to great lengths to explicate that an individual could not be assured of eternal life:

> No one, moreover, so long as he is in this mortal life, ought so far to presume as regards the secret mystery of divine predestination, as to determine for certain that he is assuredly in the number of the predestinate; as if it were true, that he that is justified, either can not sin any more, or, if he do sin, that he

[19] P. Schaff, *History of the Christian Church* (New York: Charles Scribner's Sons, 1910; repr., Grand Rapids: Eerdmans, 1995), 4:212.

[20] A. C. McGiffert, *A History of Christian Thought* (New York: Charles Scribner's Sons, 1933), 2:153.

[21] J. S. Whale, *The Protestant Tradition: An Essay in Interpretation* (Cambridge: Cambridge University Press, 1955), 67.

[22] Ibid.

[23] Ibid., 84.

[24] Seeberg, *Text-Book of the History of Doctrines*, 2:121.

[25] T. Aquinas, *Summa Theologica*, vol. 2, Great Books of the Western World, vol. 20, ed. R. M. Hutchins (Chicago: William Benton, 1952), 359–60 (Question 112, art. 5).

> ought to promise himself an assured repentance; for except by special revelation, it can not be known whom God has chosen unto himself.[26]

Moreover, the later canons on justification anathematized anyone who claimed or taught that an individual could be assured of salvation.[27]

Martin Luther

Of course this is the context into which Martin Luther was born (1483–1546) and which he would eventually challenge head-on. In fact, Luther argued that the Roman Catholic view of assurance must be eradicated since it denies the gospel itself. Luther's understanding of the believer's assurance of salvation comes directly from the pages of Scriptures, not least from 1 John. Commenting on 1 John 5:13, he says, "For contrary to the manifest understanding of all men I *must believe* and *be certain* that I must live forever, even though I see in the meanwhile that I am being consumed by worms. Indeed, I *must believe* and *be sure* that I not only shall have but do have eternal life."[28] Luther's linking of faith and certainty here demonstrates that he views the assurance of salvation to be of the essence of saving faith and thus the possession of every genuine believer.[29]

For Luther, assurance is part and parcel of saving faith precisely because it is grounded on the promises of God, which were fulfilled in the work of Christ and not on the works of man. This is evident in his comment on 1 John 1:7 when he says:

[26] P. Schaff, *The Creeds of Christendom with a History and Critical Notes* (New York: Harper & Brothers, 1877), 2:103.

[27] Ibid., 113–14. One such example is Canon XVI: "If any one saith, that he will for certain, of an absolute and infallible certainty, have that great gift of perseverance unto the end,—unless he has learned this by special revelation: let him be anathema."

[28] M. Luther, *Lectures on the First Epistle of John*, ed. J. Pelikan, trans. W. A. Hansen in vol. 30 of *Luther's Works* (St. Louis: Concordia, 1967), 320–21(emphasis mine). Compare his often cited comment on Ps 90:17: "He who prays for remission of sins and hears the absolution of Christ should be certain that truly, just as the Word declares, his sins are forgiven; and he should be assured that this is in no sense man's work but God's work. Whatever, therefore, is done in the church *must rest on certainty*" (M. Luther, *Selected Psalm II*, ed. J. Pelikan, trans. P. M. Bretscher in vol. 13 of *Luther's Works* [St. Louis: Concordia, 1956], 140).

[29] "Faith is a living and daring confidence in God's grace, so sure and certain that the believer would stake his life on it a thousand times. This knowledge and confidence in God's grace makes men glad and bold and happy in dealing with God" (M. Luther, *Word and Sacrament*, ed. E. T. Bachmann, trans. C. M. Jacobs, vol. 35 of *Luther's Works* [St. Louis: Concordia, 1960], 370–71).

> But if we cling to the Word that has been made known, we have this treasure, which is the blood of Christ. If we are beset by sins, no harm is done. The blood of Christ was not shed for the devil or the angels; it was shed for sinners. Accordingly, when I feel sin, why should I despair, and why should I not believe that it has been forgiven. For the blood of Christ washes sins away. The *main thing* is that *we cling* simply to the Word. Then there is no trouble.[30]

There is no trouble because Luther's assurance is fundamentally founded upon Christ and not one's own works.[31]

It is important to note at this point that since Luther viewed faith and assurance as so closely tied together, he can at times be found implying that a lack of assurance demonstrates that one is not a believer.[32] Luther, however, appears to qualify such statements by asserting that believers can have a weak faith and suffer from doubts from time to time for various reasons.[33] Therefore, though assurance is of the essence of faith, it is not perfect. There are times when a believer might have greater assurance and times when his assurance is weak.

So what place, if any, did Luther have for works in relation to assurance? In his comments on 1 John 2:3, he asserts that "if the true knowledge of Christ is present, it will not be without fruit or without works that are truly good."[34] Luther desires to make certain that the one who is truly a believer will have fruit/evidence of that belief in the way he lives. His comments actually resemble much of contemporary scholarship in referring to John giving *tests* or ways in which a believer might *learn* that he is genuine: "And if you do not hate your brother, *you learn* in this way that the kingdom of God is in you."[35]

[30] Luther, *Lectures on the First Epistle of John*, 228.

[31] See also his comments on 4:17 where he says, "Therefore if consciousness of a great sin weighs you down, comfort yourself with this blood of love. . . . No human religion can hold its own in the face of the judgment, but it is solely in the blood of Christ that we have confidence on the Day of Judgment" (Luther, *Lectures on the First Epistle of John*, 301–2; ibid., 236).

[32] M. Luther, *Word and Sacrament*, ed. E. T. Bachmann, trans. C. M. Jacobs, vol. 35 of *Luther's Works* (St. Louis: Concordia, 1960), 13: "Should you . . . not believe that your sins are truly forgiven and removed, then you are a heathen, acting toward your Lord Christ like one who is an unbeliever and not a Christian; and this is the most serious sin of all against God. . . . By such disbelief you make God a liar."

[33] M. Luther, *Selected Psalm II*, 138: "Therefore we become frightened at the slightest occasion. Furthermore, because sins and the punishment of sin are daily experiences, there are enough occasions for sorrow and for weakness of faith."

[34] Luther, *Lectures on the First Epistle of John*, 238.

[35] Ibid. (emphasis mine). See also his comment on 3:24, where he asserts that we know that God abides in us because his Spirit produces works in us: "For he who does not despise the

With Luther though, one must always remember that he goes to great lengths to hold the biblical tension between faith and works, even if he almost sounds contradictory at times. Perhaps the most indicative comment of Luther's understanding of this tension can be found in his commentary on 1 John 3:19–20 and is worth citing at length. Beginning in 3:19, he says:

> This is the *evidence* with which *we assure ourselves* of our calling and by which it is established that we are standing in the truth. If I am not moved by the weakness of my brother, I surely do not love him. From the *fruits* of love we can *learn* that we have love. Faith is established by its *practice*, its *use*, and its *fruit*. . . . The consciousness of a life well spent is the *assurance* that we are keeping the faith, for it is *through works* that we *learn* that our *faith is true*.[36]

One is amazed, however, to find that he immediately follows this line of thinking with this comment on 3:20:

> If you lack works, yet you should not lack faith. Even if persuasion is lacking, *yet faith and hope are greater*. For it is the *sum and substance* of the Gospel that you should *believe* and hope. Although we should consider ourselves unworthy, yet we should accept the grace that is offered and the Gospel. Even if our conscience makes us fainthearted and presents God as angry, *still "God is greater than our heart." Conscience is one drop; the reconciled God is a sea of comfort*. The fear of conscience, or despair, must be overcome, even though this is difficult. It is a great and exceedingly sweet promise that if our heart blames us, "God is greater than our heart" and "knows everything."[37]

It is therefore clear that Luther believes assurance to be of the essence of faith precisely because it is grounded on the work of Christ. In spite of this, he does appear to allow the believer's perseverance in holy living to serve as a secondary support or confirmation to this assurance. For Luther, then, the promises of God as fulfilled in the work of Christ were the absolute foundation of assurance, while one's

Word of God, to him He brings the first fruits of the Spirit, which show him how he can learn that he is in God and God is in him" (ibid., 282). Or again on 4:18, Luther says, "[E]veryone should *test* his faith. If he believes in Christ, he has love" (ibid., 302).

[36] Ibid., 279 (emphasis mine).

[37] Ibid., 280 (emphasis mine). See also his comment on 2:29, in which Luther says, "John proceeds to exhort to works and the *fruits of grace*, and he does so with various proofs, in order that he may arouse us to do good, yet in such a way that we do not put our confidence in these works. It is Christ's first aim that the tree be good, then that it bear fruit. What is the source of goodness? It does not come *from the fruits*; it comes *from the root*. It does not come from sanctification; it comes from regeneration. For he who is born of Him is righteous (v. 29)" (ibid., 264; emphasis mine).

perseverance in righteousness could provide only a supporting/confirming role.

John Calvin

It is widely recognized that Calvin, like Luther,[38] understood assurance to be of the essence of saving faith. This can be seen throughout his many writings but perhaps most clearly in book 3, chapter 2, paragraph 7 of his *Institutes of Christian Religion*,[39] where he sets forth his definition of saving faith: "Now we shall possess a right definition of faith if we call it a *firm and certain* knowledge of God's benevolence toward us, founded upon the truth of the freely given promise in Christ, both revealed to our minds and sealed upon our hearts through the Holy Spirit."[40] This definition makes clear that assurance is of the essence of saving faith because it is fundamentally grounded upon the unconditional promise of God as fulfilled in Christ.[41] Precisely because one's faith is founded on the promises of God and not on one's

[38] For a helpful discussion on the similarities of Luther and Calvin on the assurance of salvation, see R. C. Zachman, *The Assurance of Faith* (Minneapolis: Fortress, 1993). Zachman's basic thesis is that "even though Calvin and Luther do have different emphases and motifs in their theology, they agree fundamentally that the foundation of the assurance of faith lies in the grace and mercy of God toward us in Jesus Christ crucified, revealed to us in the gospel. The testimony of a good conscience confirms, but does not ground, this assurance of faith by attesting that our faith in Christ is sincere and not feigned" (*The Assurance of Faith*, vii). See also W. Cunningham, *The Reformers and the Theology of the Reformation* (London: Banner of Truth, 1862; repr., 1967), 111–48, esp. 119.

[39] J. Calvin, *Institutes of Christian Religion*, 2 vols. ed. J. T. McNeill, trans. F. L. Battles, Library of Christian Classics, vols. 20–21 (Philadelphia: Westminster, 1960). Henceforth, Calvin's *Institutes* will be cited as *Inst.* followed by book, chapter, and paragraph (e.g., *Inst.* 3.2.7.). Following Calvin's own appeal, I have interacted with Calvin's *Institutes* 1559 edition, since he states on p. 3 ("John Calvin to the Reader") that he was not satisfied with his *Institutes* until the 1559 edition. Moreover, he also notes that one should read his commentaries in light of the *Institutes* since in his publishing of commentaries he notes that he will always "condense them, because I shall have no need to undertake long doctrinal discussions, and to digress into commonplaces. In this way the godly reader will be spared great annoyance and boredom, provided he approach Scripture armed with a knowledge of the present work [*Institutes*], as a necessary tool" ("John Calvin to the Reader," 4–5).

[40] Calvin, *Inst.* 3.2.7 (emphasis mine). Portions of this definition are reiterated in John Calvin, *The First Epistle of John*, trans. John Owen, vol. 22 of *Calvin's Commentaries*, ed. D. W. Torrance and T. F. Torrance (Edinburgh: Oliver and Boyd, 1960; repr., Grand Rapids: Baker, 1999), 244.

[41] Calvin, *Inst.*, 3.2.32.

own works,[42] it is the "sure and secure possession of those things which God has promised us."[43]

It is also true that Calvin believed that the doctrine of predestination was an integral part of the believer's assurance. Contrary to later reformed theologians, he warned strongly against the idea of querying the hidden will of God,[44] teaching that believers should instead anchor their assurance in what is revealed in Scripture.[45] Assurance, then, is found in Christ as we see Him in the Word of God, so "predestination, rightly understood, brings no shaking of faith but rather its best confirmation."[46] Therefore, predestination bolsters the believer's assurance, since it elucidates the very fact that salvation and perseverance are all of grace and not works.[47]

Of course Calvin's insistence on the fusion between assurance and saving faith could lead one to believe that a lack of such assurance indicates that a person might not be a believer.[48] Like Luther, Calvin qualifies such statements throughout his *Institutes* and commentaries in his insistence that assurance is not perfect. While assurance is of the essence of faith, faith is never perfect, and he regularly speaks of such things as "weak faith," "least drop of faith," and "imperfect faith."[49] Such faith is nevertheless "real faith," and we are "illumined as much as need be for *firm assurance* when, to show forth his mercy, the light of God sheds even a *little* of its radiance."[50] Moreover, it is

[42] Ibid., 3.2.29.

[43] Ibid., 3.2.41. Cp. Calvin, *First Epistle of John*, 204.

[44] Calvin, *Inst.* 3.24.4: "Satan has not more grievous or dangerous temptation to dishearten believers than when he unsettles them with doubt about their election, while at the same time he arouses them with a wicked desire to seek it outside the way. I call it 'seeking it outside the way' when mere man attempts to break into the inner recesses of divine wisdom, and tries to penetrate even to highest eternity, in order to find out what decision has been made concerning himself at God's judgment seat. For then he casts himself into the depths of a bottomless whirlpool to be swallowed up; then he tangles himself in innumerable and inextricable snares; then he buries himself in an abyss of sightless darkness."

[45] See Calvin, *First Epistle of John*, 240; idem, *Inst.* 3.24.4–5.

[46] Calvin, *Inst.* 3.24.9.

[47] Calvin, *First Epistle of John*, 203; Calvin, *Inst.* 3.21.1.

[48] Calvin, *Inst.*, 3.2.16. Here Calvin can be found making such bold statements as, "No man is a believer, I say, except he who, leaning upon the assurance of his salvation, confidently triumphs over the devil and death. . . . We cannot otherwise well comprehend goodness of God unless we father it from the fruit of great assurance."

[49] Ibid., 3.2.18–20.

[50] Calvin, *Inst.* 3.2.19 (emphasis mine).

clear that such faith/assurance is something that believers can grow and progress in from weak to strong.[51]

The Holy Spirit also plays an essential role in the believer's assurance of salvation, according to Calvin.[52] In fact, Letham rightly asserts that "it was Calvin more than anyone else who was responsible for the emergence of the doctrine of the internal testimony of the Holy Spirit and for stressing that it was this that was the root cause of all assurance that the Christian enjoyed."[53] According to Calvin's definition of faith cited above, the certain knowledge of God's benevolence toward believers is not only founded upon the promise of Christ but also revealed to the minds of believers and sealed upon their hearts by the Holy Spirit.[54] Faith, therefore, is not something initiated by man but is clearly a "work of God" and "manifestation of God's power."[55] For Calvin, the Spirit does not work in some private mystical way apart from the Scriptures to assure the believer's heart;[56] rather, He seals the promises found in the Scriptures upon the hearts of the believers and assures them that they are true.[57] Moreover, Calvin also taught that the Spirit produces the fruit of obeying God's commands and living righteously, by which the believer might find further *confirmation* that his faith is genuine.[58]

Since Calvin teaches that the Holy Spirit produces the fruit of righteous living in the life of the believer, the believer should be able to look to such fruit and derive assurance. Interpreters of Calvin, how-

[51] This is seen in Calvin's comments on 1 John 5:13 when he says, "As there ought to be a daily progress of faith, so he says that he wrote to those who had already believed, so that they might believe *more firmly* and with *greater certainty*, and thus enjoy a *fuller confidence* as to eternal life" (emphasis mine) (Calvin, *First Epistle of John*, 264). See also Calvin, *Inst.* 3.2.19.

[52] Calvin, *Inst.* 3.1.4.

[53] Letham, "The Relationship Between Saving Faith and Assurance of Salvation," 20–21.

[54] Calvin, *Inst.*, 3.2.7.

[55] Ibid., 3.2.35.

[56] Ibid., 1.9.1–3.

[57] Ibid., 1.7; 1.9; 3.14; 3.2.36.

[58] This is clearly seen in Calvin's comments on 1 John 4:12–13: "He speaks, however, first of love, when he says, that God *dwells in us*, if we love one another; for perfected, or really proved to be, in us is then his love; as though he had said, that God shews himself as present, when by his Spirit he forms our hearts so that they entertain brotherly love. For the same purpose he repeats what he had already said, that we know by the Spirit whom he has given us that he dwells in us; for it is a *confirmation* of the former sentence, because love is the *effect* or *fruit of the Spirit*" (emphasis mine) (Calvin, *First Epistle of John*, 243). See also Calvin, *First Epistle of John*, 227.

ever, must be careful on this point, for Calvin, like Luther, is quite cautious to uphold the biblical tension between faith and works or the "basis" of assurance and its "secondary support." Against what would later be referred to as the practical syllogism,[59] Calvin writes, "For a conditional promise that sends us back to our own works does not promise life unless we discern its presence in ourselves. Therefore, if we would not have our faith tremble and waiver, we must buttress it with the promise of salvation, which is willingly and freely offered to us by the Lord in consideration of our misery rather than our deserts."[60]

On the other hand, Calvin does affirm that works are "*signs* of divine benevolence," "*fruits* of regeneration," "*proof* of the indwelling of the Holy Spirit," and "*signs* of the calling," which all serve to strengthen assurance.[61] Even here though, he is careful not to overstate the use of righteous living in assurance. To be sure, the heeding of biblical warnings and the holy living of the believer serve to bolster one's assurance of salvation but must never be viewed as the foundation of such assurance. Calvin's comment on 1 John 2:3 is insightful:

> After having treated of the doctrine respecting the gratuitous remission of sins, he comes to the exhortations which belong to it, and which depend on it. . . . For we cannot know him as Lord and Father, as he shews himself, without being dutiful children and obedient servants. In short, the doctrine of the gospel is a lively mirror in which we contemplate the image of God, and are transformed into the same. . . . But we are not hence to conclude that faith recumbs on works; for though every one receives a *testimony to this faith*

[59] The practical syllogism of the later Reformed tradition "is a conclusion drawn from an action. The basic form of the syllogism when it pertains to salvation is as follows: Major premise: Those only who do 'x' are saved. Minor premise (practical): But I do 'x'. Conclusion: Therefore I am saved" (Beeke, *Assurance of Faith*, 97 n. 153).

[60] Calvin, *Inst.*, 3.2.29. Moreover, commenting on one of Augustine's statements as to why he does not put any trust in his works, Calvin writes, "He gives two reasons why he dared not vaunt his works before God: because if he has anything of good works, he sees in them nothing of his own; and secondly, because these are also overwhelmed by a multitude of sins. From this it comes about that his conscience feels more fear and consternation than assurance" (ibid., 3.14.20). This of course is due to the fact that believers are always aware that whatever good work they do is tainted with the flesh (ibid., 3.14.19).

[61] Emphasis mine. In his commentary on 1 John 1:7, Calvin writes, "He now says, that the *proof* of our union with God is certain, if we are conformable to him; not that purity of life conciliates us to God, as the prior cause; but the Apostle means, that our union with God is *made evident by the effect*, that is, when his purity shines forth in us" (Calvin, *First Epistle of John*, 164; emphasis mine). See also ibid., 215, 217; Calvin, *Inst.* 3.14.18–20.

> from his works, yet it *does not follow that it is founded on them*, since they are *added as an evidence.*[62]

For Calvin the believer's perseverance in righteousness serves only "to *confirm confidence*, as a *prop*, so to speak, of the *second order*; but in the meantime we ought to have our *foundation on grace alone.*"[63] The foundation of assurance cannot finally be the lifestyle of the Christian since he continually struggles with sin and is in constant need of cleansing (1 John 1:7).[64] Therefore, assurance is of the essence of faith since it is fundamentally grounded on the promises of God as fulfilled in Christ, while man's heeding of biblical warnings and perseverance in holiness serve as important yet secondary support.

Later Calvinism: *Westminster Confession of Faith*

As the Reformation continued through the teachings of Calvin's successor Theodore Beza on into England through such key figures as William Perkins, the reformed doctrine of assurance continued to experience changes.[65] Following Calvin, it would appear that the secondary support of assurance, specifically sanctification, began to receive heightened emphasis. Here however, there is intense debate among Reformation and Puritan scholars as to the degree to which later Calvinists changed Calvin's view of assurance. On the one hand, there are those who would argue that there is a fundamental distinc-

[62] Calvin, *First Epistle of John*, 173–75 (emphasis mine). Or again, commenting on 1 John 3:19 he says, "We only know that we are God's children by his sealing, His free adoption on our hearts by His Spirit and by our receiving by faith the sure pledge of it offered in Christ. Therefore, love is an *accessory* or *inferior aid*, a *prop* to faith, *not the foundation* on which it rests" (ibid., 222; emphasis mine). See also ibid., 165–66, 182, 218, 222.

[63] Ibid., 246 (emphasis mine).

[64] Commenting on the fact that Jesus is our advocate in 1 John 2:2, he says, "By these words he confirms what we have already said, that we are very far from being perfectly righteous, nay, that we *contract new guilt daily*, and that yet there is a remedy for reconciling us to God, if we *flee to Christ*; and this is *alone* that which *consciences can acquiesce*, in which is included the righteousness of men, in which is *founded* the hope of salvation" (ibid., 170–71; emphasis mine). Ibid., 167.

[65] For a diverse description of the evidence, see Beeke, *Assurance of Faith*; Kendall, *Calvin and English Calvinism to 1649*; Letham, "Saving Faith and Assurance in Reformed Theology"; Bell, *Calvin and Scottish Theology*.

tion between Calvin and later Calvinists.[66] On the other hand, there are those who are just as adamant that the change was "quantitative and methodological and not qualitative or substantial."[67] A sure conclusion seems difficult and scholars on both sides appear equally immovable in their position.

Westminster Confession of Faith. Whatever conclusion one may draw on this issue, it is enough for our purpose to notice that by the time the Westminster Confession of Faith was drawn up, changes in the Reformed doctrine of assurance had most assuredly taken place. To begin with, while Calvin and Luther argued that one's assurance was of the essence of saving faith, the Westminster Confession of Faith asserts that it is something that comes later:

> This infallible assurance doth not so belong to the essence of faith but that a true believer may wait long and conflict with many difficulties before he be a partaker of it: yet, being enabled by the Spirit to know the things which are freely given him of God, he may, without extraordinary revelation, in the right use of ordinary means, attain thereunto. And therefore it is the duty of everyone to give all diligence to make their calling and election sure.[68]

Interestingly, one of the verses cited in support of the statement that assurance is not of the essence of faith is 1 John 5:13, since John says that he has written to those who believe but nevertheless appear to be in need of assurance.[69]

The other clear distinction between Calvin and Westminster was Calvin's insistence that the ground of assurance is the promises of God as fulfilled in Christ and that holy living serves as a secondary

[66] So Kendall, *Calvin and English Calvinism to 1649*; Bell, *Calvin and Scottish Theology*; A. N. L. Lane, "Calvin's Doctrine of Assurance," *VE* 11 (1979): 32–54; A. C. Clifford, *Atonement and Justification: English Evangelical Theology 1640–1790—an Evaluation* (Oxford: Clarendon, 1990).

[67] Beeke, *Assurance of Faith*, 2. So also Letham, "Saving Faith and Assurance in Reformed Theology"; idem, "The Relationship Between Saving Faith and Assurance of Salvation"; S. D. Wright, "The Pastoral Use of the Doctrine of God's Sovereignty in the Theology of Theodore Beza" (Ph.D. diss., The Southern Baptist Theological Seminary, 2001); M. E. Dever, "Richard Sibbes and the 'Truly Evangelical Church of England': A Study in Reformed Divinity and Early Stuart Conformity" (Ph.D. diss., Cambridge University, 1992); R. Lovelace, "Evangelicalism: Recovering a Tradition of Spiritual Depth," *The Reformed Journal* 40 (1990): 20–25.

[68] *Westminster Confession of Faith* (Glasgow: Free Presbyterian Publications, 1646, 1990), XX, 3 (henceforth, *WCF*).

[69] See chap. 6 where I interact with this idea in more detail.

support. In contrast, by the time of Westminster, there seems to be equality among three "grounds" of assurance:

> This certainty is not a bare conjectural and probable persuasion, grounded upon a fallible hope; but an infallible assurance of faith, founded upon the divine truth of the promises of salvation, the inward evidence of those graces unto which these promises are made, the testimony of the Spirit of adoption witnessing with our spirits that we are children of God; which Spirit is the earnest of our inheritance, whereby we are sealed to the day of redemption.[70]

Once again, a key section of this statement is supported with a passage from 1 John. Here 1 John 3:14 is cited in support of the statement that one of the three parts of the foundation is the "inward evidence of those graces unto which these promises are made." Therefore, it appears that this confession held to a three-tiered foundation as opposed to Calvin and Luther's single foundation with secondary supports.

Jacobus Arminius: A Dissenting Voice

Of course Calvin and later Calvinists were not the only voices on assurance during this time. In fact, one key voice was a student of Theodore Beza named Jacobus Arminius (1560–1609). Arminius was a contemporary of William Perkins who grew to disagree with many of the assumptions of Reformed Theology.[71] The key point of departure with which this study is interested is his view on the believer's assurance of salvation. It is important to note, however, that Arminius was in substantial agreement with much of later Calvinism's view of assurance. He agreed that assurance is to be found in Jesus as well as "the action of the Holy Spirit inwardly actuating the believer and by the fruits of faith, . . . and the testimony of God's Spirit witnessing together with his conscience."[72] Nevertheless, his point of departure on this issue was in the degree of assurance that a believer might actually have without being presumptuous. Arminius asserted that a believer

[70] *WCF*, XX, 2.

[71] For a survey of Arminius's disputes with other reformed theologians, see C. Bangs, *Arminius: A Study in the Dutch Reformation* (Grand Rapids: Francis Asbury Press, 1985); Letham, "Saving Faith and Assurance in Reformed Theology," 311–19.

[72] J. Arminius, *The Writings of James Arminius*, trans. James Nichols and W. R. Bangall (Grand Rapids: Baker, 1956), 1:255.

could have a *present assurance* of *present salvation* but not a *present assurance* of *final salvation*.[73]

Regarding assurance of present salvation, he says, "With regard to the certainty [or assurance] of salvation, my opinion is, that it is possible for him who believes in Jesus Christ to be certain and persuaded, and, *if his heart condemn him not*, he is now in reality assured, *that he is a Son of God, and stands in the grace of Jesus Christ*."[74] On the other hand, regarding present assurance of final salvation, Arminius begins by posing two questions: "Is it possible for any believer, without a special revelation, to be certain or assured that he will not decline or fall away from the faith? . . . Are those who have faith, bound to believe that they will not decline from the faith?"[75] He responds negatively to both questions: "The affirmative of either of these questions was never accounted in the church of Christ as a catholic doctrine; and the denial of either of them has never been adjudged by the church universal as a heresy."[76] Hence, for Arminius, a believer could find only present assurance of present salvation but not present assurance of final salvation.

Contemporary Views of Assurance in 1 John

Having surveyed four historical trajectories of assurance, it is now important to switch gears and briefly examine a sampling of the contemporary views of assurance that can be found in the commentaries and articles on 1 John. Every effort has been made to understand inductively the various ways in which individual scholars have interpreted John's teaching on assurance. Moreover, I have sought to evaluate where each writer falls with reference to the four historical trajectories surveyed above. This is not to say that those shown to fit within a particular category are in complete agreement, for each certainly displays his or her own nuances. The purpose, then, is not

[73] Bangs, *Arminius*, 347–48. It may be helpful to note at this point that John Wesley's view of assurance appears to be virtually identical to that of Arminius on this point. The one apparent difference might be the degree to which Wesley would stress the role of the Holy Spirit in assurance (see M. A. Noll, "John Wesley and the Doctrine of Assurance," *BibSac* [1975]: 161–77).

[74] Arminius, *Writings of James Arminius*, 1:255 (emphasis his).

[75] Ibid., 2:503.

[76] Ibid.

to establish a rigid system of classification but to demonstrate that the majority of the contemporary views of assurance in 1 John are similar to one of the four historical trajectories surveyed above. Therefore, following the ordering above, I will survey some of the contemporary literature under the headings (1) "No Assurance of Salvation," (2) "Luther and Calvin," (3) "Later Calvinism," and (4) "Arminianism."[77] Moreover, I have added a fifth category to this part of the survey ("The Grace Movement") to account for what is a rather new interpretation (historically speaking) on assurance in 1 John that has been influential in American Evangelicalism. Due to the aforementioned dearth of literature on the specific topic of assurance in 1 John, only a handful of the works in this survey are specific to this topic. Beyond these, I have also surveyed some of the more influential commentaries on 1 John with hopes of understanding their view of assurance in this epistle.[78]

No assurance of salvation. In a book as heavy laden with statements of confidence and assurance as 1 John, it is difficult to imagine that any serious interpreter of the text would argue that John does not assure his readers of eternal life (5:13). Not surprisingly, none of the interpreters surveyed here can confidently be placed under this heading. This is because, to one degree or another, all of the commentators surveyed speak of John offering "assurance" or "reassurance" and perhaps even "tests" throughout their commentaries. However, while some of the Catholic commentators use the term *assurance*, they do not seem to be referring to assurance of salvation but are simply arguing that John is giving his readers "assurance" that they are on the right side of the dispute between him and the secessionists.[79] D. A. Carson has perhaps best assessed the situation in his statement that the majority of the Catholic commentaries on 1 John "largely bypass

[77] I am not attempting to understand each writer's personal view of assurance of salvation. The goal is to understand what each writer believes John to be teaching.

[78] This survey is far from exhaustive, for that would take a book in itself. This study is not a historical survey of assurance in 1 John; rather, it is a biblical theology of assurance in 1 John, and thus the purpose of this survey is simply to overview the broad spectrum of contemporary scholarship on the nature of assurance of salvation in 1 John.

[79] See especially R. E. Brown, *The Epistles of John: Translated with Introduction, Notes, and Commentary*, The Anchor Bible, vol. 30 (New York: Double Day, 1982), 633.

the theme of assurance and see in this book a depiction of proper Christian communal life."[80] Nevertheless, none of the Catholic commentaries surveyed can be confidently placed under this rubric, since all are exegetical in their approach and appear to interpret such passages as 5:13 to be saying that John has written to give his readers assurance.

Luther and Calvin. Those who fall under this heading do not necessarily agree with every aspect of Luther and Calvin's views of assurance, for even Luther and Calvin themselves display subtle nuances. Interpreters placed here are those who understand John to be teaching that assurance is fundamentally grounded on the promises of God as fulfilled in the work of Christ and only secondarily supported by the fruit of the Spirit. Moreover, each of those in this group understands John to be teaching that those who are "born of God" will persevere to the end, so assurance in 1 John is of both present and final salvation.

The clearest illustration of this view is D. A. Carson, who asserts that in 1 John, the "objective ground of assurance" is the "finished cross-work of Christ," while the believer's diligence in good works "should be regarded as 'accessory and inferior' aids" to such assurance.[81] The letter of 1 John was written as a result of a crisis that was "precipitated by the secession of some members who have been powerfully influenced by some form of protognosticism. Their departure left behind believers who were, spiritually speaking, badly bruised. The raw triumphalism of most forms of gnosticism dented the confidence of those who refused to go along with the movement."[82] Therefore, John sets forth "tests" in order to reassure his readers that they have eternal life and that it is the false teachers who actually fail the tests and therefore do not have eternal life abiding in them.[83] Moreover, John also exhorts his readers to persevere in the faith, which is in no way contradictory, since in Johannine theology, "God's sovereign assurance does not function as a disincentive to effort, but as an incentive."[84] To be sure, in Johannine thought, those who fail to

[80] Carson, "Reflections on Assurance," 250.
[81] Carson, "Johannine Perspectives on the Doctrine of Assurance," 59.
[82] Carson, "Reflections on Assurance," 274.
[83] Carson, "Johannine Perspectives on the Doctrine of Assurance," 75–77.
[84] Ibid., 75–76.

persevere, demonstrate that they were never genuine believers to begin with (2:19). Nevertheless, this perseverance and passing of "tests" serve as a secondary support to one's assurance that is fundamentally grounded upon the cross-work of Christ.[85]

While Schreiner and Caneday's recent biblical theology of the relationship of warning passages to perseverance and assurance does not focus exclusively on 1 John, they do interact significantly with this letter. The overarching thesis of this book appears at first glance to land them closer to the view of later Calvinism since they argue that biblical warnings are a *means* to salvation[86] and the heeding of such warnings is a means of assurance. Nevertheless, the careful reader will note that such statements are periodically qualified throughout the book, for they even assert that they are right in line with Luther and Calvin.[87] In addition, they strive to make certain that "biblical assurance rests fundamentally on God and his promises"[88] and even assert that we should emulate Calvin "by also preserving the balance between the *foundation* and *confirmation* of our assurance."[89] Moreover, while using the analogy of assurance based upon a three-legged stool, which is the terminology of later Calvinists, they are nevertheless careful to clarify that it is an insufficient analogy because the primary leg is the promises of God.[90]

Commenting specifically on 1 John, Schreiner and Caneday argue that the "primary goal" of the letter is assurance and this assurance is *grounded* on the promises of God and work of Christ.[91] They go on to argue that though the promises of God are the "*fundamental leg*" of a three-legged stool, it would nevertheless be wrong for us to "conclude from this that the other legs of the stool are superfluous."[92] In fact, the idea that a transformed life is vital evidence of salvation is a theme that permeates the entire letter. Moreover, they rightly contend that John did not write these "tests" or warnings to further shake the

[85] Ibid., 71–72, 82, 96.
[86] Schreiner and Caneday, *The Race Set before Us*, 38, 269.
[87] Ibid., 268–305.
[88] Ibid., 277.
[89] Ibid., 300 (emphasis mine).
[90] Ibid., 276–77.
[91] Ibid., 278–81.
[92] Ibid., 283.

confidence of his readers but to comfort them as they came to realize their own genuineness and that it was actually the secessionists who failed to pass the tests.[93] Finally, Schreiner and Caneday argue that the third leg of the stool (the witness of the Holy Spirit) is also observable in passages like 4:13, where believers are assured that we abide in Him and He in us as a result of the Holy Spirit.[94]

Later Calvinism: Westminster Confession of Faith. This category differs from the previous one in that there is the belief that assurance is not part and parcel of saving faith and therefore is something a believer might not attain for some time. Moreover, while Calvin and Luther argued for a foundation with secondary supports, this view puts forth a multitiered foundation of assurance. The contemporary scholars I have placed under this rubric do not necessarily argue that assurance is something a believer might not attain for some time. Instead, the key delineating factor for placing interpreters under this heading is their argument that assurance in 1 John is grounded on a multitiered foundation rather than asserting that assurance is based on the foundation of Christ with secondary supports. Like the view of Luther and Calvin, all who fall in this group argue that John teaches that a genuine believer cannot lose his salvation, so assurance is of both present and final salvation.

Colin Kruse appears to be a good example of this view. He argues that the purpose of 1 John was to "bolster the assurance of his readers by the double strategy of showing the secessionists' claims to be false and showing his readers that they are in the truth."[95] Many of the "tests" are claims of the false teachers, which John turns on their heads. Commenting on the "test" in 2:3, Kruse says, "Ongoing assurance that we are people who know God is dependant upon ongoing obedience to his commands."[96] He gives the impression that John's grounds for assurance are equal: "The readers' assurance is to be

[93] Ibid., 285.

[94] Ibid., 303–4. For others who appear to fall into this overall view similar to that of Luther and Calvin, see du Toit, "The Role and Meaning of Statements of 'Certainty'"; M. M. Thompson, *1–3 John*, IVP New Testament Commentary Series (Downers Grove, IL: InterVarsity, 1992).

[95] C. G. Kruse, *The Letters of John*, PNTC (Grand Rapids: Eerdmans, 2000), 27; cf. 143, 188, 198–200.

[96] Ibid., 77.

grounded on God's testimony about His Son, their own godly living, loving action and concern for fellow believers, their obedience to the love command, and the Spirit's testimony to Christ."[97] Moreover, this assurance is of both present and final salvation, as is made clear in his rejection of the idea that the sin that leads to death can be committed by one who is truly born of God.[98] In light of this, Kruse apparently fits well in this category.[99]

Arminian. Those who fall under the Arminian heading are similar to the previous view in that they assert that John teaches that assurance comes through believing in Jesus and confirming that one passes the tests laid out in this epistle. The point of departure, however, is that those in this camp argue that genuine believers can lose their salvation. Therefore, like Arminius, these interpreters argue that assurance is only present assurance of present salvation.

I. Howard Marshall asserts time and again that John's purpose for writing this letter was to assure/reassure his readers of their salvation.[100] The primary mode of deriving such assurance through this letter is the series of "tests" set up by John. On this point Marshall says, "John is writing the present verse with a positive purpose, to reassure his readers that their experience of God was genuine. We can know by this he says: The test is whether we keep His commandments. This test is deliberately put as a condition, since it may or may not be true of each of the readers; each one must ask himself whether he fulfills the condition."[101] Hence the believer is to read the tests in 1 John and examine himself to see if he passes the test. If he does,

[97] Ibid., 33; cp. 198–200.

[98] Ibid., 202; cp. 107, 191.

[99] R. Law also appears to fall into this camp. This is perhaps best seen in his statement: "With St. John the grounds of assurance are ethical, not emotional; objective, not subjective; plain and tangible, not microscopic and elusive. They are three, or, rather, they are a trinity: Belief, Righteousness, Love. By his belief in Christ, his keeping God's commandments, and his love to the brethren, a Christian man is recognized and recognizes himself as begotten of God" (*Tests of Life*, 297). For others who seem to fall along this line of thought see Atchison, "Towards Developing a Theology of Christian Assurance"; D. L. Akin, *1, 2, 3 John*, NAC, vol. 38 (Nashville: Broadman & Holman, 2001); J. R. W. Stott, *The Letters of John*, TNTC, rev. ed. (Grand Rapids: Eerdmans, 2000).

[100] I. H. Marshall, *The Epistles of John*, NICNT (Grand Rapids: Eerdmans, 1978), 5, 55, 122–28, 156, 169, 191, etc.

[101] Ibid., 123.

he is able to walk away with assurance of his salvation. Marshall is careful, however, to make certain he is not teaching that salvation turns on works. Commenting on 1:7 he makes clear that believers will sin and must look to the blood of Jesus to cleanse them from their sin.[102] Moreover, he is clear that assurance derived from obedience alone might lead one to feel that he is not abiding in God, so it is the Holy Spirit whose presence and witness bring the assurance so dearly desired.[103] Nevertheless, Marshall gives the impression that the predominant emphasis in 1 John is assurance of salvation that comes through the heeding of John's warnings and persevering in holy living that includes obeying the commands, loving the brethren, and having a right confession of Jesus. Moreover, Marshall holds that such assurance is only assurance of present salvation in that John teaches that genuine believers can fall into apostasy.[104] This is most clear in his comments on 1 John in his book *Kept by the Power of God*.[105] Here he says, "According to 1 John, then, sin is a possibility among believers, even to the point of denial of Christ, and the teaching of the Epistle is not fully accounted for if sin is regarded as a possibility only among those who have never been truly converted."[106] It would appear then that Marshall believes that 1 John teaches that assurance of salvation comes through faith in Christ, the witness of the Holy Spirit, and the obedience that must follow to demonstrate the reality of such faith. This assurance, however, is only present assurance because the genuine believer can in fact walk away from the faith.

As noted above, some Catholic commentators seem to fall somewhere between this category and the first one. Raymond Brown is a good example of this position. Brown argues that 5:13 should be seen as the purpose statement for the entire epistle of 1 John.[107] This epistle was written as a result of the schism that had occurred in the community, and those who departed were attempting to influence others to

[102] Ibid., 112; cp. 118.
[103] Ibid., 202–3.
[104] Ibid., 152, 160–61, 249–50.
[105] I. H. Marshall, *Kept by the Power of God: A Study of Perseverance and Falling Away* (Minneapolis: Bethany Fellowship, 1974), 183–87.
[106] Ibid., 186–87. See also his comments on 184–85.
[107] Brown, *Epistles of John*, 630–33.

embrace their teaching and follow them. This epistle then is a polemic designed to help his readers understand that the secessionists are in the wrong and he is in the right. Commenting on the purpose statement of 5:13, Brown says that John "wishes to strengthen his readers in their Christology since only a faith that is correct Christologically gives life."[108]

It is somewhat puzzling to try to decipher Brown's view of the nature of assurance in 1 John. While he uses the terms *assurance* and *reassurance*, it is difficult to understand exactly what he is teaching. At times he can be seen saying that John is reassuring his readers that they know Christ, have had their sins forgiven,[109] or even that they have eternal life.[110] Moreover, Brown speaks of John "wanting his readers to face the parousia with confidence based upon their abiding in Christ."[111] Nevertheless, throughout the countless passages that most commentators want to speak of assurance of salvation, Brown tends to avoid such terminology. Instead he prefers to speak of John reassuring his readers not that they have eternal life but that they are the ones who are on the right side of the schism.[112] This is seen most clearly in his comments on 5:13, where he says "several times previously, after he has described dualistically the situation vis-à-vis the secessionists, his *pastoral sense* has led him to *reassure* his readers that they are on the *right side* and hence are not the object of his polemic."[113] Moreover, for the majority of commentators, John offers a series of "tests" by which his readers might find comfort that they are truly believers and recognize that it is the false teachers who actually fail to pass these tests. For Brown, however, such "tests" like keeping the commandments (2:3) are not tests of whether one might detect the presence of God in their lives and thus

[108] Ibid., 632.

[109] Ibid., 364: "In the next unit (2:12–17) the author turned his attention to the first group, the children of light who are his 'Children,' reassuring them that they have known Christ, have had their sins forgiven, and have conquered the Evil One." Or again commenting on 3:20, Brown says, "In 1:8–2:2 the sinner was assured that God forgives through the atonement of Christ, and that same assurance is repeated here" (477).

[110] Ibid., 635: "The readers know that they possess eternal life (5:13)."

[111] Ibid., 420–21; cf. 477, 561.

[112] Ibid., 371–76. Here he speaks of "reassurance against secessionist deception."

[113] Ibid., 633–34 (emphasis mine).

derive assurance but are the *very means* by which believers might have that relationship.[114]

Finally, Brown gives the impression that the most assurance a believer might experience is some form of assurance of present salvation but certainly not final salvation. In the context of 5:13–21, he contends that "amidst his reassurances the author mentions also a deadly sin or sin unto death (5:16)."[115] Brown believes this to be the sin of the secessionists, which could be committed by one who has actually passed over from death to life. On this point he says,

> When his readers came to faith and joined the Johannine Community of "brothers," they passed from death to life (1 John 3:14). By leaving the Community the secessionists have shown that they hate the "brothers" and have *reversed* the process by *passing from life to death*. In this sense theirs is a sin that is unto death.[116]

Hence, if one is able to "reverse the process" and "pass from life to death," then believers can lose their salvation; thus their assurance is at best an assurance of present salvation but certainly not final salvation.[117]

The Grace Movement. One final view does not fit any of the historical views surveyed above. This is the view asserted by a group known as the "Grace Movement."[118] While this group has clearly captured a following at the popular level, it has not enjoyed the same response among biblical scholars. Nevertheless, it is important to interact with this view, if only briefly, due to its popularity in many of our churches

[114] Ibid., 278–79. This is seen in his comment on 2:3 when he says, "The author argues that one cannot know God without keeping his commandments. . . . [O]ne gains a knowledge of God through behavior, when that behavior is governed by God's commandments. Keeping the commandments is *more than an external way of verifying* a claim to know God; rather it is a criterion that has an essential relationship to the claim made" (278–79; emphasis mine). Moreover, in his footnote to the last sentence of this quote this view is clarified even more when he asserts, "There is a problem with R. Law's thesis that 1 John supplies the 'tests' by which one can detect the presence of divine life, as exemplified by the many 'This is how we can be sure' sentences. . . .[F]or the Johannine writer what is offered is more than a test; *it is a means* (279; emphasis mine).

[115] Ibid., 636.

[116] Ibid (emphasis mine).

[117] For others who appear to fit into the Arminian camp, see S. S. Smalley, *1, 2, 3 John*, WBC, vol. 51 (Waco: Word Books, 1984); J. Painter, *1, 2, and 3 John*, Sacra Pagina, vol. 18 (Collegeville, MN: Liturgical, 2002).

[118] This group now has its own journal—*Journal of the Grace Evangelical Society*.

as well as the fact that they have introduced a rather novel view of assurance in 1 John. Here I will interact primarily with Zane Hodges, since he has been one of the more influential voices in this movement and has written extensively on 1 John.[119]

Hodges's overarching theology of assurance is that it is based exclusively on the promises of God and work of Christ and is therefore completely divorced from works. On this point he says, "Basically we insist that *the New Testament Gospel offers the assurance of eternal life to all who believe in Christ for that life. The assurance of the believer rests squarely on the Biblical promises in which this offer is made, and on nothing else.*"[120] Assurance is therefore part and parcel of saving faith but can have no secondary support, for that would result in righteousness or assurance based upon works.[121]

It would appear that Hodges begins with this overarching theological construct of assurance and then imposes it on the text of 1 John by way of an innovative reading of John's tests. Arguing against the overwhelming majority of New Testament scholars, he asserts that John does not give "tests of life/salvation/assurance" throughout this epistle; rather, he gives his readers "tests of fellowship."[122] Here he contends that John must be speaking about tests of fellowship,[123] since the purpose statement of 1 John comes in 1:3 as opposed to 5:13.[124] For Hodges then, 5:13 is only the purpose statement for 5:9–12, while

[119] See Z. C. Hodges, *The Epistles of John: Walking in the Light of God's Love* (Irving, TX: Grace Evangelical Society, 1999); idem, *Epistles of John*, Bible Knowledge Commentary; idem, *The Gospel Under Siege: Faith and Works in Tension*, 2nd ed. (Dallas: Redencion Viva, 1992), 51–72.

[120] Hodges, *The Gospel Under Siege*, 143 (emphasis his). See also R. T. Kendall, *Once Saved, Always Saved* (Chicago: Moody, 1983); M. Eaton, *No Condemnation: A New Theology of Assurance* (Downers Grove, IL: InterVarsity, 1995).

[121] Ibid.

[122] See Hodges, *The Epistles of John*, 34; idem, *Gospel Under Siege*, 51–52, where he boldly refers to the "tests of life" view as "hopelessly misguided" and "absurd." It would appear that the first to espouse the "tests of fellowship" view was G. H. King, *The Fellowship* (London: Marshall, Morgan and Scott, 1954). Others who hold this view include C. C. Ryrie, *I, II, and III John*, The Wycliffe Bible Commentary, ed. C. F. Pfeiffer and E. F. Harrison (Chicago: Moody, 1962); J. W. Roberts, *The Letters of John*, The Living Word Commentary (Austin: R. B. Sweet, 1968); E. M. Curtis, "The Purpose of 1 John" (Th.D. diss., Dallas Theological Seminary, 1986); J. G. Mitchell, *Fellowship* (Portland, OR: Multnomah, 1974); J. D. Pentecost, *The Joy of Fellowship* (Grand Rapids: Zondervan, 1977).

[123] Hodges says the only "test of salvation" in the whole letter is found in 5:1 (*Epistles of John*, 144).

[124] Ibid., 50–52, 226–29. See also E. M. Curtis, "The Purpose of 1 John," 161–62.

1:3 serves as the overarching purpose statement for the whole epistle.[125] Therefore, the purpose of the letter is "fellowship."

Following this line of thinking, the numerous "by this we know" passages such as 2:3 were not written to strengthen the readers' assurance of salvation but their assurance that they are currently enjoying right "fellowship" with God.[126] Here, "having come to know God" does not speak of salvation but fellowship.[127] Passages such as 3:9, then, do not present a problem since the person walking in close fellowship with God actually does not sin. When he does sin, however, he simply demonstrates that his fellowship is momentarily broken and thus temporarily conceals the fact that he is really a believer.[128] Therefore, John does not give a series of tests to demonstrate who was genuine and who was not; rather, he offers "tests" to help the readers understand that succumbing to the teaching of the false teachers could disrupt their fellowship with God.

Hodges wants to make absolutely clear that this "fellowship with God" or "abiding in God" must never be misunderstood to be referring to salvation. He argues that if one were to assert that "abiding/remaining" in God or in the community was at all tied to regeneration or salvation, then one could not be certain of his salvation until death.[129] To support this view, however, Hodges is forced to come up with some fanciful exegesis at a number of places like 2:19. Against the clear teaching of the passage, he insists that the "us" from which

[125] It should be noted here that a recent dissertation by G. W. Derickson argues that virtually everyone (with the seeming exception of him and Smalley) has misunderstood the letter of 1 John and that the correct understanding is that neither 1:3 or 5:13 should be seen as *the* purpose statement, but both should be viewed as *a* purpose statement ("An Evaluation of Expository Options of 1 John" [Th.D. diss., Dallas Theological Seminary, 1993]; idem., "What Is the Message of 1 John?" *BibSac* 150 [1993]: 89–105).

[126] This view also appears to reject completely any polemical overtones to the letter.

[127] Hodges, *Epistles of John*, 75–77. Hodges denies that "passing from death to life" in 3:14 speaks of conversion. Commenting on this verse he avows, "But it would be a mistake to read the statement as if the apostles were sure of their eternal salvation because they loved the brethren. There is no reason why this should be true for them or any other Christian. Assurance of salvation is based on the testimony of God (see 5:9–13 and discussion there). Instead, in a perfectly normal use of the word know, John declares that he and his fellow apostles have a direct and immediate knowledge of their passage from death to life through the experience of loving their Christian brothers" (*Epistles of John*, 156–57).

[128] Hodges, *The Epistles of John*, 139–46; idem, *The Gospel under Siege*, 67–68.

[129] Hodges, *The Gospel under Siege*, 51.

the false teachers have departed was not the community to which John was writing but the apostles themselves. He seems confident that these false teachers "went out" from the Jerusalem church as opposed to a secession from the community to which John has written.[130]

Plan of Procedure

There is much diversity in the way in which assurance of eternal life has been understood in 1 John. I will show how this letter teaches that assurance of eternal life is *fundamentally grounded* in the work of Christ and supported in a *vital* yet *subsidiary* way by the lifestyle of the believer.

This effort will begin in chapter 2 where I will focus on the historical setting and purpose of 1 John. I will begin with a mirror reading of the text in order to build a working hypothesis regarding the situation to which John has written. After examining the text of 1 John itself, attention will then be turned to the external evidence to establish whether any of the known false teachings (or a combination of them) that were contemporaneous with this letter might account for the problems found here. Finally, after examining each of the letter's purpose statements, I will set forth the argument that John has written the entire letter to assure his readers that they are the ones who have eternal life and concomitantly to exhort them to continue to abide in Christ.

Chapter 3 will start at the beginning of the letter and argue that John seeks to ground his readers' assurance in the cross-work of the Christ from the outset (1:1–2:2). This will be followed by an examination of the other passages where Christ's finished work on the cross is emphasized (3:5,8; 4:9–10; 5:5–7). Finally, the chapter will end with a discussion of the assurance one should have as a result of the ongoing work of Christ in His divine protection over those who have been born of God (5:18).

In chapter 4, I will examine the idea of the new covenant in 1 John. Here I will attempt to demonstrate that John has alluded to the text of Jeremiah 31:29–34 in his discussion of the χρῖσμα ("anointing") that

[130] Hodges, *The Epistles of John*, 108–9.

abides in his readers and teaches them all things (2:20,27). I will then lay out some of the promises of the new covenant and argue that the writer of 1 John understood these to be fulfilled in the community to whom he wrote.

Chapter 5 will then focus on the writer's emphasis on the lifestyle of the believer. Here I interact with his tests of righteousness, love, and belief, and argue that these tests serve as a vital support for the reader's assurance of eternal life. Moreover, this chapter will include a discussion on perseverance and apostasy in 1 John and interact with how these ideas fit within a letter that was written with the primary purpose of assuring its readers.

Finally, chapter 6 will summarize and conclude the study. Here the aim is to see how the key themes discussed in chapters 2 through 5 fit together. This will be followed by an examination of some of the pastoral implications of this study and some of the ways in which pastors and lay leaders can apply such teachings to real people in real situations in life.

Chapter 2
JOHN'S PURPOSE FOR WRITING

Introduction

Virtually everyone would agree that each New Testament epistle has a definitive purpose that stands behind its publication. It is important then for us to understand what the purpose was behind the writing of 1 John. In 5:13, the writer informs his readers that he has written so that they might know they have eternal life. While the majority of New Testament scholarship is in agreement that this is the overarching purpose statement of the letter, readers are nevertheless confronted with several other statements of purpose as they read this short epistle. Therefore, it is important to determine which of these, if any, should be viewed as John's overarching purpose. Of course questions regarding the letter's purpose inevitably lead to the probing of the text for clues about the situation in the community to which the author was writing.

To be sure, any discussion of John's[1] purpose for writing must include some sort of theory regarding the situation behind this letter.

[1] This book assumes the traditional view that John the son of Zebedee was the author of both the Fourth Gospel and the three epistles traditionally ascribed to his name and that the Gospel was written prior to the epistles. To be sure, this view is debated among scholars. Nevertheless, I believe that it is still the most persuasive interpretation of both the internal and external evidence. Space and the focus of this study preclude engaging in yet another rehearsal of the argumentation on this issue. This, however, has been done at length elsewhere, and thus I will simply point to the work of others in order to focus on the thesis at hand. For some who argue for a view similar to my own, readers should consult D. A. Carson and D. J. Moo, *An Introduction to the New Testament*, rev. ed. (Grand Rapids: Zondervan, 2005), 670–75; D. Guthrie, *New Testament Introduction* (Downers Grove, IL: InterVarsity, 1990), 858–64; R. Law, *The Tests of Life: A Study of the First Epistle of St. John*, 3rd ed. (Edinburgh: T. & T. Clark, 1914; reprint, Grand Rapids: Baker, 1968), 39–51; J. R. W. Stott, *The Letters of John: An Introduction and Commentary*, TNTC, rev. ed. (Grand Rapids: Eerdmans, 2000), 17–43; B. F. Westcott, *The Epistles of St. John: The Greek Text with Notes and Essays* (Grand Rapids: Eerdmans, 1955), liii–lv. To be sure, many argue against John the apostle as the author of both the Gospel and letters and argue that these works were written by a "community," "circle," or "school." Some of these writers include R. E. Brown, *The Epistles of John: Translated with Introduction, Notes, and Commentary*, The Anchor Bible, vol. 30 (New York: Double Day, 1982), 3–28; G. Strecker, *The Johannine Letters: A Commentary on 1, 2, and 3 John*, trans. L. M. Maloney, Hermenia (Minneapolis: Fortress, 1996), xxxv–xlii; O. Cullmann, *The Johannine Circle*, trans. J. Bowden (Philadelphia: Westminster, 1976).

This chapter will therefore begin with a working hypothesis of the historical setting before moving to an examination of John's statements of purpose. As in any attempt to reconstruct the setting, the primary source of evidence must be the document itself. Hence, the proposed background information is the result of what is hoped to be a faithful mirror reading of the text of 1 John combined with an evaluation of the external evidence of some of the known heretical teachings of the day. Such an examination will inevitably work in a circle, for the external evidence has some bearing on the internal while the internal certainly aids in one's understanding of the external.[2] Therefore, the goal of this chapter is to use both the internal and external evidence in order to best understand John's purpose for writing.[3] This will be important for the remainder of this study in that here I will argue that John's purpose is to assure his readers that they, as opposed to the secessionists, are the ones who have truly been born of God and have eternal life abiding in them. Moreover, I will argue that John pursues this purpose with single-minded devotion from the first word to the last and that each of his five purpose statements makes this abundantly clear.

Internal Evidence

A careful mirror reading of the text of 1 John is the fundamental building block by which to understand the situation behind this letter.[4] Perhaps the best way forward is to begin with some of the things that are most clear and proceed to those that are more debated. One

[2] So C. G. Kruse, *The Letters of John*, PNTC (Grand Rapids: Eerdmans, 2000), 1–2.

[3] Every attempt has been made to keep the discussion of the background issues terse since similar views to the one adopted here have been set forth in more detail elsewhere. See especially Carson and Morris, *An Introduction to the New Testament*, 677–82; Kruse, *Letters of John*, 1–4, 15–27; Stott, *Letters of John*, 44–55; I. Howard Marshall, *The Epistles of John*, NICNT (Grand Rapids: Eerdmans, 1978), 14–22.

[4] Marshall's caution is helpful at this point in that he urges that interpreters must "beware of supposing that every attitude which John condemns must necessarily be attributed to the false teachers, or that their teaching formed a coherent, complete system of thought" (Marshall, *The Epistles of John*, 15). Moreover, Burge is also correct in his assessment that outlining the teachings of the false teachers is a difficult endeavor since "writers rarely give a complete hearing to their opponents' views, and we have no first-hand information from John's adversaries" (G. M. Burge, "John, Letters of," in *Dictionary of the Later New Testament and Its Developments*, ed. R. P. Martin and P. H. Davids [Downers Grove, IL: InterVarsity, 1997], 590).

can have the highest level of certainty that a schism has occurred within the church or group of churches to which this letter was addressed (2:18–19). Beyond this, it also appears that those who have departed from the fellowship (henceforth "secessionists")[5] have done so as a result of their differing views of the person and work of Jesus Christ as seen in 2:22–23; 4:1–3,14–15; 5:1,5–12. Taken together, the false teachers seem to have denied that the divine Christ/Son of God is the man Jesus (2:22; 4:15; 5:1,5). In other words, the secessionists appear to have denied the union between the divine Christ and the human Jesus. This is perhaps most clear at 5:5–6, where John elucidates that the Son of God is Jesus who came all the way through water and blood. He came "not by water alone" (οὐκ ἐν τῷ ὕδατι μόνον), "but by water and by blood" (ἀλλ᾽ ἐν τῷ ὕδατι καὶ ἐν τῷ αἵματι). The phrase "not by water alone" indicates that the secessionists did not have a problem agreeing that He came by water. Their point of contention was the blood. They apparently denied that the Son of God came through the blood of the cross, and thus they denied the atoning sacrifice of Jesus. John, however, insists that Jesus the Son of God came both by the water of His baptism and by the blood He shed on the cross.[6] Closely tied to their faulty Christology, it also appears that the secessionists parted ways with the author and his readers regarding the necessity to live righteously (1:6–10; 2:3–6; 2:15–16; 3:3–10; 5:2). In fact, from the first chapter of this letter there are indications that they were actually indifferent to sin (1:6,8,10).

It is also plausible that the letter of 1 John includes some form of the sayings/teachings of the false teachers.[7] This, of course, is one of the reasons so many argue that this letter has such a sharp polemical edge. If this is correct, it would appear that John sometimes cites particular sayings of the false teachers and then turns them on their head by adding a condition that the secessionists fail to meet. Some of these sayings might include claims to have fellowship with God (1:6),

[5] I will use terms such as *secessionists*, *false teachers*, *antichrists*, and *heretics* interchangeably throughout this book and vary them for stylistic purposes.

[6] For a thorough defense of the view overviewed here, see chap. 5, where I treat John's test of belief and interact in some detail on each of these texts.

[7] So also Brown, *Epistles of John*, 197, 231–32; Marshall, *The Epistles of John*, 15–16.

to be free from sin (1:8,10), to know God (2:4), to abide in God (2:6), and to be in the light (2:9).[8]

Finally, it is evident from the text of 1 John that the secessionists were not content to depart and form their own group but were attempting to persuade those who had remained to follow after them (2:26; 3:7). Moreover, they may have asserted that they had a special knowledge (2:4) and an anointing (2:20,27) from God. Such claims plausibly led to a triumphal (2 John 8–9) and unloving attitude (2:11; 4:8,20) toward those they believed had failed to progress beyond the basic gospel they heard from the beginning. Therefore, those remaining in the community were left with doubts and in need of reassurance.

External Evidence

Having examined the internal evidence and set forth a working hypothesis regarding the historical background of the letter, the next step is to identify the particular heresy against which John is writing. To do this, one must seek a teaching that denied that the Christ/Son of God was Jesus who had come in the flesh and that viewed holiness and love for the brethren as inconsequential to the Christian life.[9] Therefore, it is helpful to survey briefly the external evidence in order to ascertain whether any of the known heresies that were somewhat contemporaneous with John's writing might enable us to better understand the teaching of the secessionists. Such an exercise has typically led interpreters of this letter to one of or a combination of three particular movements; namely, Gnosticism, Cerinthianism, or Docetism.[10] A brief overview of each of these might prove helpful.

[8] Each of these begins with either the conditional ἐὰν εἴπωμεν ("if we say") followed by a particular claim or the substantival participle ὁ λέγων ("the one who says") followed by the claim.

[9] So also Stott, *Letters of John*, 48.

[10] Many in contemporary scholarship have moved away from seeking John's opponents in the external evidence and seek instead to understand how different trajectories of thought have spun off from "Johannine Christianity" itself and their own understanding of the Gospel of John. Some of these include Brown, *Epistles of John*, 69–115; R. A. Whitacre, *Johannine Polemic: The Role of Tradition and Theology*, SBLDS 67 (Chico, CA: SP, 1982); P. Bonnard, *Les Épitres Johanniques*, Commentaire Du Nouveau Testament (Geneva: Labor Et Fides, 1983), 9–15; S. S. Smalley, *1, 2, 3 John*, WBC, vol. 51 (Waco: Word Books, 1984), xxiii–xxxii; J. L. Houlden, *A Commentary on the Johannine Epistles*, BNTC, rev. ed. (London: A & C Black, 1994), 1–22;

Gnosticism

Any discussion which sets forth Gnosticism as the heresy that John is combating must first acknowledge that this term is itself a modern one[11] used to describe a variegated theosophical hodgepodge of teachings.[12] While this movement was not monolithic,[13] it did appear to have at its core several key elements such as a claim to special knowledge (γνῶσις) as the basis for salvation/fellowship with God as well as a sharp neoplatonic dualism, which led to a dichotomy between matter, which was considered to be evil, and spirit, which was considered to be good.[14] Hence, for gnostics, the material world, which is evil, could not have been created by the supreme God, who is good, and therefore must have been created by some lesser god. Of course the most that can be said regarding Gnosticism as a possible background for this letter is that such a teaching appears to have existed only in kernel form during the time of the New Testament

K. Grayston, *The Johannine Epistles*, New Century Bible Commentary (Grand Rapids: Eerdmans, 1984), 14–22; J. Bogart, *Orthodox and Heretical Perfectionism*, SBLDS 33 (Missoula, MT: SP, 1977); D. B. Woll, *Johannine Christianity in Conflict*, SBLDS 60 (Chico, CA: SP, 1981). Moreover others have argued that the best explanation of the background lies in the rhetoric of 1 John itself. Those in this camp would argue that if one properly understands John's rhetoric, then he need not spend all of his time postulating who the opponents are, for the rhetoric of 1 John does not demand opponents and is not necessarily polemical. For this view, see J. M. Lieu, *The Theology of the Johannine Epistles* (Cambridge: Cambridge University Press, 1991), 8–16; R. B. Edwards, *The Johannine Epistles*, New Testament Study Guides (Sheffield: Sheffield Academic Press, 1996), 57–68; J. Painter, *1, 2, and 3 John*, Sacra Pagina, vol. 18 (Collegeville, MN: Liturgical, 2002), 87–94; T. Griffith, *Keep Yourselves from Idols: A New Look at 1 John*, JSNTSup 233 (Sheffield: Sheffield Academic Press, 2002).

[11] Yamauchi points out that "the ancient sources of these movements and their Christian critics do not use the term *Gnosticism* and rarely used the term *Gnostics*" (E. M. Yamauchi, "Gnosticism," in *Dictionary of New Testament Backgrounds*, ed. C. A. Evans and S. E. Porter [Downers Grove, IL: InterVarsity, 2000], 414.)

[12] So Dodd, *Johannine Epistles*, xvii; Yamauchi, "Gnosticism," 414; Stott, *Letters of John*, 49. It is beyond the scope of this study to enter into a description of all of the various nuances that second- and third-century gnosticism took on. One should consult the text edited by James M. Robinson where many of the gnostic writings have been brought together (*The Nag Hammadi Library*, rev. ed. [San Francisco: Harper SanFrancisco, 1990]).

[13] So D. M. Scholer, "Gnosis, Gnosticism," in *Dictionary of the Later New Testament and Its Developments*, ed. R. P. Martin and P. H. Davids (Downers Grove, IL: InterVarsity, 1997), 400.

[14] So Yamauchi, "Gnosticism," 414; idem, *Pre-Christian Gnosticism: A Survey of the Proposed Evidences* (Grand Rapids: Eerdmans, 1973), 14–15; Carson, and Moo, *Introduction to the New Testament*, 678–79; D. M. Scholer, "Gnosis, Gnosticism," in *Dictionary of the Later New Testament*, 400–2.

writings.[15] Not until the second and third centuries AD was there any hard evidence that such a heresy existed.[16] Hence, any proposal of a gnostic background to this epistle should exert extreme caution and probably speak of a proto- or incipient form of this heresy.

Cerinthianism

One such proto-gnostic teaching that has been espoused as a possibility for the false teachers is the heresy of Cerinthus, which we learn about through the writings of Irenaeus.[17] According to Irenaeus, Cerinthus taught "that the world was not made by the primary God, but by a certain Power far separated from him. . . . He represented Jesus as having not been born of a virgin, but as being the son of Joseph and Mary according to the ordinary course of human generation."[18] Moreover, Irenaeus tells us Cerinthus taught that after the baptism of the human Jesus,

> Christ descended upon him in the form of a dove from the Supreme Ruler, and that then he proclaimed the unknown Father, and performed miracles. But at last Christ departed from Jesus, and that then Jesus suffered and rose again, while Christ remained impassible, inasmuch as he was a spiritual being.[19]

It would appear therefore that Cerinthus and his followers denied the union between the divine Christ and the human Jesus. Such a heresy could certainly be understood as that which stands behind John's teaching in 5:5–6. With the Cerinthian understanding of the divine Christ coming down on Jesus at His baptism and leaving Him sometime before the cross, one could see how John's statement, "not by water alone, but by water and by blood" could have been combating such a view. Therefore, both the similarity of this Christological

[15] Marshall notes that the "false teachers were forerunners of the heretics who were responsible for the developed Gnostic sects of the second century. The seeds of Gnosticism were already to be found in the New Testament period" (Marshall, *The Epistles of John*, 15).

[16] Scholer, "Gnosis, Gnosticism," 402–3.

[17] Irenaeus preserves a report said to have come from Polycarp where the apostle John fled from the bathhouse in Ephesus when he discovered that Cerinthus was present, fearing that the bathhouse might fall in on them since Cerinthus was the enemy of God (*Against Heresies* 3.3.4; cp. 3.28.6; 4.14.6).

[18] Irenaeus, *Against Heresies* 1.26.1.

[19] Ibid. Cp. 3.11.1.

heresy with the one encountered by John and the espoused traditional link between the apostle and Cerinthus make it possible that this is the heresy of the secessionists.[20]

Docetism

Another theory is that the false teachers in 1 John are the Docetic heretics described in the writings of Ignatius of Antioch. This heresy denied the humanity of Jesus and asserted that the Son of God only "seemed" (δοκέω) to be the incarnate Jesus. Writing against such a teaching, Ignatius asserted that Jesus actually "suffered all these things for us that we might attain salvation, and he truly suffered, even as he truly raised himself, not, as some unbelievers say, that his Passion was merely in semblance."[21] Earlier in his letter he commends his readers for being "fully persuaded as touching our Lord, that he is in truth of the family of David according to the flesh . . . truly born of a virgin, . . . [and] truly nailed to a tree in the flesh for our sakes under Pontius Pilate and Herod the tetrarch."[22] Moreover, it is also believed these Docetists "so misconceived the true locus of evil that they fell into sin and puffed themselves up with Gnostic pride."[23] This would account for the lack of love described by Ignatius when he says, "For love they have no care, none for the widow, none for the orphan, none for the distressed, none for the afflicted, none for the prisoner, or for him released from prison, none for the hungry or thirsty."[24] Thus it appears that, like the Cerinthians, the Docetic heretics combated by Ignatius also have much in common with the secessionists encountered by John. Again there is a rejection of the union between the divine Christ and the human Jesus. Here there is also an account of a genuine lack of love that is similar to that addressed in 1 John.

[20] For a helpful survey of Cerinthus, see Brown, *Epistles of John*, 766–71; K. Wengst, *Häresie und Orthodoxie im Spiegel des ersten Johannesbriefs* (Gütersloh: Gütersloher Verlagshaus G. Mohn, 1976), 24–34.

[21] Ingatius, *Smyrn.* 2:1. Cp. 3:1–3; 4:1–2; 5:1–3; *Trall* 9:1–2; 10:1.

[22] Ignatius, *Smyrn.* 1:1–2.

[23] Carson and Moo, *Introduction to the New Testament*, 679.

[24] Ignatius, *Smyrn.* 6:1–7:1.

Caution against Overstating the Evidence

While each of these heresies displays some striking similarities to the false teaching in 1 John, one must be cautious not to overstate the case regarding any one of these since each suffers from various weaknesses. To begin with, while some argue that Gnosticism was the false teaching John was encountering in this letter,[25] this heresy as seen in the writings of Basilides and Valentinus did not come into existence until the second century. Moreover, this later heresy was far more developed,[26] and there is little in common between these later gnostic teachings and that found in 1 John.[27] At most, one might assert that a seed form of such later gnostic teachings can be found in this letter.

One must also be cautious in proposing the heresy of Cerinthus and his followers, for such an assertion has been challenged on at least three fronts.[28] First, there are things we know about Cerinthus that are not reflected in this letter. For instance, the writer of 1 John nowhere interacts with Cerinthus's distinction between the "primary god" and the "creative power" that was removed from Him.[29] Second, there are portions in the secessionists' teaching that are not found in what we know about Cerinthus. For example, John appears to be combating a false teaching that makes a claim of sinlessness (1:8,10), and yet such a teaching is absent from what we know about Cerinthus and his followers.[30] Third, while it is possible that John knew Cerinthus, there is no evidence that Cerinthus and his followers were ever members of the community.[31] Since John's opponents were clearly part of the community before their secession (2:19), one must be cautious in arguing that Cerinthus and his followers were the secessionists of 1 John.[32]

[25] So R. Bultmann, *The Johannine Epistles*, trans. R. P. O'Hara, L. C. McGaughy, and R. W. Funk, Hermenia (Philadelphia: Fortress, 1973).

[26] See the description found in Irenaeus, *Against Heresies* 1.24.3–4; 3.16.1.

[27] So Kruse, *Letters of John*, 24–26.

[28] Marshall, *The Epistles of John*, 18.

[29] Ibid.

[30] Ibid.

[31] Kruse, *Letters of John*, 21.

[32] D. A. Carson, however, rightly asserts that "to insist on utter alignment between 1 John and our flimsy sources for Cerinthus before one is permitted to discern any connections is

Finally, the link between the Docetists combated by Ignatius and the false teachers in 1 John also appears to fall short. While there are similarities, there are also several key distinctions. To begin with, John's opponents seem to have denied that Jesus came in the flesh (4:2), but those Ignatius wrote against were true Docetists "who reduced the existence of Jesus to mere semblance, and there is no evidence that the secessionists did this."[33] Furthermore, this particular heresy had strong ties to Judaism, whereas there is no evidence that this was the case with the secessionists.[34]

Conclusion

It may be impossible to identify the precise strain of proto-gnostic teaching that might have accounted for that which John is combating. Nevertheless, the external evidence points to several heretical teachings that bear noticeable similarities with that of the secessionists. The best conclusion is that John was combating a proto-gnostic teaching that was an early form of one or a combination of these heresies. There is no doubt that

> this form cannot be precisely identified with any of the manifestations that have come down to us independently. The point is that rather few have been preserved for us, and the most we can say is that so far as the epistles of John go, the discernable errors and abysmal practices that are being opposed have much in common with the Docetism and Cerinthianism of which we know all too little.[35]

John's Purpose for Writing

John has written to a church or group of churches in which a schism has occurred. Those who have departed appear to be a form of proto-gnostics that are somewhat docetic in their Christology,

totally unrealistic not only because of the brevity of the sources (and their secondary nature in the case of Cerinthus) but also because of the intrinsic nature of virtually all branches of gnosticism ("The Three Witnesses and the Eschatology of 1 John," in *To Tell the Mystery: Essays on New Testament Eschatology in Honor of Robert H. Gundry*, JSNTSup 100, ed. T. E. Schmidt and M. Silva [Sheffield: Sheffield Academic Press, 1994], 230).

[33] Kruse, *Letters of John*, 24.

[34] So also Schnackenburg, *Johannine Epistles*, 23. See Ignatius, *Magn.* 10:1–3.

[35] Carson and Moo, *Introduction to the New Testament*, 680.

having denied the union between the man Jesus and the divine Christ. Moreover, the secessionists appear to have claimed that they had a special knowledge, fellowship, and anointing of God, which plausibly led to a triumphal and unloving attitude toward those who have remained in the community. Hence, it would appear that John has written to a group of people who found themselves in need of both reassurance and exhortation. They needed reassurance that they were actually the ones in fellowship with God, who knew God, had an anointing, and had eternal life abiding in them. Moreover, they were in need of exhortation to hold on to the gospel that was proclaimed from the very beginning, which would actually serve to bolster their confidence that they know God and have eternal life.

At this point it is important to continue to work in a circle and turn our attention back to the text of 1 John in order to evaluate whether John's own statements of purpose corroborate the findings from the above survey of the internal and external evidence. John is helpful here in that he has actually given several purpose statements, which usually begin with "I proclaim" (ἀπαγγέλλω) or "I write" (γράφω) followed by the reason for his proclamation or writing. These include 1:3,4; 2:1,12–14,21,26; 5:13. They will now be examined in the order they are found in the text.

That You Might Have Fellowship (1:1–3)

John's first purpose statement comes in 1:3, where he asserts that he has written "what he has seen and heard" so his readers might have fellowship with him, which is actually fellowship with the Father and the Son. This statement comes at the end of the first three verses, which are actually one long complex sentence in the original Greek, where the reader does not come across the main verb ("we proclaim") until the third verse. The compound object[36] of this sentence appears to be emphatic, given that it is thrust to the beginning

[36] The object of this sentence is found in v. 1: ὃ ἦν ἀπ' ἀρχῆς, ὃ ἀκηκόαμεν, ὃ ἑωράκαμεν τοῖς ὀφθαλμοῖς ἡμῶν, ὃ ἐθεασάμεθα καὶ αἱ χεῖρες ἡμῶν ἐψηλάφησαν περὶ τοῦ λόγου τῆς ζωῆς. After the brief parenthesis of v. 2, John restates a shortened form of the object (ὃ ἑωράκαμεν καὶ ἀκηκόαμεν) before proceeding to the main verb of the sentence.

of the sentence.[37] Here John employs the sensory terms, "what we have *heard*, what we have *seen with our eyes*, what we have *beheld* and our *hands have touched*," in order to highlight his own eyewitness experience of Jesus—the Word who is Life.[38] Verse 2 is therefore an epexegetical parenthesis that goes on to explain the word *life* (τῆς ζωῆς). Like the prologue of the Fourth Gospel, 1 John 1:2 stresses the importance of the incarnation ("the life was manifested"). The purpose of such an assertion appears to be the author's attempt to counteract the teachings of the secessionists where the necessity of the incarnation was rejected.

Following this brief parenthesis, the writer returns to his eyewitness experience of the incarnate Jesus and asserts that he is proclaiming what he has seen and heard for the purpose that his readers might have fellowship with him.[39] Thus one of John's purposes for writing is that his readers might have fellowship with him, which is also fellowship with the Father and the Son. Therefore, it is important to examine what is meant by the term *fellowship* and why there is a link between fellowship with God and other believers.

The word *fellowship* (κοινωνία) is found 19 times in the New Testament and can be defined as a "close association involving mutual interests and sharing."[40] The four uses of this word in 1 John

[37] So also G. M. Burge, *The Letters of John*, NIVAC (Grand Rapids: Zondervan, 1996), 52; Marshall, *Epistles of John*, 100; Marianne M. Thompson, *1–3 John*, The IVP New Testament Commentary Series (Downers Grove, IL: InterVarsity, 1992), 36.

[38] See chap. 3, where I defend this reading (emphasis mine).

[39] Throughout the letter it seems clear that John is confident that he is writing to those who are already believers (2:12–14,21,26–27; 5:13). So it might appear as odd that he writes to those who already believe in order that they might have fellowship with him, which is also fellowship with the Father and the Son. It appears as odd, however, only if we fail to take the context into account. This is because John makes clear that he is writing to those whom the false teachers are attempting to deceive (2:26) and woo away from the true fellowship with the Father and the Son into a counterfeit fellowship with the secessionists. Hence, it would seem that John has written in order that his readers might *continue to have* fellowship with him as opposed to switching their allegiance and moving into fellowship with the secessionists. Context would therefore seem to indicate that the present tense ἔχητε should probably be viewed as having continuous aspect (so Kruse, *Letters of John*, 58, who asserts that the "author's purpose is to ensure that his readers persist in the fellowship they have with him"; cp. Smalley, *1, 2, 3 John*, 12; Marshall, *Epistles of John*, 105).

[40] W. Bauer, *A Greek-English Lexicon of the New Testament and Other Early Christian Literature*, trans. W. F. Arndt and F. W. Gingrich, 3rd ed., rev. and ed. F. W. Danker (Chicago: University of Chicago Press, 2000), s.v. "κοινωνία." Dodd further asserts those who were in

demonstrate that while it is true that fellowship involves "a close association involving mutual interests," one must assert that in this letter the "close association" is with God and other believers and the "mutual interests" in which one shares revolve around the eternal Life, who was with God and revealed to the apostles (1:2). On the one hand, what is held in common is trusting in the eternal Word, who is Life, and a lack of such trust precludes Johannine fellowship with the author and other believers.[41] On the other hand, partaking in the One who was from the beginning leads to genuine fellowship with other believers, which is also fellowship with God (1:6–7). Fellowship with other believers, then, is shared precisely because each shares in a vital union with God that is grounded in trusting in the cross-work of Christ (1:3–2:2). Hauck is therefore correct in his assertion that in 1 John, fellowship is "a favourite term to describe the living bond in which the Christian stands. . . . To be a Christian is to have fellowship with God."[42]

Of course one would be remiss to limit John's discussion of this intimate relationship with God to his use of the term *fellowship*, for John expresses this theme in various ways.[43] John apparently uses "fellowship with God" (1:6) synonymously with "knowing God" (2:3–6), and "abiding in God"[44] (2:6,24; 3:24; 4:13,15–16). This is supported by the close similarities in which he employs these terms. To begin with, 1 John 1:6 is a close parallel with 2:4.[45] Both of these

κοινωνία "are persons who hold property in common, partners or shareholders in a common concern, like the fishermen disciples in Luke v. 10, who (it is implied) were joint owners of the little fishing fleet" (Dodd, *Johannine Epistles*, 6–7).

[41] First John 1:7 is a conditional sentence. If the condition of walking in the light (God is light, 1:5) is not met, then there is no fellowship with other believers. See also chap. 3, where I argue that "walking in the light" is tied to trusting in the cross-work of Jesus Christ.

[42] F. Hauck, "Κοινωνία," in *Theological Dictionary of the New Testament*, ed. G. Kittle, trans. G. W. Bromiley (Grand Rapids: Eerdmans, 1999), 807–9.

[43] See also the helpful excurses on "fellowship" in Schnackenburg, *Johannine Epistles*, 64–65; Hauck, *TDNT*, "κοινωνία," 807–9; P. Perkins, "*Koinonia* in 1 John 1:3–7: The Social Context of Division in the Johannine Letters," *CBQ* 45 (1983): 632–33; idem, *The Johannine Epistles*, New Testament Message (Wilmington, DE; Michael Glazier, 1979), 11–12.

[44] Due to the close relationship between μένειν ἐν and εἶναι ἐν, we should probably include those passages that speak of "being in God" (2:5; 5:20) as well. See E. S. J. Malatesta, *Interiority and Covenant: A Study of* εἶναι ἐν *and* μένειν ἐν *in the First Letter of Saint John*, Analecta Biblica, 69 (Rome: Biblical Institute, 1978).

[45] 1 John 1:6—Ἐὰν εἴπωμεν ὅτι κοινωνίαν ἔχομεν μετ᾽ αὐτοῦ καὶ ἐν τῷ σκότει περιπατῶμεν, ψευδόμεθα καὶ οὐ ποιοῦμεν τὴν ἀλήθειαν.

passages begin with a claim ("if we say [1:6], "the one who says" [2:4]). In 1:6 the claim is to have "fellowship with Him" while in 2:4 it is the claim to "know Him." In both verses anyone who makes such a claim and does not support it by a lifestyle appropriate for a Christian (walking in the light [1:6], keeping the commands [2:4]) is a liar ("we lie" [1:6], "is a liar" [2:4]) and has nothing to do with the truth ("and does not do the truth" [1:6], "the truth is not in him" [2:4]). Hence, it would seem that John equates "fellowship with God" and "knowing God."[46] Also, "knowing God" and "abiding in God" are probably used synonymously in this letter.[47] This is most evident in a comparison of 2:3 with 3:24.[48] In 2:3, "keeping the commands" demonstrates that one "knows God," while in 3:24 "keeping the commands" demonstrates that one "abides in God."[49] Therefore, it would appear that "abiding in God" and "knowing God" both speak of an intimate union with God that is virtually synonymous with John's use of "fellowship with God."

Moreover, the writer of 1 John gives us an idea of what this "fellowship with God" looks like as we examine its use as well as that of "knowing God" and "abiding in God." Fellowship with God appears to include walking in the light (1:6), trusting in the cross-work of Christ for the forgiveness of sins (1:7,9; 2:1–2), keeping the commands (2:3–6; 3:24), walking as Jesus walked (2:6), loving the brethren (2:10; 3:17; 4:7–8,12,16), remaining in the community of the saints (2:19), having the message of the gospel abiding in you (2:24), having confidence in His coming (2:28), not sinning (3:6), laying down one's life for the brethren (3:16), having the Spirit abiding in us (3:24; 4:13), and having a right confession of Jesus (4:15).

1 John 2:4—ὁ λέγων ὅτι ἔγνωκα αὐτόν καὶ τὰς ἐντολὰς αὐτοῦ μὴ τηρῶν, ψεύστης ἐστίν καὶ ἐν τούτῳ ἡ ἀλήθεια οὐκ ἔστιν.

[46] So also Marshall, *Epistles of John*, 121: "The abruptness of the new idea ['knowing God'] is mitigated by the fact that the writer's earlier references to fellowship with God (1:3,6,7) are alternative ways of expressing the same reality."

[47] See also 4:7 for a possible link between "knowing God" and "being born of God."

[48] 1 John 2:3—Καὶ ἐν τούτῳ γινώσκομεν ὅτι ἐγνώκαμεν αὐτόν, ἐὰν τὰς ἐντολὰς αὐτοῦ τηρῶμεν.

1 John 3:24—καὶ ὁ τηρῶν τὰς ἐντολὰς αὐτοῦ ἐν αὐτῷ μένει καὶ αὐτὸς ἐν αὐτῷ· καὶ ἐν τούτῳ γινώσκομεν ὅτι μένει ἐν ἡμῖν, ἐκ τοῦ πνεύματος οὗ ἡμῖν ἔδωκεν.

[49] See also 3:6, where there is link between "knowing God" and "abiding in Him" in the same verse.

If this exegesis is correct, then at least one of the reasons John has penned this letter is so that his readers might have fellowship with him, which is also fellowship with the Father and the Son. This fellowship involves the closest possible abiding relationship between God and the believer and works itself out in one's love for the brethren and obedience to Christ. Of course this purpose is understandable given that the false teachers were attempting to deceive John's readers away from this fellowship into "fellowship" with them, which rejects the apostolic gospel. John therefore begins his letter by pointing back to his eyewitness experience and reminding his readers that, over and against the false teachers, his words can be trusted, for he is one of the apostles who actually heard Jesus, saw Him with his own eyes, and even touched Him. His message about Jesus was historically reliable, and fellowship with God ultimately stems from belief in this Jesus.

That Our Joy Might Be Made Full (1:4)

Interestingly, John offers yet another statement of purpose in the next sentence. Here he asserts, "These things[50] we write so that our[51] joy might be made complete." Hence, this letter was also written so

[50] The neuter plural ταῦτα ("these things") is somewhat ambiguous in that it is difficult to determine whether it refers to a near referent or to the entire letter. While an argument can be made in favor of it referring only to what precedes, there are equally strong reasons to take it as referring to the whole letter. To begin with, if it is correct to link "fellowship" with such Johannine themes as "knowing God" and "abiding in God" as was argued above, then it would appear that the rest of the letter further explicates what it looks like to have fellowship with God. Moreover, given that the purpose statement in 5:13 also employs the neuter plural ταῦτα, it is possible to see these purpose statements as bookends to this epistle (so Brown, *Epistles of John*, 172–73). For others who view ταῦτα here in 1:4 as referring to the whole letter, see A. E. Brooke, *A Critical and Exegetical Commentary on the Johannine Epistles*, ICC (Edinburgh: T & T Clark, 1912, 76), 9; Westcott, *Epistles of John*, 13; Schnackenburg, *Johannine Epistles*, 62; Brown, *Epistles of John*, 172–73. In fact, as will be seen below, it is possible that each of the four times John uses the neuter plural ταῦτα with some form of the verb γράφω, he is referring to the entire letter (so also Strecker, *The Letters of John*, 76).

[51] Some manuscripts have "your" (ὑμῶν) (A, C, K, P, 33, 81, 323, 614, 630, 945, 1505, 1739) instead of "our" (ἡμῶν) (א, B, L, Ψ, 049, 69, 1241). While the external evidence slightly favors the reading "our" (ἡμῶν), it would appear that the strongest reason for favoring this reading is that it is the more difficult reading and thus, the most likely to be changed by a scribe (so also Strecker, *Johannine Letters*, 20–21). This is especially true given the parallel text in John's Gospel (15:11), where Jesus says, "These things I have spoken to you in order that my joy might be in you and your joy might be made full."

that John and the other apostles might be full of joy.[52] This is hardly surprising given John's statement in 3 John 4, where he writes that he has no greater joy than to hear that his children are walking in the truth.[53] John wanted nothing more than to see the recipients of his letter walking in close fellowship with him since he knew that his fellowship was with God. The problem, however, was that the secessionists were attempting to deceive them and lure them into their fellowship. John therefore counters their ploy by asserting that his fellowship is actually fellowship with God. Thus, there is a close link between the purpose statements of 1:3 and 1:4, for seeing his readers reject the false fellowship of the secessionists and continue in fellowship with him would result in the utmost joy for the apostle.

That You Might Not Sin (2:1)

Yet another statement of purpose is found in 2:1.[54] Having just stated that all who claim to be free from sin (1:8,10) are liars and deceive themselves, John now turns and makes clear that he is not giving license to sin.[55] In fact, he explains that one of his purposes for writing is that his readers would not sin. Such a statement will be discussed more in our interaction with 3:4–12, but for now, it is appropriate to see that John is setting forth the ideal for the Christian life. He is writing to those who have been "born of God" (2:29) and

[52] While there has been much discussion on the first person plural verbs used throughout the prologue, the best explanation is that John is including the other apostles here since he began this letter by taking his readers back to his eyewitness experience that was shared with them (so also S. J. Kistemaker, *James and I-III John*, New Testament Commentary [Grand Rapids: Baker, 1986], 238–39).

[53] See also the parallel passage to 1:4 in 2 John 12 (cp. Phil 2:2).

[54] Here we have the second statement of purpose where John uses the neuter plural ταῦτα ("these things) plus some form of the verb γράφω ("I write"). Again I would argue this one refers to the whole letter on the grounds that avoiding sin is a key theme throughout (e.g., 3:4–11; 5:18). So also Strecker, *The Johannine Epistles*, 36 n. 4; Brooke, *Johannine Epistles*, 23; Westcott, *Epistles of John*, 42; Stott, *Letters of John*, 85; B. Weiss, *Kritisch exegetisches Handbuch über die drei Briefe des Apostel Johannes*, *KEK* 14, 6th ed. (Göttingen: Vandenhoeck & Ruprecht, 1899), 39. Against Kruse, *Letters of John*, 71; Akin, *1, 2, 3 John*, 76, who both argue that it refers only to 1:5–10.

[55] So also J. Calvin, *The First Epistle of John*, trans. J. Owen, vol. 22 of *Calvin's Commentaries*, ed. D. W. Torrance and T. F. Torrance [Edinburgh: Oliver and Boyd, 1960; repr., Grand Rapids: Baker Books, 1999], 170); Grayston, *The Johannine Epistles*, 56; Brooke, *Johannine Epistles*, 22–23; Schnackenburg, *The Johannine Epistles*, 85; Marshall, *Epistles of John*, 116; Stott, *The Letters of John*, 84.

God's seed abides in them (3:9). As such, they have a new and divine enabling to live a righteous life and should strive to live accordingly. Nevertheless, this statement of purpose is immediately followed by the coordinating conjunction καὶ ("and") and the conditional statement that if anyone does sin, they have Jesus Christ as their παράκλητος ("advocate") with the Father and He is the ἱλασμός ("propitiation") of their sins.[56] This purpose follows right in line with the purpose statement in 1:3, for it has everything to do with how those who are sinful can have "fellowship" with a God who is light. Therefore, one of John's[57] purposes for writing is to help his readers understand that they must do everything in their power to avoid sin, and yet they are not sinless and are in need of Jesus' atoning sacrifice on their behalf.[58] That avoiding sin is a key theme for John is confirmed in its recurrence throughout this letter (3:4–11; 5:18). While the secessionists appear to have made claims to be free from sin, John's readers must strive to be free from sin, and yet they will sin and must deal with it by turning back to the cross of Christ for the "forgiveness" (ἀφηῇ), "cleansing" (καθαρίζει), and "propitiation" (ἱλασμός) of such sin (1:7–2:2). A key verse for rightly understanding such texts (cp. 2:17–18; 3:2; 4:3) may be 2:8. Here John tells his readers that the darkness is in the process of passing away[59] and the true light is already shining. Hence, there is the "already but not yet" tension that is found so often in the New Testament. On the one hand, the darkness is passing away, and yet it is still present. In this state of affairs, believers will continue to struggle with sin. On the other hand, the true light has already broken through and is presently shining. Therefore, John can

[56] See chap. 3 for a discussion of Jesus as παράκλητος ("advocate") and ἱλασμός" (propitiation").

[57] Here John switches from the first person plural γράφομεν ("we write") that he used in chap. 1 to the first person singular γράφω ("I write"). Smalley is helpful in his assertion that "John appears to use the first personal *singular* for direct address or exhortation; as here, when he abandons the first person plural which he has employed throughout the first chapter, and distinguishes his audience as 'you.' He tends to use the first person *plural* ('we') either when he is associating himself with those who are the guardians of the apostolic faith in the transmission of the kerygmatic message (so 1:1–3), or when he is identifying himself with his readers in terms of basic Christian experience (see v 1*b*)" (emphasis his) (Smalley, *1, 2, 3 John*, 35).

[58] So also Calvin, *1 John*, 170; Stott, *Letters of John*, 84.

[59] The context of this verse helps us to understand the present tense παράγεται as having an ongoing aspect.

say that he writes so that his readers will not sin (2:1) and that those who are born of God do not sin (3:9). It is clear, then, that one of John's purposes for writing is to exhort his readers to strive to live a holy life.[60] Nevertheless, there will still be sin and it must be dealt with by trusting in the finished work of Christ on the cross.

Because You Are Already Believers (2:12–14;21)

Most of the discussions in the commentaries and articles on 2:12–14 revolve around such issues as whether John was referring to two groups or three, the identification of these groups, and the meaning of the change in verb tense from the first cycle to the second. While there is certainly a place for such debates,[61] it is vital that such discussions do not result in missing the writer's intention in these verses, which is almost certainly a word of assurance to his readers.[62] It is noteworthy that commentators often speak of the abruptness of this section and admit that they struggle to understand exactly how it relates to what precedes and what follows.[63] Perhaps the best solution is to view this section as a brief pause in the midst of testing (2:3–11) and exhortation (2:15–17) in order to draw his readers' attention back to their present standing with God, which certainly fits the purpose of the letter (5:13). Six times in these three verses John tells his readers why he has written to them.[64] The reasons include their sins being forgiven

[60] See discussion on "tests of life" in chap. 5.

[61] It is outside the scope of this book to rehearse all of the arguments on these issues. For a view similar to that of my own regarding the debated issues in this passage, see Marshall, *Epistles of John*, 134–38. Here I will simply try to focus on the meaning of each of the writer's statements of encouragement and understand how it fits the overarching argument of the writer.

[62] See Marshall, *Epistles of John*, 134.

[63] T. Griffith contends that "no one has advanced a satisfactory explanation of the role of 2.12–14 within the body of 1 John." As a result of such understanding he concludes his study on John's use of the vocative by asserting that the six vocatives used in 2:12–14 "must be regarded as maverick examples" (*Keep Yourselves from Idols: A New Look at 1 John*, JSNTSup, vol. 233 [Sheffield: Sheffield Academic Press, 2002], 65–66). D. F. Watson argues that one must understand the complex rhetoric used in these verses to understand what the writer was trying to say. Nevertheless, when all is said and done, he simply falls into the camp that believes John is referring to two groups here and does little to explain how this section fits the rest of the letter ("1 John 2.12–14 as *Distributio, Conduplicatio,* and *Expolitio*: A Rhetorical Understanding," *JSNT* 35 [1989], 101).

[64] I take each of the six ὅτι clauses as causal. In support of this is the fact that the only other time γράφω comes before a ὅτι clause is in 1 John 2:21 where it is clearly causal (so

(2:12), their knowledge of God (2:13–14), and their overcoming the evil one (2:13–14). With each of these statements being a word of encouragement, it is evident that John has written to reassure his readers of their present standing with God.

Likewise in 2:21, we find a similar purpose statement to those found in 2:12–14. In the context of John's description of those who have departed from the fellowship, he turns and once again reassures his readers that he is confident of better things for them since they have an "anointing" (χρῖσμα) and "know all things" (2:20). He reassures them that he has not written because they do not know the truth but precisely because they do know it. Thus, it would again appear that one of John's reasons for writing was to reassure his readers that they are already believers.[65]

Concerning Those Who Are Trying to Deceive You (2:26)

In 2:18–27, John has focused on the secessionists. Here he told his readers that the secessionists went out from the fellowship because they were never truly part of it (2:19). Moreover, he elucidated the fact that these people have denied that Jesus is the Christ (2:22–23). John therefore tells his readers that he has written these things[66] concerning those who are attempting to deceive them.[67] To be sure, this particular purpose statement includes both a message of reassurance and a message of exhortation. It is reassurance in that John is clear that it is the secessionists who have a heretical Christology (2:22–23) and were never truly part of the community (2:19). Moreover, John offers further encouragement in his assertion that it is his readers, as opposed to the secessionists, who have an anointing from the holy

also Strecker, *Johannine Letters*, 57.) Moreover, it also fits the context well, since this letter was written to offer comfort to those already believing in Jesus (2:21; 5:13).

[65] So also Stott, *Letters of John*, 112.

[66] This is the third time John has used some form of the verb γράφω ("I write") and the neuter plural ταῦτα ("these things"). It is difficult to state for certain to what the neuter plural ταῦτα refers. While most would argue that it refers only to what precedes (so Smalley, *1, 2, 3 John*, 122; Haas, *Translator's Handbook on the Letters of John*, 71), it is certainly possible that it could once again refer in some sense to the entire letter (so also Strecker, *Johannine Letters*, 76). In support of this is the fact that John refers to the false teaching of the secessionists throughout this letter and will once again exhort his readers to let no one deceive them (3:7; cp. 5:21).

[67] Πλανάω here means to lead astray or to lead away from the truth, fellowship, or salvation (BDAG, s.v. "πλανάω").

One (2:20,27). Nevertheless, there is at least an implied exhortation in this statement. One of John's reasons for writing was to warn his readers about the secessionists who were trying to deceive them so that his readers might not get sucked into this aberrant teaching. Thus, it seems best to view this statement of purpose as both an exhortation for his readers to reject the secessionists' teaching and a reassurance that his readers will not ultimately be misled because they have an anointing from God.

That You Might Know You Have Eternal Life (5:13)

Finally, in 1 John 5:13, the writer offers his last purpose statement. Here, at the conclusion of the letter, John tells his readers that he has written that they might know they have eternal life. Once again interpreters are forced to understand what John meant in his use of the verb ἔγραψα ("I have written") with the neuter plural ταῦτα ("these things"). There are at least four reasons to understand "these things" as referring to the entire letter.[68] First, if I have been correct thus far in understanding each of John's statements where he employs some form of the verb "to write" plus the neuter plural "these things" as referring to the entire epistle, then this instance may follow in the same pattern.[69] Second, the believer's assurance is the focal point of this epistle as made manifest in the fact that John has incessantly given his readers reasons that they "might know they have eternal life" (1:1–2:2; 2:12–14,21; 3:1–2,20; 4:4,17; 5:18–20). Such reasons are founded on the cross-work of Christ (e.g., 1:1–2:2,12–14; 3:5,8c; 4:9–10,14,19–20; 5:4b-13) and supported by one's actions in the pub-

[68] For others who argue that ταῦτα refers back to the whole letter, see Houlden, *The Johannine Epistles*, 137; Akin, *1, 2, 3 John*, 204; Westcott, *Epistles of John*, 188; A. Plummer, *The Epistles of John*, Pineapple Commentaries (Cambridge: Cambridge University Press, 1886; reprint, Grand Rapids: Baker, 1980), 120; R. Bultmann, *The Johannine Epistles*, trans. R. P. O'Hara, L. C. McGaughy, and R. W. Funk, Hermenia (Philadelphia: Fortress, 1973), 83; Westcott, *Epistles of John*, 188; Stott, *Letters of John*, 186–87; Strecker, *Johannine Letters*, 198. Of course, some argue that it refers only to the preceding verses in chap. 5. For this view, see Derickson, "What Is the Message of 1 John," 101–4; E. M. Curtis, "The Purpose of 1 John" (Th.D. diss., Dallas Theological Seminary, 1986), 156–61; Schnackenburg, *Johannine Epistles*, 247; Brooke, *Johannine Epistles*, 142.

[69] To be sure, this is the weakest of the arguments in support of this reading since each particular instance is debated.

lic arena (e.g., 2:3–11,15–16; 3:3–24; 4:7–13,15–21; 5:1–2).[70] Third, there are striking similarities between the purpose statement in John's Gospel (20:31) with the one found here in 5:13.[71] Both include a form of γράφω with the ambiguous neuter plural ταῦτα.[72] Moreover, both include a purpose statement describing why the writer has written, and both of these statements adequately sum up the entirety of their particular writing. Finally, Carson is correct in asserting that

> with so many "this we know" statements and their kin scattered throughout the epistle, surely this last one (5:13) cries out to be read in line with the ones that have come before it. To read it as offering for the first time assurance in a new area is extraordinary, the more so when the next verse is linked with confidence in prayer—exactly as is done earlier in this epistle (3:21,22).[73]

Therefore, if I am correct in linking 1 John 5:13 with John 20:31, then it appears John has given an overarching purpose statement at the end of both his Gospel and first epistle.[74] Consequently, while there are several statements of purpose throughout this letter, it is best to view 5:13 as *the* overarching statement of purpose. This, however, does not mean that 5:13 supercedes all of the others. Instead, it

[70] See chaps. 3 and 5 for a detailed discussion of the foundation and secondary supports of assurance in 1 John.

[71] John 20:31—ταῦτα δὲ γέγραπται ἵνα πιστεύ[σ]ητε ὅτι Ἰησοῦς ἐστιν ὁ χριστὸς ὁ υἱὸς τοῦ θεοῦ, καὶ ἵνα πιστεύοντες ζωὴν ἔχητε ἐν τῷ ὀνόματι αὐτοῦ.

1 John 5:13—Ταῦτα ἔγραψα ὑμῖν ἵνα εἰδῆτε ὅτι ζωὴν ἔχετε αἰώνιον, τοῖς πιστεύ ουσιν εἰς τὸ ὄνομα τοῦ υἱοῦ τοῦ θεοῦ.

[72] The writer of John's Gospel also uses ταῦτα (καὶ ὁ γράψας ταῦτα) to refer to the entire Gospel in 21:24 (so also D. A. Carson, *The Gospel According to John*, PNTC [Grand Rapids: Eerdmans, 1991], 683; A. J. Köstenberger, *John*, BECNT [Grand Rapids: Baker Academic, 2004], 581; L. Morris, *The Gospel According to John*, NICNT, rev. ed. [Grand Rapids: Eerdmans, 1995], 754–55; C. S. Keener, *The Gospel of John: A Commentary* [Peabody, MA: Hendrickson, 2003], 2:1213; G. R. Beasley-Murray, *John*, WBC, vol. 36 [Waco: Word Books, 1987], 387; R. V. G. Tasker, *John*, TNTC [Grand Rapids: Eerdmans, 1960, 2000], 227–28).

[73] Carson, "Johannine Perspectives on the Doctrine of Assurance," 84.

[74] Many ancient Greek writings concluded with an overarching purpose statement. Moreover, in these works there was often an epilogue after the summarizing concluding statement such as the one found in 5:13 (so H. M. Jackson, "Ancient Self-Referential Conventions and Their Implications for the Authorship and Integrity of the Gospel of John," *JTS* 50 [1999]: 1–34; Keener, *The Gospel of John*, 2:1213, 1221; R. A. Whitacre, *John*, The IVP New Testament Commentary Series [Downers Grove, IL: InterVarsity, 1999], 489). For some of the ancient Greek texts that have a summary conclusion followed by an epilogue, see Homer, *Illiad and Odyssey*; Isaeus, *Estate of Cleonymus*; Cicero, *Quinct.* 28.85–29.90; Aeschines, *Timarchus*, 177.

is best to view each of the purpose statements as complementary to 5:13.[75]

Conclusion

The internal and external evidence demonstrate that this letter was written as a result of schism that took place within a church or group of churches to which John had clear ties. It is also appears that those who departed were some form of proto-gnostics, who denied the union between the man Jesus and the divine Christ. Moreover, they seem to have made a claim to have a special knowledge and anointing of God. Such claims plausibly led to a triumphal and unloving attitude toward those they were trying to seduce away from John's fellowship. Hence, John writes to a community of believers who find themselves in need of reassurance and exhortation.

I have shown that 5:13 should be viewed as the writer's overarching purpose statement for this letter, which certainly fits our interpretation of the situation within the community. Moreover, while John has given several statements of purpose throughout, each one should probably be viewed as complementary to 5:13.

In 1:3, John says that he has proclaimed the word of life in order that his readers might have fellowship with him, which is also fellowship with the Father and the Son. There I said that the mutual interest in this fellowship was Jesus, the embodiment of eternal life. Moreover, this fellowship with God (1:6) is synonymous with "knowing" and "abiding" in God. Such fellowship is essential to one's "knowing he has eternal life," so this purpose statement is complementary to that of 5:13. Moreover, in the very next verse, John explains that he has written so that his joy might be complete (1:4). With the understanding that John "has no greater joy than hearing that his children are walking in the truth" (3 John 4), this statement of purpose is closely linked with 1:3 and 5:13, since John finds joy that his children are in fellowship with God (1:3) and such fellowship leads to confidence that they have eternal life (5:13).

[75] See also Akin, *1, 2, 3 John*, 32; Strecker, *Johannine Letters*, 20–21.

In 2:1, John says that he is writing so that his children will not sin. This statement complements 5:13 in at least two ways. First, this letter is loaded with "tests of life," which John gives in order to bolster the assurance of his readers. Therefore, if heeded, this exhortation to avoid sinning will actually serve to strengthen their assurance. Second, it is also clear that this statement complements that of 5:13 in that those born of God are living during the time when the true light is already shining, and yet the darkness has not yet passed away. This statement is immediately followed by a conjunctive καὶ ("and") and the condition that if anyone does sin, they have an "advocate" with the Father who is the "propitiation" for their sins. As will be seen in chapter 3, this unremitting looking to Christ is the foundation of one's assurance. Therefore, John has written to exhort his readers to avoid sin as well as to urge them to look back to the cross when sin occurs. If the thesis is correct—that John builds his readers' assurance on the foundation of the cross-work of Christ and supports it by the way they live their lives—then 2:1 fits seamlessly with 5:13.

Moreover, John's statements of purpose found in 2:12–14 and 2:21 also complement 5:13. In these texts John assures his readers of their present standing with God. Such teaching is a direct parallel to John telling his readers that he has written so that they might know they have eternal life (5:13).

Finally, in 2:26 John tells his readers that he has written concerning those who are trying to deceive them. As in 2:1, we find here a statement of exhortation as well as encouragement. To begin with, there is at least an implicit warning in this verse. The secessionists are attempting to deceive John's readers and lead them away from his fellowship. In this regard the heeding of such exhortation would serve as at least a secondary support to his readers' assurance of salvation. Moreover, this passage is also encouraging to John's readers in two ways. First, as I will argue in the fifth chapter of this study, John has framed his tests of life in such a way that it is those who are trying to deceive them who actually fail the tests. As John's readers think through such verses as 1:6–11 or 2:18–19, they understand that it is the deceivers who demonstrate they were never truly "of us" (2:19). Moreover, as in 2:1, John follows his statement of purpose with a conjunctive καὶ ("and") and goes on to assure his readers that he is confident that they will not be deceived because they are the ones who have an "anointing" from God, and this anointing will teach them all things.

Therefore, each of John's statements of purpose is complementary to 5:13, which should be viewed as the overarching purpose statement. To be sure, each of these offers a little more specificity as to why this letter was written. John has written to encourage his readers to remain in fellowship with him, to bring himself joy as he hears that his children are walking in the truth, to exhort them to avoid sin, to get them to look to the cross when they do sin (because they are already believers), to warn them of the teachings of the secessionists, and to assure them that they will not succumb to such false teaching. Therefore, John's letter includes both encouragement and exhortation, and each ultimately serves as a means to the end that his readers might know they have eternal life.

Chapter 3

ASSURANCE GROUNDED IN THE ATONING SACRIFICE OF JESUS CHRIST

Introduction

In the previous chapter I argued that John's primary purpose behind this letter was to assure his readers that they have eternal life (5:13). This chapter will now turn and focus on the ground of such assurance. Here I will argue that even though John's pastoral concern for his readers leads him to spend most of his efforts taking them through various tests of life, he nevertheless grounds their assurance in the person and work of Jesus Christ.[1] This is evident at the outset of the letter where Jesus is displayed as the believer's "advocate" (παράκλητος) with the Father and the "propitiation" (ἱλασμός) for their sins. Given that sin is inevitable in the life of the believer (1:8,10; 2:1; cp. 5:16–17), nothing other than the work of Christ can be viewed as the foundation of assurance, for it is the only effective remedy for their sin and thus the only ground for the believer's confidence of right standing with a God who is light. Moreover, this teaching is not confined to the beginning of the letter; the writer periodically directs his readers' attention back to the cross throughout the body of his argument (3:5,8; 4:7–10; 5:5–10).[2] Finally, I will

[1] See also J. Calvin, *The First Epistle of John*, trans. John Owen, vol. 22 of *Calvin's Commentaries*, ed. D. W. Torrance and T. F. Torrance (Edinburgh: Oliver and Boyd, 1960; repr., Grand Rapids: Baker Books, 1999), 165–66, 173–75, 182, 218, 222; D. A. Carson, "Johannine Perspectives on the Doctrine of Assurance," in *Explorations: Justification and Christian Assurance*, ed. R. J. Gibson (Adelaide, South Australia: Openbook Publishers, 1996), 71–72, 82–83. B. A. du Toit, "The Role and Meaning of Statements of 'Certainty' in the Structural Composition of 1 John," *Neot* 13 (1979): 95.

[2] See also du Toit, "The Role and Meaning of Statements of 'Certainty' in the Structural Composition of 1 John," 95: "The theme of certainty and knowledge is founded in the person of Jesus Christ and the authentic apostolic testimony about him. This is the source and foundation of certainty. It *figures prominently* in the first and final main parts of the writing as a framework for the entire writing, and therefore it must be constantly kept in mind. If this basis should be removed, the entire message of salvation of the writing would fall apart" (emphasis mine). See also C. G. Kruse, *The Letters of John*, PNTC (Grand Rapids: Eerdmans, 2000), 34, who argues that the atonement is a major theme in 1 John, citing 2:2; 3:8b; 4:10; and 5:6.

conclude by arguing that this assurance is supported with the promise of the ongoing work of Christ in protecting those who have been born of God (5:18).

The Centrality of the Identity of Christ: The Foundation of the Cross (1:1–4)

The identity of the historic Jesus Christ is the starting point to understanding His work on the cross and thus one's standing with God. If the man Jesus was not also fully divine, then His death would have been no different from that of any other man crucified on a Roman cross. This is precisely the issue John expounds in the opening verses. Here his argument is double-edged. First, he makes some vital assertions about the identity of the Christ by explaining that Jesus was the Word of life, who had existed eternally with the Father. Second, he assures his readers that his words can be trusted since he had eyewitness experience of the eternal life when He was revealed to men.

The flow of thought in the first four verses is somewhat difficult to follow since the writer begins with a long complex sentence in which the main verb is not introduced until the third verse ("we proclaim"). Moreover, he begins with the object of the sentence, which is a string of four relative clauses ("What was from the beginning, what we have heard, what we have seen with our eyes, what we have beheld and our hands have touched") followed by a modifying prepositional phrase ("concerning the Word of life"), a parenthesis to further explicate the prepositional phrase (1:2), a restating of the object in truncated form ("that which we have seen and heard"), and finally the main verb. The object has been thrown forward for emphasis, since it is the object of the message that the author wants to accentuate.[3] In short, the focus of this sentence is the object, so it is vital to have a clear understanding of what the writer is proclaiming to his readers.

[3] So also G. M. Burge, *The Letters of John*, NIVAC (Grand Rapids: Zondervan, 1996), 52; J. Painter, *1, 2, and 3 John*, Sacra Pagina, vol. 18 (Collegeville, MN: Liturgical, 2002), 127; I. H. Marshall, *The Epistles of John*, NICNT (Grand Rapids: Eerdmans, 1978), 100; M. M. Thompson, *1–3 John*, The IVP New Testament Commentary (Downers Grove, IL: InterVarsity, 1992), 36.

The first of the four relative clauses that make up the object is, "what was from the beginning" (ὃ ἦν ἀπ᾽ ἀρχῆς).[4] The expression "from the beginning" (ἀπ᾽ ἀρχῆς) is used eight times in this epistle (1:1; 2:7,13–14,24 [2x]; 3:8,11), and its meaning depends on the context of the statement in each case. There is no doubt that there are instances where this phrase means something along the lines of the beginning of the proclamation of the gospel or the beginning of the readers' Christian experience (2:7,24; 3:11).[5] Nevertheless, there are other instances that do not appear to carry the same meaning. For instance, John asserts that the Devil has sinned "from the beginning" (3:8). Whatever is meant by this phrase in relation to the Devil, it is certain that it does not mean that he has only sinned from the beginning of the readers' Christian experience or the beginning of the proclamation of the gospel. Likewise, here in 1:1 as well as in 2:13–14, the writer seems to be speaking of the beginning similar to his usage in the prologue of the Gospel, thus emphasizing the eternality of Christ.[6] The key contextual clue is that he also asserts that Jesus "was with the Father" (ἦν πρὸς τὸν πατέρα) and then "revealed" (ἐφανερώθη) to us (1:2).[7] The fact that the One "who was from the beginning" was "with the Father" before being "revealed to us" in the incarnation indicates that there is more in mind here than the beginning of the proclamation. Moreover, the apparent link between the prologue of

[4] John's use of the neuter relative pronoun is best understood as a neuter of abstraction. See J. L. Boyer, "Relative Clauses in the Greek New Testament: A Statistical Study," *GTJ* 9 (1988): 247. He argues that this type of neuter relative pronoun "is frequently used of a person when he is best thought of in an abstract way." In the case of this passage, Boyer says that the neuter "may refer in an abstract way to 'all He was and did, abstract Deity.'"

[5] Some argue that this is the way each of John's usages of ἀπ᾽ ἀρχῆς in this letter should be taken as opposed to understanding it to refer to the eternality of Christ. So H. H. Wendt, "Der 'Anfang' am Beginn des 1 Johannesbriefes," *ZNW* 21 (1922): 38–42; R. A. Culpepper, *1 John, 2 John, 3 John*, Knox Preaching Guides (Atlanta: John Knox, 1985), 7; R. E. Brown, *The Epistles of John*, The Anchor Bible, vol. 30 (New York: Doubleday, 1982), 158.

[6] So H. Conzelmann, "Was von Anfang war," in *Theologie als Schriftauslegung: Aufsätze z. Neuen Testament* (München: Kaiser, 1974), 207–14; R. Schnackenburg, *The Johannine Epistles: Introduction and Commentary*, trans. R. Fuller and I. Fuller (New York: Crossroad, 1992), 57; J. Bonsirven, *Epitres de Saint Jean: Introduction, Traduction et Commentaire*, Verbum Salutis, vol. 9 (Paris: Beauchesne, 1936), 69–70; G. Delling, "ἀρχή," in *TDNT*, trans. G. W. Bromiley, ed. G. Kittle (Grand Rapids: Eerdmans, 1964), 481–82; D. L. Akin, *1, 2, 3 John*, NAC, vol. 38 (Nashville, Broadman & Holman, 2001), 51–55; Marshall, *Epistles of John*, 99–104.

[7] So also A. Plummer, *The Epistles of St. John*, Pineapple Commentaries (Cambridge: Cambridge University Press, 1886; repr., Grand Rapids: Baker, 1980), 15.

the Gospel and the prologue of this letter adds further support for this interpretation.[8] In the Gospel of John, "the beginning" refers to the time before creation, so if John is purposefully picking up on the same language,[9] then it would appear that he is once again emphasizing the eternality of Jesus the Son. If this is correct, then John begins his letter with a bold assertion about the divinity of Jesus.

The following three relative clauses go on to proclaim the validity of the writer's eyewitness experience with this One who was from the beginning.[10] First, he asserts that the One from the beginning is "that which we heard" (ὃ ἀκηκόαμεν). It is possible to argue that this statement, taken by itself, does not necessitate actual eyewitness experience but could refer to the later hearing of the message that was from the beginning of the community.[11] The context, however, stands against such an interpretation, for in the next relative clause John says, "what we have seen with our eyes" (ὃ ἑωράκαμεν τοῖς ὀφθαλμοῖς ἡμῶν), which clearly describes an eyewitness account. This is evident in that while this is the only time this expression is found in the NT, it is found 91 times in the LXX, where all but one point to a direct eyewitness experience with whatever object is said

[8] So also J. R. W. Stott, *The Letters of John*, TNTC, rev. ed. (Grand Rapids: Eerdmans, 2000), 64; Marshall, *Epistles of John*, 100–1; Akin, *1, 2, 3 John*, 51–53. Against Kruse, *Letters of John*, 51–52, who argues that it is speaking of the incarnation. Kruse does, however, state that "the echoes of the prologue of the Gospel found in this statement may imply an identity between the Word of life incarnate in Jesus Christ and the one whom the Fourth Gospel speaks of as being with God in the beginning before the foundation of the world."

[9] In the second chapter of this study, I asserted that John the son of Zebedee is the writer of both the Fourth Gospel and this epistle. If this is true, it would seem somehow odd to argue that John's reference here in the prologue of the epistle was not an allusion back the prologue of the Gospel.

[10] Of course, much of contemporary scholarship rejects the idea that such sensory language demonstrates eyewitness testimony. See especially Brown, *Epistles of John*, 158–61, who cites several ancient writers (Tacitus, *Agricola* 45; 2 Peter 1:18; Polycarp, *Philippians* 9:1; Irenaeus, *Against Heresies*, 5.1.1; Gregory Nazianzen, *Oration*, 39:1–4; Amos 2:6–16) in an attempt to prove that the language of sense perception does not necessarily express eyewitness experience. Moreover, he argues that the "we" of 1 John does not speak of eyewitness experience but a Johannine School who simply bear the tradition of the eyewitness from which their group got its start. Against such a view, see Kruse, who meticulously interacts with each of the texts cited by Brown and demonstrates that none of them support Brown's thesis that John is not providing eyewitness testimony (Kruse, *Letters of John*, 52–56).

[11] So J. M. Lieu, *The Theology of the Johannine Epistles* (Cambridge: Cambridge University Press, 1991), 23–24; Brown, *Epistles of John*, 161–62.

to have been seen.[12] Moreover, the eyewitness motif is reinforced in the next relative clause where John says, "what we have beheld and our hands have touched" (ὃ ἐθεασάμεθα καὶ αἱ χεῖρες ἡμῶν ἐψηλάφησαν). While it is unclear what nuance John intended in his use of θεάομαι ("to behold") immediately following ὁράω ("to see"), it is evident that this term typically points to eyewitness experience.[13] Outside of the three usages in this letter, θεάομαι is found in 19 other occurrences in the NT. In each instance outside of 1 John as well as the one in 1 John 4:12, there is no doubt that it denotes someone personally viewing something with his or her own eyes. Therefore, the burden of proof lies with those who argue that John's other two uses of this verb in 1:1 and 4:14[14] should be understood differently. Finally, this clause also asserts that John has not only seen Jesus, but his hands have even touched Him. While this is the only time the phrase "to touch with the hands" is used in the NT, the verb ψηλαφάω ("to touch") is used three other times; in two of them it refers to a literal touching with the hands (Luke 24:39; Heb 12:18), and in Acts 17:27 it refers to a "metaphorical sense of feeling after God."[15] Thus the phrase "and our hands have touched" is probably best understood as an actual reference to the literal touching of Jesus. Therefore, when all of the relative clauses are taken together, there is little doubt that the writer is referring to anything short of the actual eyewitness experience he and the other apostles[16] had with the One who was from the beginning.

As noted above, the four relative clauses are modified by the prepositional phrase "concerning the Word of life" (περὶ τοῦ λόγου τῆς ζωῆς). While it is somewhat difficult to determine how this phrase functions in the sentence, it is probably best to view it as modifying

[12] So also Kruse, *Letters of John*, 52.

[13] This is perhaps another allusion back to John 1, where this word was used of "beholding" the glory of Christ (1:14).

[14] In both 1:1 and 4:14, John claims to have personally seen Jesus.

[15] Kruse, *Letters of John*, 53.

[16] I interpret the writer's use of the first person plurals in these verses as his way of reminding his readers that he was a member of the group of eyewitnesses of Jesus' earthly ministry. So also Marshall, *Epistles of John*, 106–7; Stott, *Letters of John*, 61–63. Against C. H. Dodd, *The Johannine Epistles*, The Moffatt New Testament Commentary (New York: Harper and Brothers, 1946), 9–16, who argues that this language signifies the church in solidarity with the eyewitnesses.

the four preceding relative clauses. If this is correct, then all of the four relative clauses are statements in reference to "the Word of life."[17] Hence, John is proclaiming to his readers "the Word of life," that was from the beginning, that he heard, saw with his own eyes, beheld, and even touched with his own hands.

If each relative clause is in reference to "the Word of life" (τοῦ λόγου τῆς ζωῆς), then it is important to comprehend what this phrase means. Perhaps the best way forward is to begin by examining each of the words individually and then analyze how they relate to one another syntactically. While the λόγος ("word") could refer to the message of the Gospel,[18] it is probably best understood as a personal reference to Jesus. There are at least two key reasons for this interpretation. First, I have already noted the link between the prologue of 1 John and the prologue of the Gospel. In the Gospel, the "Word" is clearly a reference to Jesus, which might lead one to believe that the author was doing the same thing here unless there was compelling evidence to the contrary.[19] Second and clearly the most important evidence that the "Word" is a personal reference to Jesus is the fact that it would be odd for the writer to describe a "message" with such sensory terms as "seen with our eyes," "beheld," and "touched with our hands."[20]

What then does John mean in his use of "life" (ζωή) as a further description of the "Word" (λόγος)? To answer this question, one

[17] Dodd, *Johannine Epistles*, 3, is helpful in his assertion that "the clause 'concerning the word of life' indicates the *theme* of the announcement, and the clauses 'that which was from the beginning . . . our hands felt' state the *contents* of the announcement." See also S. S. Smalley, *1, 2, 3 John*, WBC, vol. 51 (Waco: Word Books, 1984), 6; Marshall, *Epistles of John*, 102. Of course, there are several commentators who reject this view and argue that the phrase should be viewed as summing up the relative clauses and serve as a second object to the verb ἀπαγγέλλομεν (so C. Haas, M. de Jonge, and J. L. Swellengrebel, *A Translator's Handbook on the Letters of John*, vol. 13 [London: United Bible Societies, 1972], 21, 29; Schnackenburg, *Johannine Epistles*, 60). The difference between these two interpretations is not that great, but taking the prepositional phrase with the four relative clauses seems to make the most sense of the flow of John's argument.

[18] So B. F. Westcott, *The Epistles of St. John: The Greek Text with Notes and Essays* (Grand Rapids: Eerdmans, 1955), 6–7; Culpepper, *1 John, 2 John, 3 John*, 8–9; Dodd, *Johannine Epistles*, 3–5; Brown, *Epistles of John*, 164–65.

[19] So also Haas, *Translator's Handbook* on the Letters of *John*, 29; Burge, *Letters of John*, 54; Akin, *1, 2, 3 John*, 53; Marshall, *Epistles of John*, 101.

[20] So also J. E. Weir, "The Identity of the Logos in the First Epistle of John," *ExpTim* 86 (1974–75): 118–20; K. Grayston, "'Logos' in 1 John 1," *ExpTim* 86 (1974–75): 279.

must look to the parenthetical note found in verse 2, where John further explicates this term. Here he says that "the eternal life" (τὴν ζωὴν τὴν αἰώνιον)[21] "that was with the Father" (ἥτις ἦν πρὸς τὸν πατέρα) was also "revealed to us" (καὶ ἐφανερώθη ἡμῖν). The fact that the "life" was "with the Father" and "revealed to us" indicates that the "life" should be understood as a personal reference and not simply a reference to an impersonal quality of life. Again, standing in support of this interpretation is the fact that this appears as yet another allusion to the prologue of John's Gospel where the "Word" was said to be "with God" (πρὸς τὸν θεόν [1:1–2]). In both the prologue of the Gospel and the prologue of the epistle, the "Word" (John 1:1–2; 1 John 1:1) and the "life" (John 1:4; see also 5:26; 11:25; 14:6; 17:2; 1 John 1:2) are personal references to Jesus. Hence, John is referring to Jesus as the eternal Word of life that was with the Father from the beginning and now revealed to John and the other eyewitnesses. This analysis finds confirmation in the conclusion of the letter when John asserts that Jesus Christ "is the true God and eternal life" (5:20). This passage therefore reveals that Jesus *is* eternal life or, better yet, that eternal life is embodied in Jesus Christ.[22] This is the reason John is able to say, "The one who has the Son has life" (5:11–12).

Finally, having argued that both the "Word" and the "life" are personal references to Jesus, then the best way to understand τῆς ζωῆς ("of life") is that it is in apposition to τοῦ λόγου (i.e., "the Word who is life").[23] Such a reading certainly corresponds to the understanding of "Word" and "life" explicated above. If this is correct, then the message John is proclaiming is that Jesus is the eternal Word (as in the

[21] The terms "life" and "eternal life" are used interchangeably throughout the writings of John (so also Marshall, *Epistles of John*, 103) and serve as a key theme in this letter (1:1–2; 2:25; 3:14–15; 5:11–13,16,20).

[22] This idea is supported in the Gospel of John in at least five passages (1:4; 5:26; 11:25; 14:6; 17:2).

[23] So also Schnackenburg, *Johannine Epistles*, 59; Plummer, *Epistles of St. John*, 16; D. W. Burdick, *The Letters of John the Apostle* (Chicago: Moody, 1970), 19; R. Law, *The Tests of Life: A Study of the First Epistle of John*, 3rd ed. (Edinburgh, T. & T. Clark, 1909; repr. Grand Rapids: Baker, 1968), 370. Against M. M. Culy, *I, II, III John: A Handbook on the Greek Text* (Waco: Baylor University Press, 2004), 5; K. Grayston, *The Johannine Epistles*, New Century Bible Commentary (Grand Rapids: Eerdmans, 1984), 40; F. F. Bruce, *The Epistles of John: Introduction, Exposition and Notes* (Grand Rapids: Eerdmans, 1970), 36–37.

prologue of the Gospel) as well as the embodiment of eternal life (1:2) that has been revealed to men.

In 1:3, John states that his purpose in proclaiming the eternal Word, who is life, is that his readers might have fellowship with himself and the other apostles, which is nothing short of fellowship with the Father and His Son Jesus Christ.[24] The second chapter of this study described fellowship as "a close association involving mutual interests." Thus the mutual interest or that which is held in common in this fellowship is the object of John's proclamation: the eternal Word who is life.[25] It is therefore the person and work of Jesus that is the mutual interest that John shares with his readers, uniting them with the Father and the Son. Therefore, while he will go on to further elucidate the basis of his readers' fellowship with God in the coming verses (1:5–2:2), John clearly begins his letter by asserting that one's understanding of the person of Jesus is central to the believer's fellowship with God.[26]

The Centrality of the Cross in the Believer's Fellowship with God, Who Is Light (1:5–2:2)

To be sure, 1:1–4 lays the foundation for what is said in 1:5–2:2. By the time John moves to 1:5, he has already stated that he has proclaimed the eternal Word, who is life, so that his readers might have fellowship with him, which is indeed fellowship with God. In 1:5–2:2, he now moves the argument forward by describing the basis of such fellowship. Here he contends that the only way sinners can have fellowship with God is to confess their sins and trust in the work of

[24] See chap. 2, for more detail on the two purpose statements found in 1:3–4.

[25] So also Akin, *1, 2, 3 John*, 57.

[26] So also du Toit, "The Role and Meaning of Statements of 'Certainty' in the Structural Composition of 1 John," 88–89: "It is significant that the prologue which designates the basis of certainty is converged upon the person of Jesus Christ, whom the disciples have seen, heard, and touched. Knowledge of God, and thus community with God, as well as certainty, are possible only because of and through Jesus Christ. . . . Furthermore, it can be continued only on condition that the facts are being carried forward authentically. This is the reason why reliable testimony is the guarantee for certainty. . . . [T]he prologue is of the utmost importance to the rest of the writing, because the entire theme of certainty is based upon it. The Christ-event and the apostolic testimony about it must therefore be kept in mind throughout the rest of the document."

Jesus for the forgiveness and cleansing of such sins and their right standing before God.

God Is Light (1:5)

In 1:5 the writer sets forth "the message" (ἡ ἀγγελία)[27] he heard directly from Jesus;[28] "God is light and in Him there is no darkness at all." The profundity of this statement must not be lost in its brevity, for not only does it inform the reader about the character of God, it should probably be understood as the thesis of this section (1:5–2:2), given the fact that the writer proceeds to interact on the issue of how sinful people can have fellowship with this God who is light.[29] It is therefore vital that we begin by seeking to understand what John meant when he described God as light.[30]

Light in the Old Testament. Most interpreters would agree that while there are affinities with John's use of light in the writings of the Dead Sea Scrolls,[31] as well as some of the gnostic literature,[32] the clearest background for John's use of light is found in the Old Testament.[33] Even though there are no instances where the Old Testament

[27] Law (*Tests of Life*, 56) argues, "What is asserted is that the whole purport of the Christian Revelation, from a certain point of view, may be said to be this—God is light." He points to 3:11 as a support to such a statement in that here the ἀγγελία is that "we love one another."

[28] Once again the writer points back to his eyewitness experience of Jesus to further validate the veracity of his message: "the message which we heard from Him and proclaim to you."

[29] So also Thompson, *1–3 John*, 40–41: "In many ways the statement that *God is light* is the thesis of the epistle. It includes a definition of God's character as well as implications for the life of Christian discipleship. In fact, to lay bare the relationship between the character of God as light and Christian life as 'walking in the light' is the whole point of the first part of the epistle" (emphasis hers). See also Law, *Tests of Faith*, 59; Burge, *Letters of John*, 64; Brown, *Epistles of John*, 225; Plummer, *Epistles of John*, 23; Schnackenburg, *Johannine Epistles*, 73.

[30] A number of helpful studies have been written on the light/darkness motif in ancient literature. See for example H. Conzelmann, "φῶς," in *TDNT*, 310–58; G. Strecker, *The Johannine Letters*, trans. L. M. Maloney, ed. H. Attridge, Hermeneia (Minneapolis: Fortress, 1996), 25–28; Dodd, *Johannine Epistles*, 18–19.

[31] Strecker is helpful in his assertion that while there are certainly similarities between John and Qumran in their light/darkness motif, "one should not overlook the difference: an identification of God with 'light' is absent from Qumran, as is the idea that at the center of theology must stand a revealer who mediates access to God. For this reason alone, one may not assert any dependence of the Johannine writings on the Qumran literature" (*Johannine Letters*, 26).

[32] See especially R. Bultmann, *The Johannine Epistles*, trans. R. P. O'Hara with L. C. McGaughy and R. W. Funk, ed. R. W. Funk, Hermenia (Philadelphia: Fortress, 1973), 16–17.

[33] So also Burge, *Letters of John*, 65–66; Thompson, *1–3 John*, 41; Bruce, *Epistles of John*, 40–41; Strecker, *Johannine Letters*, 26.

specifically says, "God is light" as is found in 1 John 1:5, there are nevertheless multiple passages where the metaphor of light is used for God. A brief survey of such texts demonstrates that this metaphor is flexible and varies in emphasis. Thompson is helpful here in that she has broken down the Old Testament imagery of light into three categories, namely, light as a symbol of (1) God's self-manifestation, (2) God's revelation, and (3) God's salvation.[34]

First, several passages characterize God's self-manifestation as light (Exod 3:1–6; 13:21–22; Ps 104:2,4). In these passages it is evident that such a description is an appropriate metaphor for the holiness, purity, and righteousness of God, for in these texts the metaphor of light points to the moral perfection of God.[35] Second, light is used to describe the revelation of God through the spoken or written word: "Your word is a lamp to my feet and a light to my path" (Ps 119:105; see also Pss 36:9; 43:3; 56:13; 119:130; Prov 6:23; Job 24:13; 29:3; Isa 2:5; Dan 5:11,14). Such texts demonstrate that God's written or spoken word illuminates how men should live. Finally, light is also used as a symbol for the salvation of God (Pss 18:28; 27:1; Isa 9:1; 58:8,10; 60:1,19–20). This is perhaps most clear in the book of Isaiah. In Isaiah 49:6, we see that the "Servant of the Lord" is made to be "a light of the nations." The text goes on to say that the purpose behind the servant as a light to the nations is that the salvation of the Lord may extend to the ends of the earth. Hence, the metaphor of light is frequently employed in reference to God in the Old Testament, and the context always determines how to understand the metaphor.

Light in John's Gospel. The metaphor of light is used in various ways in the Fourth Gospel as well. As might be expected in John's writings, one would be remiss in just about every occurrence of this metaphor in the Gospel to try to limit it to either one meaning or the other, given his proclivity for double entendre. A helpful example can be found in the prologue (1:4–5,9; see also 8:12; 11:9–10; 12:35–36). Here the emphasis seems to be on "light" as God's revelation of truth. Nevertheless, light could also be understood as God's salvation in this context since it is a metaphor of God's revelation of truth as

[34] Thompson, *1–3 John*, 41.
[35] See Marshall, *Epistles of John*, 109.

manifested in His Son, whom many will receive and be saved (John 1:12).[36] Moreover, it is also plausible that while the emphasis is on light as God's revelation or salvation, there could also be a moral side to the metaphor as well. Carson's argument is compelling:

> Any reader who had read through this Gospel once and was now re-reading it, could not fail to see in v.5 an anticipation of the light/darkness duality that dominates much of the rest of the book. The 'darkness' in John is not only absence of light, but positive evil (cf. 3:19; 8:12; 12:35,46; 1 Jn. 1:5,6; 2:8,9,11); the light is not only revelation bound up with creation, but with salvation. Apart from the light brought by the Messiah, the incarnate Word, people love darkness because their deeds are evil (3:19), and when the light does put in an appearance, they hate it, because they do not want their deeds to be exposed (3:20).[37]

This kind of difficulty is actually present in each of John's usages of light in the Gospel. Even though there might be an emphasis at times on light as revelation of truth, the moral element appears to be present as well. There is, however, at least one instance in the Gospel where the light metaphor is used with a clear focus on the moral side. This is found in John 3:19–21, where we read that men love darkness instead of light because their deeds are evil and that those who do evil actually hate the light. Here the relationship between light and purity on the one hand and darkness and evil on the other is explicit. Again, therefore, the metaphor of light is seen to be flexible, and the context must ultimately guide one's interpretation.

Light in 1 John 1:5. In 1 John 1:5, the first thing one should notice is that the metaphor is applied directly to God. In the Fourth Gospel, Jesus was said to be *the* light of the world (8:12; 9:5), but here, "God *is* light" (ὁ θεὸς φῶς ἐστιν). This statement therefore appears to tell us something about the nature of God. A couple of parallel statements about God are found in John's writings and are actually helpful in understanding 1:5. Elsewhere, John says, "God is love" (1 John 4:8,11) and "God is spirit" (John 4:24). In each of these "God is" statements, the predicate nominative clearly describes a quality or

[36] D. A. Carson, *The Gospel According to John*, PNTC (Grand Rapids: Eerdmans, 1991), 119.
[37] Ibid., 119–20.

something about the nature of God.[38] Perhaps it is telling that John draws moral implications in each of the "God is" statements found in the Gospel and epistles (God is spirit, John 4:24; God is light, 1 John 1:5; and God is love, 1 John 4:8,11). If God is spirit, then true believers will worship God in spirit and in truth (John 4:24). If God is love, then those born of God will love one another (3:10; 4:7). Likewise, if God is light, then those who have fellowship with God will walk in the light and avoid the darkness (1:7).[39] Thus, it would appear that the statement "God is light" should be taken ethically, which clearly fits one of the ways in which the whole light motif is used in both the Old Testament and the Gospel of John as seen above.[40]

Light is the absence of darkness. It symbolizes purity, perfection, and holiness. "God is light" is therefore best understood as synonymous with other biblical statements such as "God is holy" (Lev 11:44–45; 1 Pet 1:16).[41] This interpretation is substantiated by the context itself. John's assertion that "God is light" is immediately followed by the supporting statement, "and there is no darkness in Him at all" (καὶ σκοτία ἐν αὐτῷ οὐκ ἔστιν οὐδεμία).[42] Moreover, the next verse further demonstrates the moral emphasis of John's statement in that he asserts that anyone who makes a claim to fellowship with such a God and yet walks in the darkness is a liar (1:6). Since the remainder of the letter focuses on how one can know he is in fellowship with this God who is light, it appears that John begins with a

[38] See D. B. Wallace, *Greek Grammar Beyond the Basics: An Exegetical Syntax of the New Testament with Scripture, Subject, and Greek Word Indexes* (Grand Rapids: Zondervan, 1996), 45.

[39] So also Westcott, *Epistles of St. John*, 17; Brown, *Epistles of John*, 230.

[40] So also S. A. Hunt, "Light and Darkness," in *The Dictionary of the Latter New Testament and Its Development*, ed. Ralph P. Martin and Peter H. Davids (Downers Grove, IL: InterVarsity, 1997), 657–59; G. L. Borchert, "Light," in *New Dictionary of Biblical Theology: Exploring Unity and Diversity of Scripture*, ed. T. D. Alexander, Brian S. Rosner, D. A. Carson, and Graeme Goldsworthy (Downers Grove, IL: InterVarsity, 2000), 645.

[41] So also Schnackenburg, *Johannine Epistles*, 73: "The author of John uses the term 'light' to speak of the reality of God—not, however, in the sense of revelation, but in the sense of his heavenly fullness of being and moral holiness." So also A. E. Brooke, *The Johannine Epistles*, ICC (Edinburgh: T. & T. Clark, 1912, 1976), 12; Plummer, *Epistles of John*, 23; Westcott, *Epistles of St. John*, 17; Thompson, *1–3 John*, 42–43; Marshall, *Epistles of John*, 109; Stott, *Letters of John*, 76–77; Smalley, *1, 2, 3 John*, 20. Against Akin, *1, 2, 3 John*, 62–71; Law, *Tests of Life*, 60, who argue that God as light signifies that the divine nature is "self-revealing."

[42] Note the emphatic double negative in this verse (καὶ σκοτία ἐν αὐτῷ οὐκ ἔστιν οὐδεμία) employed to highlight the fact that there is absolutely no darkness in God.

message about God precisely because his focus is on how sinners can have fellowship with a God who is completely holy. Therefore, John's purpose was not to enhance one's doctrine of God but to point to His nature and character in order to help his readers understand the basis for their assurance of fellowship with a holy God.[43]

Fellowship with the God Who Is Light

After establishing the fact that God is perfectly holy (φῶς), the writer focuses his attention on how individuals can have fellowship with such a God. This is accomplished by three pairs of alternating third-class conditional sentences found in 1:6–2:2[44] that should probably be viewed as inferential to 1:5. They alternate in that each pair begins with a negative statement of how not to have fellowship with God followed by a positive proclamation of how such fellowship is to be attained. It is plausible that all of the negative examples were either real statements of the secessionists or a summary of some of their teachings.[45] In each instance John provides a claim of the secessionists in the protasis ("if" clause) followed by the apodosis ("then" clause), where the claim is demonstrated to be fraudulent. Following each of the negative conditional sentences, the reader finds a positive example of what true fellowship with God actually looks like. This interplay between negative and positive is extremely helpful for our purposes since it illuminates how one does and does not have fellowship with God and therefore serves to bolster the confidence of the one who walks in the light.

As one reads through these alternating pairs of conditional sentences, it becomes obvious that the negative examples are parallel to one another as are the positive examples. Moreover, it would

[43] See Dodd, *Johannine Epistles,* 19; Hunt, "Light and Darkness," 657; Conzelmann, "φῶς," 354; Marshall, *Epistles of John,* 108.

[44] For others who view 1:5–2:2 as a single unit with three sets of antithetical claims, see E. Malatesta, *Interiority and Covenant: A Study of* εἶναι ἐν *and* μένειν ἐν *in the First Letter of Saint John,* Analecta Biblica 69 (Rome: Biblical Institute, 1978), 95; Bonsirven, *Epitres de Saint Jean,* 83–84; Brown, *Epistles of John,* 224; Marshall, *Epistles of John,* 108; Stott, *Letters of John,* 75. Against J. C. O'Neil, *The Puzzle of 1 John: A New Examination of Origins* (London: S.P.C.K., 1966), 13–15; Westcott, *Epistles of St. John,* 14; Brooke, *Johannine Epistles,* 10–11, who all argue that 2:1 should be seen as a break in the pattern and thus, the beginning of a new section.

[45] So also Kruse, *Letters of John,* 62; Thompson, *1–3 John,* 44.

also appear that there is a heightening of emphasis with each of the negative examples given. It is therefore advantageous to examine the negative examples together followed by the positives. Moreover, examining the negatives and positives separately will enable a better understanding of what John is referring to when he speaks of walking in the darkness (1:6) and walking in the light (1:7).

Negative examples. The first negative example is found in 1:6. As noted above, I take each of these conditional sentences to be inferential to the thesis statement found in 1:5. Hence, *precisely because* God is light and there is no darkness in Him, those who make a claim to have fellowship with Him[46] while walking in darkness are liars and do not do the truth. John is unambiguous in his assertion that people cannot have fellowship with a holy God when they themselves are living in the sphere of moral darkness. The word περιπατέω ("to walk") denotes more than a simple moral lapse but actually refers to the lifestyle of the individual.[47] Hence the protasis of this sentence points to those who are making claims to fellowship while seemingly having little concern with the way they live their lives.

John goes on to assert that if the protasis is true of an individual, then he is guilty of two things.[48] First, since there is absolutely no fellowship between light and darkness, such an individual is a liar, for his lifestyle does not support his claim. Second, these individuals are not only liars but have failed to "do the truth." The expression "do the truth" (ποιέω + ἀλήθεια) occurs in the Hebrew Old Testament at 2 Chronicles 31:20 and Nehemiah 9:33.[49] In the first

[46] See chap. 2, where I argued that fellowship with God is synonymous with knowing God and abiding in God.

[47] The word περιπατέω has a continual aspect in and of itself and can be translated "to walk," "to go about," "conduct one's life," "behave," or "live" (so W. Bauer, *A Greek—English Lexicon of the New Testament and Other Early Christian Literature*, trans. W. F. Arndt and F. W. Gingrich, 3rd ed., rev. and ed. F. W. Danker [Chicago: University of Chicago Press, 2000], s.v. "περιπατέω" [BDAG]). It is actually a popular Jewish metaphor for the way people live their life whether positively or negatively (e.g., Pss 1:1; 15:2; 56:13; 82:5; Job 29:3; Eccl 2:14; Isa 2:5; 9:2 [see Brown, *Epistles of John*, 197]). Therefore, the lexeme itself coupled with John's choice of the present tense calls for a durative understanding here (so also G. S. Ebel, *NIDNTT*, s.v. "περιπατέω"; Smalley, *1, 2, 3 John*, 23; Brooke, *Johannine Epistles*, 15).

[48] Note the double apodosis in each of the negative examples.

[49] To "do the truth" is actually a little more common in the LXX but has roughly the same range of meaning as in the Hebrew Old Testament (see Gen 32:10; 47:29; Isa 26:10).

instance it refers to Hezekiah's doing truth in relation to following the Law, and in the second it speaks of God's faithfulness in all His ways. To "do the truth" is a common phrase in both the Hebrew Qumran literature (1QS 1:5; 5:3; 8:1–2; 1QpHab 7:10–11) and some of the Greek intertestamental works (Tob 4:6; 13:6; *T. Reub.* 6:9; *T Benj.* 10:3). Here to "do the truth" often refers to one of the virtues to be done but is commonly "colored by the view that what is found in the law (or in the interpretation of it) is truth."[50] Similarly, in Johannine thought, the truth refers not to the revelation in the Law but the revelation that comes in and through Jesus, who is the embodiment of truth.[51] Moreover, each of the nine occurrences of "truth" (ἀλήθεια) in 1 John (1:6,8; 2:4,21; 3:18,19; 4:6; 5:6) appears to be a reference to the truth that comes through the revelation in Christ. If this is correct, then the secessionists are liars because their claim to have fellowship with God does not match their lifestyle and they fail to do the truth as found in the revelation of Jesus Christ.[52]

The second negative example is found in verse 8. Here it would appear that John is once again quoting either a false claim or a synopsis of a false claim of the secessionists in the protasis. The claim is literally "to have no sin" (ἁμαρτίαν οὐκ ἔχομεν), which appears to be referring to a *state* in which the false teachers are claiming to live. That this is true is supported by an examination of the many other phrases where John employs the verb ἔχω ("to have") to govern an abstract noun. These include the instances where this verb is used with "fellowship" (1:3,6,7), "confidence" (2:28; 3:21; 4:17), "hope" (3:3), "life" (3:15; 5:12–13), "love" (4:16; John 5:42; 13:35; 15:13),

[50] Brown, *Epistles of John*, 200: "This is implied in 1QpHab 7:10–11: 'The men of truth, those who do the Law'; and it is explicit in 1QS 8:1–2, which speaks of the community officers as 'perfectly knowledgeable in all that is revealed of the Law in order to do truth.' In *T. Benj* 10:3 there is the instruction 'to do the truth, each one to his neighbor, and to keep the Law of the Lord and His commandments.'"

[51] For an extensive defense of this view, see I. de la Potterie, *La verite dans Saint Jean*, vol. 2, Analecta Biblica 73–74 (Rome: Biblical Institute, 1977), 479–535. So also Burge, *Letters of John*, 68–69; D. Rensberger, *1 John, 2 John, 3 John*, Abingdon New Testament Commentaries (Nashville: Abingdon, 1997), 52; Brown, *Epistles of John*, 199. Against Bultmann, *Johannine Epistles*, 19, who argues for a Greek background for John's use of ἀλήθεια.

[52] If we take into account the rest of the context of this section, it is possible that the ἀλήθεια that these individuals fail to do is the truth of trusting in the cross-work of Christ.

"joy" (3 John 4; John 17:13), and "peace" (John 16:33).[53] Each refers to being in a particular state (e.g., state of fellowship, confidence, hope, etc.). The particular phrase "to have sin" (ἔχω + ἁμαρτία) is found only in the Johannine literature (four occurrences in the Gospel and one in the epistles). The usages of this phrase in the Gospel (9:41; 15:22,24; 19:11) are helpful, for in each instance it carries the meaning of being in a state of guiltiness for one's sins.[54] If we allow this evidence to aid our understanding here at 1:8, then the claim of the secessionists appears to be that they are not in a *state* of guiltiness for their sins. In other words, whatever their conduct might appear to be on the outside, there is really no inherent sin in their nature, so they are without guilt.[55] Hence, they are able to claim that they "have no sin." Such a claim is probably the result of their proto-gnostic understanding of how one enters into fellowship with God. For them, being right with God is found by way of "knowledge," and therefore sin is not the major problem but rather ignorance or lack of knowledge.[56] It is plausible they believed that those who were enlightened with this special knowledge and anointing from God experienced an eradication of the sin nature, and they claimed this form of sinlessness as a result.[57] Perhaps their dualistic understanding of light and darkness that led them to believe that since God is light, those who are His children (3:1–2) are children of light and are therefore completely pure

[53] See Brown, *Epistles of John*, 205, for a helpful discussion on this point.

[54] Ibid., 205–6: "The expression 'have sin' occurs four times in GJohn (9:41; 15:22,24; 19:11), always in a situation in which a wrong action has already been committed or there is a wrong attitude already existing, and in which something further has occurred to underline the evil of that action. . . . In 1 John 1:8, which is the only instance of 'have sin' in the Epistles, the meaning seems to be the same. The author is warning people who have sinned that they cannot claim, 'we are free from the guilt of sin.'" So also G. B. Christie, "An Interpretive Study of 1 John 1:9" (Th.M. thesis, Dallas Theological Seminary, 1975), 45.

[55] So also Stott, *Letters of John*, 82.

[56] See Carson, "Johannine Perspectives on the Doctrine of Assurance," 69.

[57] So also Dodd, *Johannine Epistles*, 21–22: "The heretics (if we may read between the lines, with the support of what is known about 'Gnostic' teaching) take their stand upon the belief that Christians have been given a new nature superior to that of other men. Consequently, they affirm, Christians are already sinless beings; or if not all Christians, at least those who have attained to superior enlightenment. They have no further need for moral striving: they are already perfect. Indeed, some appear to have held that if the enlightened do things which in other men would be counted sinful, they are not sinners. Their mystical communion with God in itself removes from them the category of sinful men."

and righteous and reflect the character of God. In that sense they have a share in God's state of purity.[58]

John, however, forbids such thinking. Not only has he shown them to be liars and those who do not do the truth in 1:6; he now further asserts that they have deceived themselves and the truth is not in them. The apodoses of 1:6 and 1:8 are closely linked, but the wording is heightened in 1:8. Not only are they deliberate liars (1:6); they are actually self-deceived (1:8). The verb πλανάω ("to deceive") is used two other times in 1 John (2:26; 3:7) and the noun πλάνη ("deceit") is used once (4:6). The context is identical in each occurrence. In 2:26 and 3:7, John warns his readers concerning those who are trying to deceive them. Even when the noun is employed, it is in the context of offering criteria by which to discern the spirit of truth and the spirit of deceit. Hence, John argues that these people are not only attempting to deceive his readers but have actually deceived themselves. Likewise, he goes on to assert that they have not only failed to "do the truth" (1:6), but the truth has no place in them. In other words, they have completely missed the truth that has been revealed by Christ, as ultimately made evident in their rejection of their need for His work on the cross.

Finally, the third negative example shares much in common with the second. Here again there is a claim in the protasis to be free from sin (οὐχ ἡμαρτήκαμεν). While much time and effort have gone into various attempts to understand the different nuances that John might have intended in 1:8 and 1:10,[59] these two statements are probably virtually synonymous.[60] John is constantly saying the same thing in different ways, and here it is no different. The one who denies he is a sinner not only lies (1:6) and deceives himself (1:8) but also makes

[58] See Thompson, *1–3 John*, 46–47.

[59] Some argue that v. 8 refers to a principle of sin and v. 10 refers to sinful actions (so Brooke, *Johannine Epistles*, 17; Smalley, *1, 2, 3 John*, 29, 33; Haas, *Translator's Handbook on the Letters of John*, 32, 39; Stott, *Letters of John*, 82–84). Another position is offered by Brown, who argues that v. 8 refers to the guilt incurred by sin and v. 10 refers to the actual acts of sin (Brown, *Epistles of John*, 204–5; 211–12).

[60] So also Marshall, *Epistles of John*, 115; Dodd, *Johannine Epistles*, 22–23; Grayston, *Johannine Epistles*, 52; Akin, *1, 2, 3 John*, 74; Thompson, *1–3 John*, 46–47; Schnackenburg, *The Johannine Epistles*, 84 n. 56; Kruse, *Letters of John*, 66–70.

God a liar.[61] Here the writer makes his strongest argument against the false teachers. It is bad enough to lie (1:6); it is worse to deceive oneself to the point where the truth completely disappears (1:8), and yet nothing could be more despicable than calling God Himself a liar, which is what the secessionists ultimately did.[62] The denial that they have sinned makes God a liar precisely because it completely rejects both the biblical truth that all men are sinners before God (see 1 Kgs 8:48; Ps 14:3; Job 4:17; 15:14–16; Prov 20:9; Eccl 7:20; Isa 53:6; 64:6) and His provision of Christ's atoning sacrifice for their sins.[63]

Moreover, there is also a possible heightening of the charges against the heretics in the second portion of the apodosis. In 1:8 John said that the truth was not in them. Here in 1:10, we are told that "the word" (ὁ λόγος) is not in them. The question, then, is what does John mean in his use of "the word" in this context? With the understanding espoused above that the "truth" in 1 John is the truth of God as revealed through Christ, it would appear that we have at least three options. First it is possible that John is referring to the spoken word of Christ, for we saw at the beginning of this section that he is conveying the very message (1:5) he heard from Him. Second, it is also possible that John is speaking about the written words of Christ. Given the understanding proposed above that the Gospel was written prior to the epistles, it is probable that John's readers were familiar with at least the Fourth Gospel and possibly some of the other Gospels as well. Hence, "the word" could be understood as the words of Christ as found in the written Gospel(s). Finally, it is possible that John is referring to Christ Himself in his use of "the word,"[64] where indeed truth is embodied. Such an interpretation is possibly supported by the fact that John has already referred to Jesus as "the Word, who is life" (τοῦ λόγου τῆς ζωῆς) (1:1–2). Perhaps a distinction between these three should not be forced here, given that

[61] Context indicates that αὐτὸν refers to God the Father. God is the One who is light (1:5). The secessionists made claims to fellowship with God. There is nothing in this context that would indicate that anyone else would be in view in the writer's use of αὐτὸν here.

[62] See Brown, *Epistles of John*, 231.

[63] So also Thompson, *1–3 John*, 48.

[64] John's use of λόγος in the prologue of the Gospel as well as this epistle adds plausibility to this idea. See above for a defense of ὁ λόγος as a personal reference to Christ in this letter.

Jesus is the eternal Word and the embodiment of truth. Regardless, those who deny that they have sinned do not have "the word" of God in them at all.

Positive examples. Interspersed with the three negative examples are three positive examples of what fellowship with God does in fact look like. As with the negatives each positive example is phrased in the form of a conditional sentence. The first is found in 1:7 where John informs his readers that if they walk in the light they not only have fellowship with one another but can also trust that the blood of Jesus cleanses them from every sin. As in 1:6, the verb περιπατέω ("to walk") signifies the lifestyle of the individual. Therefore, the protasis of this example describes one whose manner of life is conducted in the light in the same way that God is in the light.[65]

There are two positive consequences for those who walk in the light. First, they have fellowship with one another, which actually comes as a bit of a surprise in that one might have expected the writer to say they have fellowship with God[66] since this is the claim made by the secessionists in 1:6. Nevertheless, readers of this letter have already seen in the flow of John's argumentation that fellowship with one another is in fact fellowship with God (1:3).[67] In other words, the writer understands these two to be inextricably tied together so that the one who walks in the light enjoys fellowship with other believers, which is nothing short of fellowship with the Father and the Son. In fact John contends throughout the remainder of the letter that there

[65] I take αὐτός here to be the ὁ θεὸς of v. 5. This is somewhat difficult, since in 1:5 God is light and here He is said to be in the light. Notwithstanding, the context never gives any indication that someone else is in view other than the God who is light. John's imagery is flexible and can certainly refer to God as light and being in the light. Haas (*Translator's Handbook on the Letters of John*, 35) asserts, "[O]ne should bear in mind that John does not intend to give logical definitions but is hinting at aspects of a reality that by definition is undefinable" (see also Smalley, *1, 2, 3 John*, 23).

[66] An evaluation of the critical apparatus in Nestle Aland, 27th ed., indicates that some of the scribes struggled with this phrase, as seen by the textual variant where the more expected ἀυτοῦ has been inserted (so A^{vid}, t, w, vgmss; Tert, Cl, Hier). Clearly ἀλλήλων ("one another") is the best attested reading externally and has the most in its favor internally, given that it is the more difficult reading and yet makes good sense within the context (1:3).

[67] See chap. 2.

is no such thing as genuine fellowship with God that does not include fellowship with the brethren.[68]

The second consequence for those who walk in the light is that the blood of Jesus cleanses them from every sin. Immediately readers are confronted with the fact that walking in the light is not a synonym for walking in perfection. In actuality, it would appear that when an individual does walk "in the light" he becomes all the more aware of his own sin and imperfection and must therefore trust in the blood of Jesus for the "cleansing" (καθαρίζει) of every sin.[69] This thought is vital to John's argument and one's understanding of walking in the light, for it is the dominant theme that permeates each of the positive examples of fellowship with God. On the one hand, John is adamant that those who have fellowship with God have a changed life as seen in his description that they walk in the same sphere God walks (i.e., in the light). On the other hand, it is assumed that walking in the light includes sin and that those who walk in the light do not deny their sin like the heretics (1:8,10) but look to the cross-work of Christ for the cleansing thereof.[70] *Only* through the blood of Jesus can individuals find cleansing of sin and continue to walk in the light.

The second positive example is closely tied to the first. Again in 1:9, the atoning work of Christ on the cross is the preeminent focus. Over and against the false claim of being sinless (1:8), it is actually those who confess their sins before God that are in right standing with Him. Those who confess[71] their sins find that God is both "faithful" and "just" to forgive their sins and cleanse them of all unrighteousness. The two coordinate adjectives chosen to speak of God must not

[68] See the numerous tests of love throughout this letter.

[69] Smalley is correct when he says, "The 'blood' of Jesus occupies an important place in NT thought, and must be interpreted above all against the specific background of the cultic observances on the Day of Atonement (Lev 16; but cf. also the Passover story and ritual, Exod 12). In his suffering and death, the NT writers claim, Jesus in perfect obedience offered the *true* and lasting sacrifice for sin (cf. Rom 3:25; Heb 9:12–14; 10:19–22; Rev 1:5; also 1 Cor 5:7). Thus to say here that the blood of Jesus 'purifies us from every sin' means that in the cross of Christ our sin is effectively and repeatedly (καθαρίσῃ, 'purifies,' is a continuous present) removed; although John does not explain how this happens" (*1, 2, 3 John*, 25).

[70] So also Schnackenburg, *Johannine Epistles*, 79.

[71] The context as well as John's use of the present tense verb would seem to indicate that the confession of sins is an ongoing activity for the believer.

be missed, for they are essential to understanding how forgiveness and cleansing are possible with a God who is light.

First, John asserts that God is "faithful" (πιστός). Three other places in the New Testament refer to God in this way (1 Cor 1:9; 10:13; 2 Cor 1:18). Each of these speaks of God's faithfulness in various ways including His faithfulness in confirming His own to the end and presenting them blameless on the Day of the Lord Jesus (1 Cor 1:8–9), not allowing any temptation to overcome them, but providing a way of escape in order that they might endure (1 Cor 1:13), and being faithful to fulfill His promises, which are all "yes" in Christ (2 Cor 1:18).[72] With the context of this passage referring to the believer's forgiveness and cleansing of sin, God's faithfulness here is best understood as a reference to His faithfulness in forgiving sins. This would certainly fit the Old Testament theme that God is faithful to His covenant promise to forgive His people (Jer 31:34; Mic 7:18–20) and cleanse them of all unrighteousness (Ezek 36:25).[73] Throughout the Old Testament there are quotations and allusions back to the quintessential promise of God to forgive His people found in Exodus 34:6–7:

> The Lord, the Lord God, compassionate and gracious, slow to anger, and abounding in lovingkindness and truth; who keeps lovingkindness for thousands, who forgives iniquity, transgression and sin; yet He will by no means leave the guilty unpunished, visiting the iniquity of fathers on the children and on the grandchildren to the third and fourth generations

(see Num 14:18; Neh 9:17; Pss 86:15; 103:8; 145:8; Dan 9:9; Joel 2:13; Jonah 4:2; Nah 1:3; Sir 2:1; 1 QH 6:8–9).[74] It is probably best then to understand John's use of πιστός here as reference to God's faithfulness to His covenant promises to forgive and cleanse His people, which ultimately finds its fulfillment in and through the work of Jesus on the cross.

Interestingly, in Exodus 34:7, God is shown as both gracious to forgive and resolute that the guilty not go unpunished. Here too, John

[72] So also Kruse, *Letters of John*, 69.

[73] So also Smalley, *1, 2, 3 John*, 31; Stott, *Letters of John*, 82–83; Schnackenburg, *Johannine Epistles*, 83

[74] See J. Lieu, "What Was from the Beginning: Scripture and Tradition in the Johannine Epistles," *NTS* 39 (1993): 461–67, who argues that 1 John 1:9 reflects the influence of Exod 34:6 and the numerous quotations and allusions.

is interacting along the same lines in his assertion that God is not only "faithful" to His promises to forgive but also "righteous." The word *righteous* (δίκαιος) is found in five other occurrences in this letter (2:1,29; 3:7 [2X]; 3:12). In each of these instances, the word refers to acting in a righteous manner.[75] Of course, the question that surfaces is, How can God be acting righteously in failing to punish sinners? The answer is found both in 1:7 where John says that the blood of Jesus is the way in which sins are dealt with and in 2:1–2 where he says that "Jesus Christ the righteous One" (Ἰησοῦν Χριστὸν δίκαιον) is the "propitiation" (ἱλασμός) for all sins. Therefore, while phrased differently, it would appear that John is arguing along similar lines as Paul in Romans 3:21–26, where God is shown to be both the just and the justifier. Here God is both faithful to His covenant promises to forgive sinners and being righteous in punishing sin. The only way both can be true simultaneously is in the cross of Christ where His covenant promises to forgive and cleanse His people are fulfilled and His righteous punishment of sin is exacted.

The result[76] of God's being both faithful and righteous is that sins are forgiven and all unrighteousness is cleansed.[77] The verb ἀφίημι ("to forgive") is a forensic term that literally means "to release" or "let go"[78] and is often used in reference to debt or trespass (see Luke 7:43).[79] Thus, through the blood of Christ our sins are completely "let go" or "released" from God's accounting. Furthermore, the verb καθαρίζω carries the meaning "to cleanse" or "to purify,"[80] which appears to nuance the idea of forgiveness. Marshall notes that "to

[75] See Kruse, *Letters of John*, 70.

[76] I take the ἵνα plus the subjunctive ἀφῇ as a result here.

[77] Note the play on words between God's "righteousness" (δίκαιος) and the cleansing of our "unrighteousness" (ἀδικίας). Moreover, two verses later we are told that Jesus is the "righteous One" (δίκαιον). Smalley is insightful here when he says, "Therefore, on the basis of his own righteousness, manifested above all in the righteous act of the cross (cf. v 2), Jesus is supremely able to ask for that righteousness to be *extended to all God's children* who are in fellowship with him. On that ground, also, God (who is himself 'righteous,' v 9a) can 'purify us of every kind of *un*righteousness' (v 9b; cf. Rom 3:26)" (Smalley, *1, 2, 3 John*, 37–38).

[78] BDAG, s.v. "ἀφίημι."

[79] See Brown, *Epistles of John*, 211, who notes that "in the LXX it appears in a cultic setting as well: 'The priest will make atonement for sin, and the sin will be forgiven' (Lev 4:20; 19:22). A covenant setting is apparent in Num 14:19: 'Forgive the sin of your people according to the abundance of your covenant mercy.'"

[80] BDAG, s.v. "καθαρίζω."

purify is to remove the defiling effects of sin, either by the avoidance of sinful acts (2 Cor 7:1; Jas 4:8) or by the pardon of sins already committed (Eph 5:26; Heb 1:3; 10:2). The thought here is primarily of pardon through Christ's atoning blood, but the fact that John speaks of *both* forgiveness *and* cleansing may suggest that he is also thinking of the destruction of sinful desires which defile us in God's sight."[81] Therefore, the interplay set up by the author between 1:8 and 1:9 presents the reader with a great paradox. The false teachers made claims regarding fellowship with God and sinlessness, yet they are actually shown to be self-deceived, while John's readers confess their sins and actually become as sinless in God's sight as a result of His forgiveness/cleansing, and thus they enjoy fellowship with Him.

Finally, the third and most comprehensive of the positive statements is found in 2:1–2. Not only is this example parallel to the first two, but it further explicates the teaching found in both of them. Having just stated that all who claim to be free from sin (1:8,10) are liars and deceive themselves, John now turns and asserts that he is not giving license to sin (2:1).[82] Nevertheless, he understands that sin is a real possibility for believers and contends that it must be taken seriously and dealt with through the work of Jesus. Hence, immediately following the statement that he has written so his readers will not sin, he adds a coordinating conjunction and asserts that if anyone does sin, Jesus Christ, the righteous One, is their advocate with the Father (2:1b).

The word translated "advocate" (παράκλητος) is found in the New Testament exclusively in the Johannine literature (John 14:16,26; 15:26; 16:7; 1 John 2:1) and is completely absent from the LXX. This limited usage makes it somewhat difficult to understand the meaning of the word. Deissmann examines the New Testament passages where παράκλητος is used and concludes that it refers to an advocate speaking on behalf of one who is accused of something.[83]

[81] Marshall, *Epistles of John*, 114 n. 14. See also Calvin, *The First Epistle of John*, 241; Westcott, *Epistles of St. John*, 25; Smalley, *1, 2, 3 John*, 32.

[82] So Calvin, *The First Epistle of John*, 170; Grayston, *The Johannine Epistles*, 56; Brooke, *Johannine Epistles*, 22–23; Schnackenburg, *The Johannine Epistles*, 85; Marshall, *Epistles of John*, 116; Stott, *The Letters of John*, 84.

[83] A. Deissmann, *Light from the Ancient Near East: The New Testament Illustrated by Recently Discovered Texts of the Graeco-Roman World* (London: Hodder and Stoughton, 1927), 336–37.

More recently, debate has stirred as to whether this is a technical term derived from a legal context or a more general term that can be used in legal contexts.[84] Grayston, in his helpful article, "The Meaning of Parakletos," is probably correct in his assertion that "*parakletos* was a word of general meaning which could appear in legal contexts, and when it did the *parakletos* was a supporter or sponsor."[85] In his discussion on this passage, he argues that it is used in a legal context and

> corresponds to the situation described by Philo where a person who had displeased the emperor needs a sponsor to propitiate him. In John's teaching, when a Christian has sinned the Father observes that the sinner is sponsored by Christ, and is persuaded not to reject him and withdraw his truth.[86]

Such an explanation fits the context of this passage and is right at home elsewhere in the biblical witness, where the idea of an advocate is present even when the word itself is not employed.[87] As always, context must guide our interpretation and here the context is dealing with a sinner in need of outside help ("and if someone sins"). In the midst of such sin, there is need for another to intercede before a holy God. Since sinners are unable to plead for themselves, they are in need of a "righteous" advocate to plead with the "righteous" Father on their behalf. Jesus is therefore the only One capable of serving in such a role. Moreover, John's use of πρὸς ("with") here harkens back to John 1:1 where the eternal Word was said to be "with God" (πρὸς τὸν θεόν) and 1 John 1:2, where eternal life was said to be "with the Father" (πρὸς τὸν πατέρα). Here then it is clear that Jesus Christ, the advocate, is literally in the presence of the Father pleading on behalf of sinners.

The fact that Jesus is referred to as "righteous" (δίκαιος) provides further insight as to why He is able to stand as the "advocate" before the Father. In 1:9, God was said to be "righteous" (δίκαιος) and the

[84] Some who see this as a technical term include Behm, "παράκλητος," in *TDNT*, 800–14; H. G. Liddell and R. Scott, *A Greek-English Lexicon*, 9th ed., rev. H. S. Jones and P. G. W. Glare (Oxford: Clarendon, 1996), s.v. "παράκλητος"; Law, *Tests of Life*, 168; Westcott, *Epistles of St. John*, 42–43.

[85] K. Grayston, "The Meaning of *PARAKLETOS*," *JSNT* 13 (1981): 75. So also Strecker, *Johannine Letters*, 36–39; Akin, *1, 2, 3 John*, 77–80; Kruse, *Letters of John*, 72–73.

[86] Grayston, "The Meaning of *PARAKLETOS*," 80.

[87] E.g., Matt 10:32; Rom 8:26,34; Heb 7:25. See also Exod 32:30–32, where Moses intercedes for the people of Israel and Job 42:7–10, where Job intercedes for his friends.

One who cleanses His people from all "unrighteousness" (ἀδικίας). Jesus is able to stand as our "advocate" before the "righteous" Father precisely because He Himself is "righteous." As noted above, the word *righteous* (δίκαιος) is found in five other occurrences in this letter (2:1,29; 3:7 [2X]; 3:12) and refers in each case to one's acting in a righteous manner. This word, then, is used in reference to Jesus in order to demonstrate that He is the righteous One, who has no sins of His own and is therefore the only One who can stand in the presence of the righteous Father and intercede for those who have not acted righteously.[88] "He can, as it were, plead his own righteousness before God and ask that sinners be forgiven on the basis of his righteous act."[89]

In 2:2, John moves the discussion forward by pointing back to the reason Jesus is able to stand as our "advocate"; namely, because He is the "propitiation" (ἱλασμός) for our sins.[90] The word ἱλασμός occurs only here and at 4:10 in the New Testament, and there is considerable debate as to whether it (as well as the entire ἱλάσκομαι word group in both the LXX and New Testament) should be understood as denoting "expiation"[91] or "propitiation."[92] Since there are places in

[88] So also Kruse, *Letters of John*, 73; Smalley, *1, 2, 3 John*, 37–38.

[89] Marshall, *Epistles of John*, 117. Schnackenburg (*Johannine Epistles*, 86–87) is probably correct in his assertion that Jesus' role of high priest stands behind this verse. "The whole picture is strikingly reminiscent of Heb. 7:25. The high priest, who is 'holy, blameless, undefiled, separated from sinners,' has offered himself once and for all and now lives forever to be the advocate of those who 'by him draw near to God.' . . . In addition to the idea of God as faithful and merciful (1:9), we now have Jesus Christ as the priestly advocate and mediator. He relieves the faithful of all their anxiety about their salvation, now once more endangered by sin, and he assures them that in spite of their weakness they can draw near to the throne of grace (Heb. 4:16; 10:19ff.)."

[90] See Strecker, *Johannine Letters*, 39; Akin, *1, 2, 3 John*, 82; Schnackenburg, *Johannine Epistles*, 86; Marshall, *Epistles of John*, 117; Westcott, *Epistles of St. John*, 44.

[91] It is beyond the scope of this study to rehearse all of the arguments on both sides on this issue. For a clear argument in favor of "expiation" as the meaning, see C. H. Dodd's influential work "Hilaskesthai: Its Cognates, Derivatives, and Synonyms in the Septuagint," *JTS* 32 (1931): 352–60. Dodd surveys the entire ἱλάσκομαι word group and argues that in both the LXX and the New Testament, God should not be viewed as the object of a sin offering and thus His wrath propitiated but should instead be viewed as the subject of the action where He removes the defilement of sin or "expiates" it. It is also evident that most who argue for this view either minimize or completely reject the idea of the personal wrath of God towards sinners. For others who fall into this category, see Westcott, *Epistles of St. John*, 87; Brooke, *Epistles of John*, 28; T. C. G. Thorton, "Propitiation or Expiation?" *ExpTim* 80 (1968–69): 54–55.

[92] For an excellent defense of "propitiation" as the primary meaning here, readers should consult L. Morris's excellent book, *The Apostolic Preaching of the Cross*, rev. ed. (Grand Rapids:

the LXX where this word might mean either expiation or propitiation, the context must determine the meaning.

The context of 1:5–2:2 as well as that of 4:10 points toward the idea that the death of Jesus on the cross propitiates the righteous wrath of God.[93] To begin with, the writer of this letter asserts that there will be a final "day of judgment," where he hopes his readers will be able to stand without fear (4:17–18). At the very least, the wrath of God is implicit when referring to a final day of judgment, given that fear is involved for those not abiding in God (4:15–18). Moreover, within the specific context of 1:5–2:2, there are several indicators that propitiation is the best translation. In 1:7, John asserts that the blood of Jesus cleanses us from every sin. Of course those who argue against the idea of Jesus' death propitiating God's wrath look to this verse as a support for their argument that John is speaking only of expiation.[94] This notwithstanding, Morris is helpful when he ponders the question, "Why should sin be expiated?"

> What would be the consequences to man if there were no expiation?' . . . It seems evident on the scriptural view that if sin is not expiated, if men "die in their sins," then they have the divine displeasure to face, and this is but another way of saying that the wrath of God abides upon them. It seems that expiation is necessary in order to avert the wrath of God, so that nothing seems to be gained by abandoning the concept of propitiation.[95]

Moreover, in 1:9 God is said to be both faithful to His covenant promises to forgive His people and righteous in all His actions. Above the question was asked, "How can God be completely righteous if He allows the guilty to go free?" The answer again points to the idea

Eerdmans, 1965), 144–213. Here Morris convincingly argues that God does have wrath toward sinners and it is in the cross-work of Christ that God's wrath is placated or "propitiated." It should also be noted that the majority of those who argue for propitiation as the primary meaning here argue for both the propitiation of God's wrath and the expiation of sins as two sides of the same coin. For others that argue for propitiation, see D. Hill, *Greek Words and Hebrew Meanings: Studies in the Semantics of Soteriological Terms* (Cambridge: Cambridge University Press, 1967), 37–38; R. R. Nicole, "C. H. Dodd and the Doctrine of Propitiation," *WTJ* 17 (1954–55): 117–57; idem, "Hilaskesthai Revisited," *EQ* 49 (1977): 173–77.

[93] It is interesting that, while rejecting the idea of "propitiation," even Dodd is forced to say that "in the immediate context it might seem possible that the sense of 'propitiation' is in place: if our guilt requires an advocate before God, we might, logically, need to placate His righteous anger" (*Johannine Epistles*, 26).

[94] So Dodd, *Johannine Epistles*, 26–27.

[95] Morris, *Apostolic Preaching of the Cross*, 211.

of Jesus' death as the propitiation of God's wrath.[96] God both fulfills His covenant promises to forgive His people and yet is completely righteous in that He diverted the punishment due to sinners onto His Son, whereby God is seen as both the just and the justifier (see Rom 3:25). Finally, in 2:1, Jesus is said to be the "righteous One" who is able to stand before the righteous Father and plead the case of sinners as their "advocate." Here the thought of individuals being in need of an "advocate" before God further demonstrates their desperate state and need of intervention, given that their sin stands against them. Jesus thus pleads their case and can do so because He is righteous and because He Himself is the offering (1:7) whose blood not only cleanses their sin but also renders God favorable towards them.[97] Of course, the biblical concept of propitiation is different from the pagan understanding where the people offer sacrifice to the gods in hope of propitiating an arbitrary deity. Here God is the One who took the initiative (4:10) in providing the sacrifice of His Son, so He is both the subject and object of the propitiation.[98] Therefore, the context of this verse indicates that through the cross-work of Christ, God showed Himself to be both faithful and righteous when His wrath toward His people was propitiated and their sins forgiven.

Excursus on "the whole world" (2:2b). The precise meaning of John's statement that Jesus was the propitiation "not for ours [sins] alone, but also for the whole world" (2:2b; cp. 4:14) is difficult to understand and hotly debated. Perhaps the best way forward is to begin with what is most certain. Virtually all interpreters would agree that the writer was not arguing that the sins of the whole world were *effectively* dealt with on the cross so that all men have eternal life even if they do not believe in Jesus. Such a teaching is clearly rejected by John, for in 5:11–13, he contends that only those who have the Son have life and those who do not have the Son do not have life.

[96] Morris asserts that we also have "a reference to Christ as 'the righteous,' and a few verses earlier there is mention of His blood (1 John 1:7). In these things we may discern a striking coincidence with Romans 3:25, where the propitiation occurs in a passage which several times refers to God's righteousness, and which says the propitiation is in Christ's blood" (ibid., 207).

[97] See Marshall, *Epistles of John*, 118; Morris, *Apostolic Preaching of the Cross*, 206–7.

[98] So also Kruse, *Epistles of John*, 73–74.

It is, however, much more difficult when the discussion moves to what John actually meant by "the whole world."[99] Some contend that this passage speaks of God's redemption with a universal scope in its *potential*. In this interpretation the "whole world" should be understood as "all inclusive," thus Jesus is the propitiation for all men without exception.[100] Nevertheless, since John is clear that only those who have the Son have life and those who do not have the Son do not have eternal life (5:12), it is said that Christ's propitiation was *sufficient* to deal with the sins of the whole world but only becomes *effective* if one believes (i.e., "sufficient for all and effective for the elect").[101]

Others argue that when John speaks of the "whole world," he is referring to all the elect of both Jews and Gentiles. In other words, in 2:2b, John is making the point that Jesus' death did not apply to Jewish believers only (i.e., "ours") but also to the elect Gentiles (i.e., "the whole world"). Such an argument flows from much time and effort in the Fourth Gospel, where the particular redemption of the elect is so prominent (e.g., John 5:21; 6:37,44,65,70; 8:47; 10:26,29; 12:32; 13:18; 15:16,19; 17:6,9,12,24). Here then the inclusive phrase "the whole world" serves John's purpose in demonstrating that Jesus died not only for the Jews but for "all types of people" (i.e., "the whole world"). According to this interpretation, virtually all of John's usages of the terms *all* and *world* in both the Gospel and epistles should be understood along the lines of "all" without distinction, not "all" without exception.[102]

While both of the above positions are possible interpretations of 1 John 2:2, neither is without problems. In the first instance, to assert that Jesus' death was sufficient to deal with the sins of all people but only becomes effective if one believes is actually difficult to support theologically. To my knowledge no one has adequately refuted John

[99] For a helpful survey of the various historical positions on this passage, see G. D. Long, *Definite Atonement* (Frederick, MD: New Covenant Media, 1977, 2006), 101–20.

[100] So Akin, *1, 2, 3 John*, 84; Smalley, *1, 2, 3 John*, 40.

[101] So Kruse, *Letters of John*, 74–75; Akin, *1, 2, 3 John*, 84–86. Cp. Carson, *The Difficult Doctrine of the Love of God* (Wheaton, IL: Crossway, 2000), 16–21, 73–79.

[102] For the classic defense of this position see J. Owen, *The Death of Death in the Death of Christ* (Edinburgh: Johnstone & Hunter, 1852; repr., Carlisle, PA: The Banner of Truth Trust, 2002), 218–26. See also Long, *Definite Atonement*, 115–19.

Owen's definitive statement on this issue and is therefore worth quoting in its entirety. Here Owen asserts:

> God imposed his wrath due unto, and Christ underwent the pains of hell for, either all the sins of all men, or all the sins of some men, or some sins of all men. If the last, some sins of all men, then have all men some sins to answer for, and so shall no man be saved; for if God enter into judgment with us, though it were with all mankind for one sin, no flesh should be justified in his sight. . . . If the second, that is it which we affirm, that Christ in their stead and room suffered for all the sins of all the elect in the world. If the first, why, then, are not all freed from the punishment of all their sins? You will say, "Because of their unbelief; they will not believe." But this unbelief, is it a sin, or not? If not, why should they be punished for it? If it be, then Christ underwent the punishment due to it, or not. If so, then why must that hinder them more than their other sins for which he died . . . ? If he did not, then did he not die for all their sins. Let them choose which part they will.[103]

While I would argue that Owen's logic here is irrefutable, his view of 1 John 2:2b falls short in that he imposes the context of the Fourth Gospel onto the context of the first epistle. The argument that "not for ours alone" refers to Jewish believers and "the whole world" refers to Gentile believers loses it force here. Keep in mind that John is writing to a congregation of both Jews and Gentiles. Hence, when he says, "not for ours alone," the "our" almost certainly includes himself and all the recipients of the letter (i.e., both Jews and Gentiles in this particular fellowship). This view then fails to adequately explain John's dichotomy between "ours" and the "whole world," since "ours" appears to include both Jews and Gentiles.

The best explanation of this text must interact with some sort of working hypothesis regarding the background of the letter. In the second chapter of this study I argued that John wrote to a group of believers who were struggling with doubts and were in need of reassurance after the departure of the secessionists, who were identified as some form of proto-gnostics, and I argued that the very nature of such proto-gnostic thinking caused most of these groups to be sectarian. These proto-gnostics believed that *they* were the ones who had a special knowledge (2:4) and an anointing from God (2:20,27). It also appears that such beliefs likely led to a triumphal (2 John 8–9) and unloving attitude (2:11; 4:8,20) toward those they felt had failed to

[103] Owen, *The Death of Death*, 61–62.

progress beyond the basic gospel they heard from the beginning. Such a background is helpful here in that John is combating the sectarian mind-set of the secessionists throughout the letter. Thus, even though the secessionists rejected the cross-work of Christ, John nevertheless wants to obliterate any such sectarian thinking and therefore seeks to demonstrate the broad scope of the atoning sacrifice of Christ. Jesus did not die for our sins alone. Here, then, the "our" would include John and his recipients. The "whole world" would include all believers everywhere throughout the world. Therefore, Jesus was not only the propitiation for the sins of one little group of believers in Asia Minor but for the children of God all over the world.[104]

Such a teaching would have been a huge encouragement to John's readers on at least two fronts. First, nothing could be more reassuring to a struggling believer than to ponder the reality that Jesus' death on the cross has completely propitiated God's wrath toward every single sin. No doubt as John's readers pondered this theological truth, they were greatly encouraged and their confidence strengthened. Second, John's teaching that Jesus was the propitiation for the whole world also would have been helpful in serving as yet another reminder that it is not only a few "enlightened" ones in this little group who have fellowship with God. Quite the contrary, because of Jesus' atoning sacrifice, there is a great multitude of believers all over the world whose sins have been propitiated and who therefore have fellowship with God.

Summary of Walking in the Light and Walking in the Darkness

In 1:5–2:2, the writer has set forth three alternating pairs of conditional sentences that move from negative to positive examples of how to and how not to have fellowship with God. Above I noted that each of the negative examples is parallel to the others as is each of the positive examples. The negatives were examined together followed by an examination of the positives.

[104] Note the parallel in John 11:51–52. While the context is different, the wording is similar, which would seem to support the interpretation I have just offered. 1 John 2:2b—οὐ περὶ τῶν ἡμετέρων δὲ μόνον ἀλλὰ καὶ περὶ ὅλου τοῦ κόσμου. John 11:52—καὶ οὐχ ὑπὲρ τοῦ ἔθνους μόνον ἀλλ᾽ ἵνα καὶ τὰ τέκνα τοῦ θεοῦ τὰ διεσκορπισμένα συναγάγῃ εἰς ἕν.

The negative examples of how not to have fellowship with God are not only parallel but may have a genuine heightening of emphasis in each of the apodoses. In 1:6 those who make false claims to have fellowship with God lie and do not practice the truth. In 1:8 they not only lie; they deceive themselves and the truth is not in them. Finally, in 1:10, not only have they deceived themselves, but they make God a liar, and His word is not in them. This link between the apodoses and the clear link between the last two protases alert us to the fact that all three of the protases should probably be viewed as parallel as well. It would appear then that the second and third protases found in 1:8 and 1:10 further explicate what is meant in the first (1:6).[105] If this is correct, then walking in the darkness is not only walking in the sphere where God does not dwell (1:5) but also a denial that one is a sinner. In other words, walking in the darkness entails a complete rejection of one's need for the cross-work of Christ in His life.[106]

On the other hand, all of the positive examples are also parallel, with the atoning sacrifice of Christ standing as their common theme. The three positive examples of how one can be in fellowship with God (1:7,9; 2:1–2) are extremely enlightening in that they elucidate the fact that walking in the light does not mean living a sin free life. Quite the contrary, walking in the light includes sin and the cleansing thereof.[107] While John does not specifically define what it means to walk in the light, the context is helpful. It appears that walking in the light involves living in a righteous lifestyle (1:6a; 2:1a), which nevertheless seems to assume sin (1:7c, 9), confession (1:9), and trusting in the work of Christ on the cross as the propitiation of God's righteous wrath (2:2) and the cleansing of all unrighteousness (1:7,9). Moreover, both the context of this passage and John's use of the present tense verbs περιπατέω, ὁμολογέω, and καθαρίζω indicate that the walking, the confessing, and the cleansing are all continual

[105] This is strengthened in the fact that John never comes right out and gives a definition of what it means to walk in the darkness, which is more than likely because he defines it in the remainder of the negative examples.

[106] So also C. P. Baylis, "The Meaning of Walking 'in the Darkness' (1 John 1:6)," *BibSac* 149 (1992): 222.

[107] So also Conzelmann, "φῶς," 355: "The walk is paradoxical in structure. Part of walking in the light, in sinlessness, is continually confessing one's sins."

activities of the one who walks in the light.[108] Hence, walking in the light should be seen not only as a lifestyle of obedience and love for the brethren but fundamentally a lifestyle of trusting in the work of Christ for one's forgiveness of sins and right standing with God.

Therefore it is clear that John has begun his letter by making it absolutely certain that fellowship with God and the assurance thereof are fundamentally grounded in the atoning sacrifice of Christ. Such assurance does not ultimately stem from a claim to fellowship with God, a false claim of being sinless, or even the discernment that one is passing the various tests of life that are found throughout the letter. In fact, it will be argued in chapter 5 that all of John's "tests" must be read in light of 1:5–2:2.[109] Assurance of fellowship with God finds its foundation ultimately in trusting in the work of Christ on the cross for the forgiveness of sins and cleansing of all unrighteousness, whereby the sinner is made right with God. Such assurance is realized in those who live in the light, which involves living righteously, loving the brethren, and continually trusting in Christ's work on the cross for every sin.

The Centrality of the Cross Corroborated in Subsequent References

While 1:5–2:2 is the clearest instance where John grounds his readers' assurance of eternal life in the cross-work of Christ, this theme resurfaces on several occasions throughout the body of the letter. Here I will focus on 4:7–10 and 5:5–10, which appear to be two of the clearest allusions back to the cross.[110]

[108] So also Kruse, *Letters of John*, 64.

[109] See especially 3:6,9, which appear to contradict 1:8.

[110] Other allusions to the cross-work of Christ include each of John's tests of belief (2:22–23; 4:1–3,15; 5:1,5–6), with which I will say more in chap. 5. Each of these tests stresses the importance of the unity between the man Jesus and the divine Christ, which is vital to one's understanding of the atonement. Marshall is correct in insisting that as soon as we deny the union between the divine Christ and the human Jesus, "we lose the cardinal point of the New Testament doctrine of the atonement, that *God* was in Christ reconciling the world to himself; in the last analysis, the doctrine of the atonement means that God himself bears our sins and shows that the final reality in the universe is his sin-bearing, pardoning love, but if Jesus is not the Son of God, his death can no longer bear this significance" (Marshall, *Epistles of John*, 233–34). Moreover, there are also two key allusions to the cross that are found in the midst of John's test of righteousness in 3:4–10. To be sure, the emphasis in both of these is parenetic,

Not that We Loved God (4:7–10)

An important text for understanding John's teaching of the atoning sacrifice of Jesus Christ can be found in 4:7–10, which is located in the middle of one of the writer's tests of love (4:7–13). There is no doubt that the primary purpose in pointing to the cross was to give his readers an example to follow (4:11). Nevertheless, this text illustrates the importance of the cross and serves to complement John's earlier teaching in 2:1–2. Here the writer unambiguously asserts that Jesus' sacrificial death was the result of God's loving initiative.

Beginning in 4:7, John makes the case that those born of God love one another because love is from God. Moreover, the converse is also true in that the one who does not love does not know God because God is love. The statement "God is love"[111] refers to God's loving nature and is explicated in the next two verses. In verse 9, the love of God[112] is clearly demonstrated in His initiative in sending His One and Only Son into the world (4:9) so that His people might live through Him. This is the only usage of the verb "to live" (ζάω) in this letter, but the noun "life" (ζωή) is employed frequently in reference to life or eternal life, and this life is always found in Jesus (see 5:11–12).[113] Elsewhere, the writer said that one is able to know he has passed from death to life by seeing the fruit of the love of the brethren (3:14). While the fruit of passing from death to life is the love for the brethren, 4:9 helps us see that this "life" is the direct result of God's sending His Son.

using the cross as the impetus for holy living. Nevertheless, each is a link back to the atoning sacrifice. Here John tells his readers that Jesus came for the purpose of removing sin (3:5) and destroying the work of the Devil (3:8), which were two clear results of His atoning sacrifice (cp. John 12:31; Col 2:14–15; Heb 2:14).

[111] In my discussion above on "God is light," I noted that the three Johannine "God is" statements are parallel to one another and tell us something about the nature of God. Nevertheless, the emphasis in each of these statements was not to build his reader's doctrine of God but to exhort them to live holy (see also 1 Pet 1:15–16).

[112] The context demonstrates that John is referring to God's love for us and not our love for God. God is clearly the One who took the initiative in sending His Son (τὸν υἱὸν αὐτοῦ τὸν μονογενῆ ἀπέσταλκεν ὁ θεὸς εἰς τὸν κόσμον). Moreover, in the following verse (4:10), John says that it is not because we loved God but that He loved us. Therefore, τοῦ θεοῦ in the phrase ἡ ἀγάπη τοῦ θεοῦ should be understood here as a subjective genitive.

[113] See Smalley, *1, 2, 3 John*, 242; Kruse, *Letters of John*, 158; Westcott, *Epistles of St. John*, 149.

The following verse goes on to explicate how one has spiritual life through the Son (4:10). Again, John puts on display the truth that God took all the initiative in bringing sinners from death to life. It was not because we loved God but because He loved us and sent His Son as the "propitiation" (ἱλασμός) for our sins. As noted above, the word ἱλασμός describes the work of Jesus on the cross, where the righteous wrath of God was exacted on His Son in place of sinners. This verse clearly distinguishes the biblical notion of propitiation from that seen in pagan writings, for sinners did not love God or seek to appease His wrath (4:10,19). Here God demonstrates His love by taking all the initiative in bringing the spiritually dead into spiritual life by providing the sacrifice of His Son. Therefore, He is both the subject and the object of the propitiation. Moreover, this loving initiative resulted in nothing less than sinners being made right with God. Hence, this passage further supports our thesis of the centrality of the cross-work of Christ in that sinners did not love or seek God, which left God to take the initiative in sending His Son, knowing that it was the only effective remedy for their sins.

Not by Water Alone (5:4b–10)

Another instance where the writer points back to the atoning sacrifice of Jesus comes in the test of belief found in 5:4b–10. While more will be said about this text in chapter 5, it is certainly appropriate to include a few statements here, for it is perhaps the clearest indicator that John's tests of belief at least implicitly demonstrate the importance of the cross. To be sure, the primary purpose of this passage is to assure the children of God that they have overcome the world by distinguishing between the heresy of the secessionists and the message heard from the beginning. Nevertheless, in this process the centrality of the person and work of Jesus is again in view and would therefore add support to the thesis stated above.

The Son of God is Jesus (5:4b–5). Beginning in 5:4a, John says that everyone born of God overcomes the world. Then in 5:4b,[114] he

[114] I understand 5:4b to be a transition sentence similar to the way John has transitioned from one topic to the next throughout this letter (e.g., 3:10, where he moves from the moral

declares that faith (πίστις) is the victory that overcomes the world.[115] The nature of the victory that comes through faith is debated. Some argue that it is the victory believers have through faith at conversion.[116] Another proposal is that this victory is the believer's victory over the false teachers.[117] Still others have asserted that the victory is referring to the victory over sin, Satan, and the world that took place on the cross.[118] A decision among these options is perhaps reductionistic, given the fact that it is one's faith that brings about conversion and gives the believer victory over false teaching, sin, Satan, and the world.[119] Therefore, it is probably best to understand these elements as parts that make up the whole of the final victory.

The object of faith (5:5–6). Verse 5 moves the discussion forward by stressing the *object* of the faith that overcomes the world. Here John poses the rhetorical question, "Who is the one who overcomes the world?" He is not content with a nebulous answer. This faith has a clear object, and it is not a special knowledge from the divine Christ or even some form of teaching about Christ that in the end is nothing short of idolatry (5:21). Quite the contrary, the faith that overcomes the world is that which has as its object the historic God-man: Jesus the Son of God.[120] Given that his readers were apparently abiding in the gospel of eternal life, which they were taught in the beginning (2:24–25), this test of life would have strengthened their assurance. The one who overcomes the world is none other than he who believes

test to the love test). For a similar interpretation, see Strecker, *Johannine Letters*, 181; Brown, *Epistles of John*, 592.

[115] Even though John regularly uses the cognate πιστεύω ("to believe"), this is the only time the noun πίστις ("faith") is used in John's Gospel or epistles (4b). Some argue that πίστις is not simply an internal act of believing but carries the idea of "the public profession of what one believes" (Brown, *Epistles of John*, 571; cp. Westcott, *Epistles of John*, 180; Bultmann, *Johannine Epistles*; Smalley, *1, 2, 3 John*, 271). Regardless of whether one agrees that the idea of public profession is present here, context clearly indicates that the content of this faith is what is important.

[116] Heibert, "An Exposition of 1 John 5:1–12," 221; Brooke, *Johannine Epistles*, 131.

[117] So Stott, *Letters of John*, 177.

[118] So Schnackenburg, *Johannine Epistles*, 230; Westcott, *Epistles of John*, 180.

[119] See Brown, who works through these options and concludes by saying, "I see no way to be certain as to which past action 1 John means here" (*Epistles of John*, 571).

[120] It is important to note that 5:1a and 5:5a appear to be parallel passages. Thus it seems best to understand John's description as ὁ Χριστὸς and ὁ υἱὸς τοῦ θεοῦ as virtually synonymous descriptions of Jesus (see chap. 5).

that the Son of God is Jesus, who came through water and blood (5:5–6; cp. 2:22; 4:15).[121]

The test of 5:5 is expanded in the next few verses where the focus is on the person and work of the historic Jesus Christ. To be sure, it is best understood as yet another instance where John is countering the false teachings of the secessionists[122] by emphasizing the importance of the atoning sacrifice of Jesus the Son of God. Here he contends that Jesus came through water and blood.[123] He did not come by water alone but by water and by blood. The secessionists apparently agreed that Jesus came by water but rejected that He came by blood. Therefore, before going any farther, it is important first to seek to understand what is meant by the terms *water* and *blood*. Throughout the history of the church, there have been three primary ways in which the water and blood have been understood.[124] (1) First, the water and blood have been taken as a reference to the two sacraments of baptism and the Lord's Supper.[125] There are a number of problems with this

[121] See chap. 5, where I argue that Ἰησοῦς is the complement and not the subject in John's statements such as ὁ πιστεύων ὅτι Ἰησοῦς ἐστιν ὁ υἱὸς τοῦ θεοῦ.

[122] Against T. Griffith, *Keep Yourselves from Idols: A New Look at 1 John*, JSNTSup 233 (Sheffield: Sheffield Academic Press, 2002), 153, who argues that there is no polemic here at all.

[123] This passage is somewhat obscure for the modern reader as seen in the fact that virtually every point is debated. In fact, Plummer asserts that this passage "is the most perplexing passage in the Epistle and one of the most perplexing in the N.T." (*Epistles of St. John*, 113). Nevertheless, since there is no attempt on the part of the writer to explain the testimony of the Spirit, the water, and the blood, it would appear as though the original readers would have known precisely what the writer was referencing.

[124] I use the term "primary" to signify that there are certainly others outside of these three. For instance, B. Witherington argues that water refers to the physical birth of Jesus ("The Waters of Birth: John 3.5 and 1 John 5.6–8," *NTS* 35 [1989]: 160). Kruse interprets the water not as Jesus' baptism by the Baptist but as His baptizing ministry (*Letters of John*, 178). M. C. de Boer argues that "through water and blood" should be understood epexegetically (e.g., "through water, that is blood") ("Jesus the Baptizer: 1 John 5:5–8 and the Gospel of John," *JBL* [1988]: 103).

[125] While this view was common in the early church and Reformation, it is now held by only a few (O. Cullmann, *Early Christian Worship* [London: SCM Press, 1953], 110 n. 1; O. S. Brooks, "The Johannine Eucharist: Another Interpretation," *JBL* 82 [1963]: 293–300; P. Grech, 'Fede e sacramenti in Giov 19,34 e 1 Giov 5.6–12," in *Fede e sacramenti negli Scritti giovannei*, ed. Puis-Ramn Tragon [Rome: Abbazia S Paulo, 1985], 149–63). Most contemporary scholars who hold this view usually reserve it for the second reference to water and blood and point to the change in preposition from διά to ἐν to support their claim. Strecker argues this view as follows: "What is more important is that, apparently, the shift of the διά construction to one with ἐν also introduces a change in the system of theological coordinates, and that in the phrase ἐν

interpretation, not least that it does not do justice to the purpose of John's writing in that he is not dealing with issues of sacramental theology but arguing against a Christological heresy.[126] Moreover, using the term *blood* by itself as a reference to the Lord's Supper is without parallel.[127] (2) The second interpretation of the water and the blood is that it is parallel to John 19:34–35 where Jesus' side is pierced by the Roman soldier and the text says that blood and water flowed from His side.[128] Again, this view is not without problems. First, it is difficult to see how this verse explains John's clarifying phrase, "not by water alone." Second, if John were alluding back to the pierced side, one wonders why he would change the order from blood and water to water and blood.[129] (3) Finally, the interpretation that best fits the context of the passage is the view that the water and the blood refer to two key points in Jesus' early ministry; namely, His baptism and His atoning sacrifice on the cross.[130] This interpretation best fits the context in that it understands John to be arguing against a proto-gnostic false teaching similar to that of Cerinthus which espoused that the divine Christ came upon the human Jesus at His baptism and left Him sometime before the cross.[131] Thus He came by water only when the

τῷ ὕδατι καὶ ἐν τῷ αἵματι it is no longer simply the baptism and death of Jesus (including its atoning effect) but also the two community sacraments of baptism and the Lord's Supper that are the object of instruction" (*Johannine Letters*, 183). See also Westcott, *Epistles of John*, 182. Moreover, while some argue for the water and blood as baptism and death in v. 6, they assert that in v. 8 water and blood refer to the sacraments (so Schnackenburg, *Johannine Epistles*, 235–38; Bultmann, *Johannine Epistles*, 80–81). Still others argue that even though the primary meaning is Jesus' baptism and death, there is at least a secondary allusion to the sacraments in v. 8 (so Stott, *Letters of John*, 182; Brown, *Epistles of John*, 584–85; Dodd, *Johannine Epistles*, 130–31; Bruce, *Epistles of John*, 212).

[126] So H. Venetz, "'Durch Wasser und Blut gekommen:' Exegetishce Überlegungen zu 1 Joh 5,6," in *Die Mitte des Neuen Testaments: Einheit und vielfalt neutestamentlicher Theologie. Festschrift für Eduard Schweizer zum siebsigsten Geburtstag*, ed. Ulrich Luz and Hans Weder (Göttingen: Vandenhoeck & Ruprecht, 1983), 357–58.

[127] This view also fails to interact on the aorist participle ὁ ἐλθὼν, which would appear to govern each of the instances of water and blood in this verse and more than likely refers to an event that has happened and not something that is ongoing like the sacraments (so Brown, *Epistles of John*, 573; Smalley, *1, 2, 3 John*, 277).

[128] So Thompson, *1–3 John*, 134; Brown, *Epistles of John*, 578.

[129] See Carson, "The Three Witnesses," 221–24, for a convincing rebuttal of this view.

[130] So Marshall, *Epistles of John*, 231–34; Smalley, *1, 2, 3 John*, 278–80; Akin, *1, 2, 3 John*, 196–97.

[131] So Akin, *1, 2, 3 John* 197; Marshall, *Epistles of John*, 233; Carson, "The Three Witnesses," 228–30.

divine Christ came upon the human Jesus at His baptism but not by blood. Contrary to such a heretical teaching, John intends to demonstrate that Jesus was the Son of God all the way through[132] both the water at His baptism and through the blood He shed on the cross.[133] This teaching is of course vital in John's mind as seen in his numerous tests of belief because if there is a denial of the union between the divine Christ and the human Jesus, then there is a wholesale rejection of the atonement for which He came, and there is then no reconciliation between sinful humans and the God who is perfectly light.

The threefold testimony. John's claim that Jesus was the Son of God all the way through the baptism and atoning sacrifice is then buttressed with the assertion that the Spirit is the One who bears witness (μαρτυρέω) to these things and the Spirit is truth (ἀλήθεια).[134] In chapter 5, I will argue that this probably refers back to the Spirit's witness to John the Baptist that Jesus was the Son of God (John 1:32–34). Moreover, the motif of witness continues through verses 7–10, where we see that not only does the Spirit testify that Jesus is the Son of God, but there are actually three who testify to this same truth: the Spirit, the water, and the blood. To be sure, there is no reason to view this threefold witness as either an interpolation or a contradiction of the single witness of the Spirit found in verse 6.[135] Instead, it would appear that John is simply seeking further support for this testimony much in line with what is taught in Deuteronomy 19:15, where a matter is to be established by two or three witnesses. There is some debate as to whether these three should be understood as independent witnesses or that the Spirit should be viewed as the One who bears witness *through* the water and the blood.[136] Even though the Spirit is listed individually in 5:6c as well as taking first place in the list in 5:8,

[132] See chap. 5 for a detailed analysis of the grammar of this passage.

[133] The only other instance where blood is used in this letter is in 1:7, where it clearly refers to Jesus' atoning sacrifice.

[134] The interplay between the one bearing witness/testifying (μαρτυρέω) and the witness/testimony (μαρτυρία) throughout 5:4b-12 should not be missed. See Kruse's helpful excurses on John's use of "witness" in both his Gospel and epistles (Kruse, *Letters of John*, 183–84). He argues that the witness motif in the letters of John "serves the purpose of distinguishing the errors of the secessionists from the truth of the message of the gospel as it was heard from the beginning" (184).

[135] Against Bultmann, *Johannine Epistles*, 80.

[136] So Akin *1, 2, 3 John*, 198; Marshall, *Epistles of John*, 237.

there does not appear to be any grounds for arguing that the Spirit is the One who witnesses through the water and blood.[137] It seems best to view all of these as complementary witnesses all pointing to the same reality,[138] namely, that the Son of God is Jesus.

The theme of the threefold witness to Jesus is moved forward in 5:9–10 via an argument from lesser to greater. Here the flow of thought is that if we receive the testimony of men, then we should accept the testimony of God all the more,[139] given that the testimony of God is greater than that of men. This verse therefore demonstrates that this[140] threefold testimony to Jesus is nothing short of God's own testimony regarding His Son. Furthermore, verse 10 goes on to state that the one who believes in the Son of God has this threefold testimony in Himself (5:10). On the contrary, the one who does not believe God's testimony regarding His Son has "made Him a liar" (ψεύ στην πεποίηκεν αὐτόν). This phrase is striking in that it may point back to chapter one where those who claimed to be without sin were said to "make Him a liar" (ψεύστην ποιοῦμεν αὐτὸν) (1:10). These are the only two instances where John asserts that someone makes God a liar, which would appear to be a lexical link between the two passages. Hence, in 1:10, they denied they had sinned, thus denying their need of Jesus' atoning death. Here, they are denying the threefold witness that the divine Christ and the man Jesus were one and the same all the way through the baptism and the cross. In both instances, it is the one who denies God's testimony about His Son's atoning sacrifice that makes Him a liar. In the first, there is a false

[137] Grammatically the three witnesses are simply linked by coordinating conjunctions: τὸ πνεῦμα καὶ τὸ ὕδωρ καὶ τὸ αἷμα.

[138] The "three are one" (καὶ οἱ τρεῖς εἰς τὸ ἕν εἰσιν) (v. 8) because they are all bearing witness to the same thing. Moreover, while some see a change in meaning in the water and blood in v. 8 from v. 6 (so Schnackenburg, *Johannine Epistles*, 235–38; Bultmann, *Johannine Epistles*, 80–81), there is no good reason for doing so. The context would again seem to argue for the water as a sign that Jesus was already the Son of God (Matt 3:17) and the blood as reference to His atoning sacrifice on the cross whereby He is clearly seen to be the Son of God (Matt 27:54). So also Heibert, "An Exposition of 1 John 5:1–12," 227; Brooke, *Johannine Epistles*, 137; Plummer, *Epistles of St. John*, 116; Smalley, *1, 2, 3 John*, 282; Marshall, *Epistles of John*, 237; Akin, *1, 2, 3 John*, 197.

[139] The apodosis is implied in the original in that the author gives us an incomplete conditional sentence (so Kruse, *Letters of John*, 180).

[140] I take the αὕτη as a referent back to the threefold testimony (see also Stott, *Letters of John*, 184; Dodd, *Johannine Epistles*, 132; Westcott, *Epistles of John*, 185).

claim to be without sin and thus a denial of one's need for the atoning sacrifice of Christ in one's life (1:10). In the second there is a rejection of God's threefold testimony regarding His Son, which certainly focuses on His atoning sacrifice on the cross whereby He came through blood. Therefore, through this test of belief, John is alluding back to the centrality of the cross-work of Christ for believers. The secessionists denied the union between the man Jesus and the divine Christ, and thus denied the importance of His atoning sacrifice.

Summary

In this section I have argued that the centrality of the cross is not only found in the beginning of the letter but also revisited throughout. Throughout the letter John elucidates that through the cross of Christ man's sins are propitiated (4:10), forgiven (3:5), and the works of the Devil destroyed (3:8). Moreover, in contradistinction to the heretics who denied the union of the divine Christ and human Jesus and the importance of His atoning sacrifice, the writer demonstrates that Jesus was the Son of God all the way through the water of His baptism and His atoning death on the cross (5:5–10). This truth is testified by three witnesses: the Spirit, the water, and the blood. Those who reject this testimony of God about His Son reject God and call Him a liar. Those who embrace this teaching about Jesus, who believe in the apostolic gospel they were taught from the beginning, can actually know and have confidence that they have eternal life.

Assurance in the Promise of the Future Work of Christ (5:18)

Finally, John not only assures his readers by looking back to the past work of Christ on the cross but also seeks to bolster their confidence by pointing them toward the promise of Christ's ongoing work of protecting those who are born of God. In 5:18 he informs his readers that no one who has been born of God sins (see also 3:9). The second part of this verse sets forth the ground for such a statement and is a message his readers would surely find comforting. The reason no one born of

God sins is because Jesus[141] keeps him from sin and the clutches of the evil one.[142] The term ὁ πονηρὸς ("the evil one") is used throughout this letter (2:13–14; 3:12; 5:18,19) and is best understood as interchangeable with "the Devil" (3:8,10).[143] Hence, this verse makes clear that John not only assures his readers regarding the past work of Jesus on the cross but also His ongoing work of divine preservation of His own.[144] Those born of God can have great assurance that they will persevere to eternal life because of the wonderful promise that Jesus will keep them from sin and the clutches of the Devil. Assurance, therefore, is not only grounded in the past work of Christ on the cross but also on the promise of His ongoing work in preserving those who are His own (cp. John 17:12; 1 Pet 1:5; Jude 24; Rev 3:10).

Conclusion

In this chapter I have argued that John grounds his readers' assurance of eternal life in the cross-work of Christ. Such an argument is confirmed at the outset of the letter (1:5–2:2). He begins with a word about the identity of Jesus. Here readers are assured that Jesus is the eternal Word, who was with the Father and revealed to John and the other eyewitnesses. Moreover, this Jesus is the embodiment of life that John has proclaimed so that his readers might have fellowship with him, which is also fellowship with God. Finally John supports his claims about the person of Jesus with a word of assurance that his teaching could be trusted, for he was the one who had actually seen Jesus with his own eyes, listened to Him with his own ears, and even touched Him with his own hands (1:1–4). Thus, John begins

[141] See Appendix 1 for a thorough defense of this reading.

[142] The word ἅπτω means "to touch" but can also carry such meanings as "to make contact with a view to causing harm" (so BDAG, s.v. "ἅπτω" [cf. Job 2:5; Ps 105:15; Zech 2:8; T.Jud 3.10; 1 Esdr 4.28]).

[143] So also Kruse, *Letters of John*, 195.

[144] See chap. 5 of this study for a thorough discussion of sin and sinlessness and the difficult interplay between 3:9; 5:18 and 1:8,10. For now it must suffice to say that John is here making a statement that those born of God fundamentally do not sin. He has just finished saying that there is a sin that is not to death and that brothers can in fact commit such a sin (5:16–17). Moreover, in 1:8,10, he makes clear that those who deny they sin are liars and the truth is not in them. The point, then, is not an ontological statement of the impossibility of sin for believers but that those born of God are fundamentally characterized by living like the One who begat them and they do so as a result of the ongoing work of Christ.

with both a word of encouragement regarding the historic person of Christ and a word of reassurance that his eyewitness teaching could be trusted.

The opening section (1:1–4) therefore lays the foundation for what is argued in 1:5–2:2, where John proceeds to assure his readers that their fellowship with God is ultimately grounded in the cross-work of Christ. Such assurance does not ultimately stem from a claim to have fellowship with God, a false claim of being sinless, or even the discernment that one is passing the tests of faith that can be found in 2:3–5:4a. Assurance of fellowship with God finds its foundation in trusting in the work of Christ on the cross for the forgiveness of sins and cleansing of all unrighteousness, whereby the sinner is made right with God. Such assurance is realized in those who walk in the light, which includes living righteously and continually trusting in Christ's atoning sacrifice for their sin.

Moreover, the centrality of the cross is not only found in the beginning of the letter but revisited throughout. In the body of the letter, John explains that through the cross of Christ man's sins are propitiated (4:10), forgiven (3:5), and the works of the Devil destroyed (3:8). Moreover, in contradistinction to the heretics who denied the union of the divine Christ and human Jesus and the importance of His atoning sacrifice, the writer demonstrates that Jesus was the Son of God all the way through the water of His baptism and His atoning death on the cross (5:5–10). This truth is testified by three witnesses: the Spirit, the water, and the blood. Those who reject this testimony of God about His Son reject God and call Him a liar. Those who embrace this teaching about Jesus, who believe in the apostolic gospel they were taught from the beginning, can actually know and have confidence that they have eternal life.

Finally, John not only grounds his readers' assurance in the past work of Jesus on the cross but also points towards the promise of His ongoing work of preserving those who have been born of God. Those born of God can have great assurance that they will persevere to eternal life because of the promise that Jesus will keep them from sin and the clutches of the Devil.

Therefore, it is clear that John grounds his readers' assurance of eternal life in the person and work of Jesus the Son of God. To be sure, we will see in the next chapter that believing in Jesus brings about new birth, and the new birth brings forth a changed life that can be tested, and such testing serves as a vital support to ones' assurance. Nevertheless, the firm foundation of the believer's assurance is in the cross-work of Christ.

Chapter 4

THE WORK OF CHRIST AND THE FULFILLMENT OF NEW COVENANT PROMISES

Introduction

The previous chapter examined the centrality of the cross-work of Christ to one's assurance of eternal life. Chapter 5 will concentrate on the vital support of such assurance, which comes from the manner in which believers conduct their lives. To be sure, the lifestyle of the believer is a major emphasis throughout this letter as evidenced by the writer's series of recurring tests. Nevertheless, before examining the tests themselves, it is important first to focus on the foundation for such testing, which is the writer's understanding that the work of Christ has ushered in the new covenant and that his readers are partakers in all of its promises and obligations. Hence, those born of God have God's own Spirit abiding in them and empowering them to walk in the light, which includes believing in the historic person of Jesus Christ, loving the brethren, and obeying the commands.

Some reject the idea that this letter or any of the other Johannine writings should be viewed through a new covenant framework due to the fact that John nowhere employs the term *covenant* (διαθήκη) in either his Gospel or his epistles.[1] Nevertheless, such a denial is reductionistic, for a new covenant motif can certainly be present even when the term *covenant* is not used.[2] I will support the thesis that

[1] See J. Painter, *1, 2, and 3 John*, Sacra Pagina, vol. 18 (Collegeville, MN: Liturgical, 2002), 101, 129. So also J. Schmid, "Bund," in *Lexicon Für Theologie und Kirche*, vol. 2, ed. M. Buchberger (Freiburg: Verlag Herder, 1958), 778: "In den übrigen Schriften des NT fehlt der B.es-gedanke vollständig, od. Er spielt wenigstens keine Rolle, so namentlich bei Jo[hannes]."

[2] For a sampling of interpreters who see a new covenant motif in 1 John, see H. A. A. Kennedy, "The Covenant Conception in the First Epistle of John," *ET* 28 (1916): 23–26; E. S. J. Malatesta, *Interiority and Covenant: A Study of* εἶναι ἐν *and* μένειν ἐν *in the First Letter of Saint John*, Analecta Biblica 69 (Rome: Biblical Institute, 1978); I. de la Potterie, "La Connaissance de Dieu dans le Dualisme eschatologique d'apres I Jn 2:12–14," in *Au service de la parole de Dieu* (Gembloux: J. Duculot, 1969), 77–79; R. E. Brown, *The Epistles of John*, The Anchor Bible, vol. 30 (New York: Double Day, 1982), 267, 279–80, 284, 349, 370, 375, 390, 410, 415, 470–72,

John writes through a new covenant framework by first making a case that his teaching on the anointing (2:20,27) is an allusion to Jeremiah 31:29–34. After that, I will lay out some of the promises and obligations of the new covenant in order to demonstrate John's assumption that these have been fulfilled through the work of Christ, and thus his readers were the recipients of the new covenant promises and were expected to keep its obligations.

The "Anointing": An Allusion to Jeremiah 31:29–33

In the context of exposing the true identity of the secessionists as antichrists, liars, and deceivers who were never really "of us" (2:18–19,22–23,26), John reassures those who remain in the fellowship that they will not succumb to such heresy because they all have the "anointing" (χρῖσμα) from the Holy One, who teaches them regarding all things.[3] It is vital, therefore, to understand what John meant in his usage of the word *anointing* and why such a teaching serves to reassure his readers in this context.

The only three occurrences of χρῖσμα ("anointing") in the New Testament are found in 1 John (2:20,27 [2x]), so it is somewhat difficult to determine its meaning. In the Pentateuch the anointing was used for the consecration or setting aside of an individual or object for sacred use (Exod 29:7; 30:25; 40:15). Later it came to symbolize the reception of the Spirit so that the individual might govern God's people or prophesy (1 Sam 16:13; Isa 61:1). This latter Old Testament usage provides the most plausible background for the act of anointing described in the New Testament. While the noun χρῖσμα is found only in 1 John, the cognate verb χρίω ("to anoint") is used five times

478–79, 484, 633–35, 639–40, 682; C. G. Kruse, *The Letters of John*, PNTC (Grand Rapids: Eerdmans, 2000), 104.

[3] It is difficult to decipher who the "Holy One" refers to in this context. It could be a reference to the Father, who is often referred to in the Old Testament as the "Holy One of Israel" (2 Kgs 19:22; Pss 71:22; 78:41; 89:18, etc.). Moreover, it could also be a reference to Jesus, who is referred to as the "Holy One of God" (Mark 1:24; John 6:69). The fact that the only other time the label "the Holy One" is found in the Johannine literature (John 6:69) is a reference to Christ tips the scales in this direction. Perhaps a distinction should not be forced, however, given that the Fourth Gospel itself can at one point say that the Father gives the Spirit (14:16,26) while at another point Jesus gives the Spirit (15:26; 16:7). Regardless of the decision, the meaning is basically the same.

in the New Testament (Luke 4:18; Acts 4:27; 10:38; 2 Cor 1:21; Heb 1:9). With the exception of one metaphorical usage in Hebrews 1:9, this verb is consistently used in reference to the anointing of the Holy Spirit. This suggests that the "anointing" in 1 John is a reference to the Holy Spirit. Such an interpretation finds corroboration in John's Gospel. Like 1 John, the Fourth Gospel describes the Spirit as One "received" by John's readers (John 14:17; 1 John 2:27a), One who abides in them (John 14:17; 2:27b), and One who teaches them all things (John 14:26; 1 John 2:27). The combination of this parallelism with the consistent usage of χρίω in the New Testament makes the Holy Spirit the most plausible interpretation of the χρῖσμα.[4]

It should not go unnoticed, however, that the exhortation to let the "message" heard from the beginning "abide in them" (2:24) is located between the two references to the anointing (2:20,27). This teaching in 2:24 appears to be parallel to that in 2:27 due to the fact that both the message heard from the beginning and the anointing abide (μένω) in the believer. It is best, then, to understand the χρῖσμα as primarily a reference to the Holy Spirit but also to acknowledge the close association between the Spirit and the Word in Johannine thought, given that the Spirit's role is not a source of new revelation but to testify to the words and work of Jesus (John 14:26; 15:26; 16:13).[5] John's readers are therefore those who do not need anyone to teach them because

[4] So also G. M. Burge, *The Anointed Community: The Holy Spirit in the Johannine Tradition* (Grand Rapids: Eerdmans, 1987), 174–75; D. W. Mills, "The Holy Spirit in 1 John," *Detroit Baptist Seminary Journal* 4 (1999): 43; R. Schnackenburg, *The Johannine Epistles: Introduction and Commentary*, trans. R. Fuller and I. Fuller (New York: Crossroad, 1992), 141–42; Brown, *Epistles of John*, 345–47; Kruse, *Letters of John*, 103; A. E. Brooke, *A Critical and Exegetical Commentary on the Johannine Epistles*, ICC (Edinburgh: T & T Clark, 1912, 1976), 55–56. Against C. H. Dodd, who argues that the anointing should be understood as the "word of God" (*The Johannine Epistles*, The Moffat New Testament Commentary [New York: Harper & Brothers, 1946]. Readers should also consult the detailed study of I. de la Potterie, who appears to combine both views (word of God and Holy Spirit) but gives priority to the word of God (the word interiorized in the heart by the Holy Spirit). ("Anointing of the Christian by Faith," in *The Christian Lives by the Spirit*, ed. I. de la Potterie and S. Lyonnet [New York: Alba House, 1971], 114–15. Cp. Malatesta, *Interiority and Covenant*, 204; M. Vellanickal, *The Divine Sonship of Christians in the Johannine Writings*, Analecta Biblica 72 [Rome: Biblical Institute, 1977], 274–75; I. H. Marshall, *The Epistles of John*, NICNT (Grand Rapids: Eerdmans, 1978), 155, who all appear to follow de la Potterie). See also Kruse, *Letters of John*, 109–110, for an excellent excurses against the view of de la Potterie.

[5] See Kruse, *Letters of John*, 155. This view is almost the reverse of de la Potterie in that there is an understanding that both are involved but that the primary reference is to the Spirit (cp.

they already know all things (2:27) due to the Spirit, who abides in them (cp. Jer 31:33–34).

As a result of the gift of the Spirit, John is able to reassure his readers that they "all" know (2:20). There is, however, a textual variant here that is important to this discussion. The debate is over the form of πᾶς ("all") that should be read in this verse. Is the best reading the nominative πάντες ("you *all* know"), or is the accusative πάντα ("you know *all things*") to be preferred? An examination of the external evidence does not provide a clear answer, for while πάντες has the support of some of the important early Alexandrian texts (א, B), this evidence alone is not decisive.[6] Perhaps the strongest argument in favor of the accusative πάντα is that nowhere in either John's Gospel or epistles is the verb οἶδα used without an object.[7] Of course such an argument cuts both ways since one could make a case that a scribe would likely change the original πάντες to πάντα to simplify the construction by making it follow this more normal pattern. Additionally, one could argue that the parallel 2:27 and John 14:26 would also lead to a scribal alteration from the original πάντες to the more familiar πάντα.[8] Hence, the more difficult reading is that of πάντες.

Not only does πάντες appear to be the more difficult reading, it also best fits the context of the passage, where John is attempting to reassure his readers in the face of the false teaching of the secessionists. Brown is almost certainly correct when he asserts that

> it would seem logical for him to derive from the *chrisma* received by his adherents the fact that therefore all of them have knowledge, so that they need not feel ashamed in the face of the Antichrists' claims. In other words, the fact

Smalley, *1, 2, 3 John*, 107–8; Brown, *Epistles of John*, 346; D. L. Akin, *1, 2, 3 John*, NAC, vol. 38 [Nashville: Broadman & Holman, 2001], 118).

[6] Πάντες is supported by א, B, P, Ψ, 104*, 398, 459, 1838, 1842, 1852, Coptic: Sahidic, Syriac: Philoxeniana, Armenian, Georgian:A1. Πάντα is supported by A, C, D, 33, 61, 81, 94, 104C, 181, 206V, 218, 254, 307, 321, 323, 326, 378, 429, 436, 442, 453, 467, 522, 614, 621, 623, 629, 630, 642, 720, 808, 915, 918, 945, 1067, 1127, 1243, 1292, 1359, 1409, 1448, 1490, 1505, 1523, 1524, 1563, 1611, 1678, 1718, 1735, 1739, 1799, 1831, 1837, 1844, 1875, 1881, 2138, 2147, 2200, 2243, 2298, 2344, 2374, 2412, 2464, 2492, 2541, 2544, 2652, 2805, 2818, Byz [180V], CyrH, Did, Old Church Slavonic:Ch,M,Si,S.

[7] See also D. A. Black, "An Overlooked Stylistic Argument in Favor of *panta* in 1 John 2:20," *Filologia Neotestamentaria* 5 (1992): 205–8, who argues for the πάντα reading more on the grounds of the overall structure of the passage. Cp. J. Breck, "The Function of PAS in 1 John 2:20," *St. Vladimir's Theological Quarterly* 35 (1991): 187–206; Kruse, *Letters of John*, 103–4.

[8] So also Brown, *Epistles of John*, 349.

of their knowledge (*pantes*), not the extent of its object (*panta*), seems best to fit the reassurance.[9]

Such an understanding emphasizes that the "anointing" is the possession of all believers and not just a select few (cp. Jer 31:34).[10]

Therefore, there seem to be at least three reasons for viewing John's teaching on the "anointing" in 1 John 2:20–28 as an allusion to the promise of Jeremiah 31:33–34.[11] First, both passages refer to the importance of God's interior working in the lives of the people. In Jeremiah 31:33, the Law will be placed within them and written on their hearts. In 1 John 2:20–27, the anointing and the message abide within John's readers. Second, the result of this inner working is that "all" have knowledge and not just a select few (Jer 31:34; 1 John 2:27). Third, the interior work in the lives of the people results in the fact that they no longer need anyone to teach them (Jer 31:34; 1 John 2:27).

Therefore, because there is reason to believe that John has alluded to this new covenant promise, it is vital to understand this prophecy in Jeremiah in order to better ascertain his purpose in alluding to it. The new covenant promise of Jeremiah 31:29–34 will now be examined followed by a brief discussion of how John's allusion to this text serves to strengthen his argument in 2:19–27.

The Parable of the Sour Grapes (Jer 31:29–30)

Many interpreters skip over the parable of the sour grapes in their discussion of the new covenant promise of Jeremiah 31.[12] Such an oversight, however, misses an important key to comprehending the

[9] Ibid., 348–49. See also B. M. Metzger, *A Textual Commentary on the Greek New Testament*, 2nd ed. (Stuttgart: Biblia-Druck, 1998), 641, who claims that πάντες was argued for by the majority of the committee "understanding the passage to be directed against the claims of a few to possess esoteric knowledge."

[10] So also Brooke, *Johannine Epistles*, 57; Brown, *Epistles of John*, 349.

[11] For others who view this passage as an allusion to the new covenant promise of Jer 31:29–34, see Brooke, *Johannine Epistles*, 56–57; Smalley, *1, 2, 3 John*, 104; Brown, *Epistles of John*, 349, 370, 375; Akin, *1, 2, 3 John*, 125–26; Kruse, *Letters of John*, 104.

[12] For a few examples of such oversight, see W. C. Kaiser, "The Old Promise and the New Covenant: Jeremiah 31:31–34," *JETS* 25 (1972): 11–23; W. Brueggemann, *A Commentary on Jeremiah: Exile and Homecoming* (Grand Rapids: Eerdmans, 1998), 289–95; W. L. Holladay, *Jeremiah 2*, Hermenia (Minneapolis: Fortress, 1989), 197–98; J. A. Thompson, *The Book of Jeremiah*, The New International Commentary on the Old Testament (Grand Rapids: Eerdmans, 1980), 578–81.

message of this promise.[13] Here Jeremiah asserts that in this coming day, the recipients of this promise will most assuredly cease[14] in their quotation of the proverb, "The fathers have eaten sour grapes and the teeth of the sons are set on edge."[15] The reason this proverb will no longer be quoted among the children of Israel is found in verse 30.[16] It is precisely because the children will no longer be punished for the iniquity of their parents as in the past. In the day of the new covenant, each man will die for his own sin.[17]

While there is diversity in the Old Testament teaching on responsibility for sin,[18] an important aspect of the old covenant was the corporate responsibility for sin (Josh 7:24–26; 1 Sam 22:16–19; 2 Sam 21:1–9) or the idea that guilt and punishment were inherited from the previous generations (Exod 20:5; 34:7; Num 14:18; Deut 5:9; Pss 79:8; 109:14; Job 21:19). Of course both of these ideas are present in Jeremiah (2:5–9; 5:1–8; 18:21; 32:18) where it is evident that Judah came under judgment as a result of the sins of Manasseh (15:4; cp. 2 Kgs 21:10–15).[19] It appears, then, that in the day of the new covenant there would be a radical shift from corporate responsibility to individual responsibility, and verses 33–34 provide the reason for such a change. The interrelation of this proverb (31:29–30) with what

[13] See D. A. Carson, "The Johannine Letters," in *New Dictionary of Biblical Theology: Exploring Unity and Diversity of Scripture*, ed. T. D. Alexander, B. S. Rosner, D. A. Carson, and G. Goldsworthy (Downers Grove, IL: InterVarsity Press, 2000), 354.

[14] Strong negation לֹא + the imperfect יֹאמְרוּ seems to accentuate a major turn of events. It is emphatic that God's people will never again quote this proverb.

[15] It appears that such a proverb was common among the Israelites in this time. See Lam 5:7 and Ezek 18:2 for the Israelites quoting proverbs similar to the one here. However, the eschatological focus of this parable in Jeremiah causes it to function differently from the usage in Ezek 18:2 (see R. P. Carroll, *The Book of Jeremiah: A Commentary* [Philadelphia: Westminster, 1986], 608–9).

[16] I take כִּי here as indicating the ground of v. 29.

[17] This same idea is repeated after the athnach. In this future day it will be the actual culprit who eats sour grapes that will ultimately find his teeth set on edge.

[18] See Deut 24:16, for an example of individual accountability. Even here though, some want to argue that this passage is speaking specifically about blood guiltiness (so H. J. Boecker, *Law and the Administration of Justice in the Old Testament and Ancient East*, trans. J. Mosier [London: SPCK, 1980], 37).

[19] See also J. R. Lundbom, *Jeremiah 21–36: A New Translation with Introduction and Commentary*, The Anchor Bible, vol. 21B (New York: Doubleday, 2004), 462, who draws the same conclusion but nevertheless fails to link them to the new covenant.

follows (31:31–34) is important for a proper understanding of this new covenant promise.

The New Covenant (Jer 31:31–32)

There is a clear link between verses 27–30 and 31–34. To begin with, the forward-looking aspect, which is focused upon a coming day, is still at the forefront.[20] Additionally, the writer is still proclaiming a direct word from the Lord.[21] Moreover, there is a connection in some of the key words such as fathers (31:29,32) and iniquity (31:30,34).[22] Finally, verses 33–34 share a common interest with and even help explicate verses 29–30 as to why a major emphasis of the new covenant involves a shift from corporate retribution to individual retribution.

Beginning in verse 31, Yahweh declares through His prophet that in this coming day, He will cut a "new covenant" with the house of Israel and the house of Judah. While this is the only time the phrase "new covenant" is used in the Old Testament, the idea is clearly present elsewhere in Jeremiah (24:7; 32:38–40; 50:5) as well as other places in the Old Testament (Isa 42:6; 49:8; 54:10; 55:1–5; 59:21; 61:8; Ezek 16:60; 34:25; 36:27–28; 37:26; Hos 2:16–25; Mal 2:1–9; 3:1).[23] While some interpreters wish to argue for a "renewed" covenant in this passage,[24] there is no conclusive evidence that the word חָדָשׁ ever means anything other than "new" in the Old Testament.[25] Perhaps this is why Kaiser's

[20] Verse 27 is the first time in chap. 31 that the phrase הִנֵּה יָמִים בָּאִים is used, and it is picked up again in v. 31.

[21] The phrase נְאֻם־יְהוָה appears in each of the remaining verses (31–34).

[22] So also Lundbom, *Jeremiah 21–36*, 460.

[23] Not to mention the fact that Jesus sees Himself as inaugurating this new covenant (Luke 22:20) and this idea is picked up by several of the NT writers (1 Cor 11:25; 2 Cor 3:6; Heb 8:8,13; 9:15; 12:24).

[24] A sampling of such interpreters include Kaiser, "The Old Promise and the New Covenant," 11–23; N. Lohfink, *The Covenant Never Revoked*, trans. J. J. Scullion (New York: Paulist, 1991), 45; F. C. Holmgren, *The Old Testament and the Significance of Jesus* (Grand Rapids: Eerdmans, 1999), 75–95; R. Rendtorff, *Canon and Theology* (Minneapolis: Fortress, 1993), 198.

[25] Against Kaiser, "Old Promise and the New Covenant," 16–17. After surveying the 53 uses of חָדָשׁ in the Hebrew Bible, there does not appear to be a single usage where the word חָדָשׁ unambiguously carries the meaning "renewed." See F. Brown, *The Brown-Driver-Briggs Hebrew and English Lexicon*, ed. S. R. Driver and C. A. Briggs (Boston: Houghton, Mifflin and Company, 1906; repr., Peabody, MA: Hendrickson, 1996), s.v. "חָדָשׁ" [henceforth *BDB*], and Ludwig Koehler and Walter Baumgartner, *The Hebrew and Aramaic Lexicon of the Old Testament*, trans. M. E. J. Richardson (Leiden: Brill, 2000), s.v. "חָדָשׁ" [henceforth, *KB*], who both offer no instances of this word meaning "renewed."

word study of חָדָשׁ appeals so quickly to the Greek words for "new" (καινός and νέος), as opposed to focusing on the Hebrew word that occurs 53 times in the Masoretic Text.[26] With the bulk of evidence lying in favor of the word meaning "new," the ambiguity of any reference in the Hebrew ever actually meaning "renewed," and the context of the passage, which clearly underscores a major disjunction between the old covenant and the one that was to come, the burden of proof lies with those who wish to argue for a "renewed covenant."[27]

Moreover, if debate over "new" or "renewed" covenant were still open for discussion, 31:32 is perhaps the linchpin for the argument that this oracle is speaking of a "new covenant." In this verse there is great emphasis placed on the discontinuity between the old and new covenants, which is accentuated by the structure of this sentence. The whole of verse 32 modifies the phrase בְּרִית חֲדָשָׁה ("new covenant") from verse 31. Here it begins with the strong negative לֹא ("not") followed by כַּבְּרִית, ("like the covenant"),[28] in order to imply that this new covenant is qualitatively different in kind from the old one. The discontinuity between these two covenants is strengthened by the author's use of a "virtual casus pendus" construction.[29] The use of

[26] It is also worthy of note that Kaiser's word study falls prey to at least two word study fallacies (cp. D. A. Carson, *Exegetical Fallacies*, 2nd ed. [Grand Rapids: Baker, 1996], 27–64). To begin with, he appeals to a "selective and prejudicial use of evidence." This is evident in the fact that he jumps so quickly to the Greek words for "new" and completely fails to survey the word in the Hebrew Old Testament, where the predominant meaning of the term means nothing other than "new." Likewise, he also stumbles into the pitfall of appealing to "unknown or unlikely meanings." Here again, while failing to interact with the 53 usages of חָדָשׁ in the Old Testament, Kaiser attempts to support his thesis by appealing to Akkadian, noting that the Hebrew "*hadas* is cognate to Semitic roots like Akkadian *edesu* meaning 'to restore' ruined altars or cities" (Kaiser, "Old Promise and the New Covenant," 17 n. 34).

[27] So also P. A. Verhoef, *New International Dictionary of Old Testament Theology and Exegesis*, ed. W. A. VanGemeren (Grand Rapids: Zondervan, 1997), s.v. "חָדָשׁ."

[28] The כ before בְּרִית should be seen as a כ of comparison, expressing a comparison in kind. For this use of the כ, see BDB, s.v. "כ". See also *KB*, s.v. "כ"; B. K. Waltke and M. O'Connor, *An Introduction to Biblical Hebrew Syntax* (Winona Lake, IN: Eisenbrauns, 1990), 203.

[29] I have used the term "virtual casus pendus" as a result of the fact that the normal casus pendus construction is resumed by means of a retrospective pronoun. This designation was decided upon during a conversation with Russell Fuller in March 2005 as a result of its affinities to the normal casus pendus constructions. One does wonder if it is not even more emphatic given the fact that it is not resumed with the expected pronoun but rather the head noun is brought back for added emphasis. For examples of the typical casus pendus constructions, see P. Joüon, *A Grammar of Biblical Hebrew*, trans. and rev. T. Muraoka (Rome: Editrice Pontificio Istituto Biblico, 2003) [henceforth *JM*], 586–88.

the strong disjunctive accent (כַּבְּרִית) followed by a series of modifying clauses describing the old covenant allows the word *covenant* to "stand aloof from what follows"[30] until it is emphatically resumed by the same word. Hence, Jeremiah is clear in his assertion that the old covenant, which Yahweh made with the people of Israel when He rescued them out of Egypt, is qualitatively different from the new covenant.

Interiority of the New Covenant (Jer 31:33)

What is new about the covenant was not only alluded to in 31:29–30 but is now explained in verses 33–34. The law will be placed בְּקִרְבָּם ("in their inward parts"/"within them"), which should be understood as the innermost being or the "seat of life" in a similar way that נֶפֶשׁ ("soul") would be used.[31] In the following parallel phrase, it is also asserted that it will be written on their heart. Thus in the new covenant the people of God will no longer have to rely on someone else to teach them the law. In this coming day the prophet exclaims that the law will be placed in their innermost being. This verse, therefore, emphasizes the interiority of the law, which is the quintessential distinction between the new covenant and that of the old.

No Need for Teachers? (Jer 31:34)

The inference drawn in 31:34 is vital to one's understanding of the uniqueness of the new covenant.[32] Since the Lord will internalize His law on the heart of His people, participants in this covenant will no longer need to be taught to "know the Lord." This is made clear by Jeremiah with the strong negation[33] of the idea of one man teaching his neighbor or brother to "know the Lord." So what does this mean? Are we to conclude that in the new covenant there will no longer be "teachers" of any kind with the exception of God Himself?[34]

[30] *JM*, 586.

[31] So *KB*, s.v. "קרב."

[32] I take וְלֹא as an energic vav of logical consecution (see *JM*, 636).

[33] I am taking וְלֹא with the piel imperfect יְלַמְּדוּ followed by the adverb עוֹד to emphasize the fact that they will *never* again have to have someone teach them to "know the Lord."

[34] So J. D. Derrett, "Mt 23,8–10 a Midrash on Is 54,13 and Jer 31,31–34," *Biblica* 62 (1981): 372–86, esp. 377.

Assuming that Jesus instituted the new covenant in the upper room (Luke 22:20), this interpretation flies in the face of the rest of the New Testament, given that the early church was continually devoting themselves to the apostles' teaching (Acts 2:42), there are those who are appointed as "teachers" (1 Cor 12:28), there is teaching throughout the books of the New Testament, and such teaching is a direct command of the Lord Jesus Himself (Matt 28:20).

What then is Jeremiah talking about when he says that there will be no need for teachers? There are two helpful clues within the passage itself. First, the immediate context makes clear that the result of the law being internalized in the heart of the people is that they will no longer need anyone to teach them to "know Yahweh" (31:34). The text itself does not say there will be no "teachers" in general but that there will be no teachers specifically to teach the people to "know the Lord." To be sure, knowing Yahweh and the teaching of Torah are inextricably bound together in the Old Testament. Under the old covenant, the priests were the ones who were primarily given the task of teaching the Torah. Moreover, the prophets can be found indicting the priests when the people failed to know the Lord. Hosea, for one, attributes the peoples' lack of knowledge of God to the priests' dereliction of their duty. In Hosea 4:6, the prophet asserts, "My people perish for lack of knowledge, because you [priests] have rejected the knowledge [i.e., Torah], so I have rejected you from being a priest for Me, and you forgot the Torah of your God, and I Myself have forgotten your sons." Hence, this passage makes clear that the knowledge of Yahweh and the teaching of Torah go hand in hand in the old covenant. All of this changes, however, in the coming of the new covenant because now the Torah is internalized within the believer. With the link between the teaching of Torah and knowing God, it is clear that they no longer need anyone to teach them to know Yahweh because the Torah is internalized within their hearts. Knowing God is therefore covenantal language, for when they enter into the new covenant and the Torah is written upon their hearts, they know God. Hence, they do not need any kind of teacher to tell them to know Yahweh.

Moreover, a second clue as to Jeremiah's meaning comes in the aforementioned proverb of verses 29–30, which provides further insight as to why new covenant believers would no longer need anyone to teach them to "know the Lord." In the old covenant, individuals did not have the law written on their hearts. In fact, as noted above, they were forced to trust in mediating tribal representative teachers such as kings, priests, and prophets. Unfortunately, when these teachers went astray, the people followed.[35] Thus the teeth of the children were set on edge because of the sins of their fathers. Jeremiah, however, makes clear that the people of the new covenant will no longer quote this proverb because the Torah will be written upon their hearts.[36] As a result, there is no longer a need for tribal representative teachers such as the priests, kings, or prophets to teach them to "know the Lord" because[37] they will all know Him. Therefore, errant priests and false prophets can no longer lead genuine new covenant believers astray, and each individual will set his own teeth on edge and die for his own sin.[38]

John's Use of Jeremiah 31

This interpretation of Jeremiah is helpful for understanding how John's allusion to this passage in 1 John 2:26–27 strengthens his argument against the secessionists and bolsters the assurance of his readers. In 2:26, he makes clear that he is warning his readers about the false teachers who are trying to deceive them. From the context of 1 John, it is most plausible that the false teachers have made claims to some special revelation from God (and therefore place themselves in the position of special authoritative teachers) with which they were attempting to mislead John's readers. It is therefore in the context of protecting his readers from these false teachers that John alludes to Jeremiah 31:27–34. Here the false teachers' ploy to lead the people astray is countered by John's reminder that all his readers already

[35] See, for example, the books of Kings and Chronicles, where the people follow the leadership of both the godly and the ungodly kings.

[36] As a result of the interior witness of the law, the idea of corporate responsibility for sin is wiped away. This is not to deny that there will still be social implications to sin. When a father lives continually in a particular sin, it is often passed on to the son. This, however, does not appear to be the primary issue in this passage.

[37] I take this כִּי as the ground of the first clause of v. 34.

[38] I am indebted to Carson, "Johannine Letters," 354, for my understanding of the proverb in this passage.

know all things (20,27) because of the "anointing" (Holy Spirit) abiding in them. The Holy Spirit, then, dwells within individual believers and teaches them all things (2:27). Hence, in the midst of the false teaching of the secessionists, John reminds his readers that they are members of the new covenant community and therefore do not need a teacher who has put himself in a special place of authority (in the likeness of the tribal representative teachers of the old covenant) by appealing to some special revelation or knowledge. This passage therefore serves to reassure his readers that they will not be led astray because the anointing abides in them.

Other Promises and Obligations of the New Covenant Found in 1 John

While the anointing pericope is perhaps the clearest allusion to a particular new covenant passage, there are several other indicators throughout this letter that John views his readers as a new covenant community. I will demonstrate this by laying out some of the promises and obligations of the new covenant[39] and then evaluating the ways in which John sees his readers living in the fulfillment of such promises.

In the new covenant passage of Jeremiah 31:29–34, there are at least four key promises. These include (1) the internalization of the Law; (2) God will be their God, and they will be His people; (3) the knowledge of God; and (4) the forgiveness of sins. In addition to the promises found in Jeremiah are those found in Ezekiel (11:18–21; 36:27–28; 37:26–28).[40] These include (5) a new and united heart, (6) the reception and interiority of God's own Spirit, and (7) God's dwelling with His people. Furthermore, the fulfillment of the new covenant in the life of the believer brings with it covenantal obligations. These include the fact that (1) the people will be God's people, and (2) they will walk in His statutes and keep His ordinances/commands.

[39] I say "some" because I am well aware that I am not interacting with every passage that is considered to be a new covenant passage. Such a study is beyond the scope of this book. Here I am simply attempting to demonstrate that John sees his readers as the fulfillment of some of these promises.

[40] I am not here noting the overlap between the two books.

God Dwelling with His People

One of the fundamental promises of both the old[41] and new covenants is the promise that God would dwell with His people. This new covenant promise is made clear in Ezekiel 37:26–28. Here God tells His people that His dwelling place will be with them and that He will set His sanctuary in their midst forever. Such a promise was fulfilled in the Gospel of John (1:14) when the incarnate Son of God comes and tabernacles (ἐσκήνωσεν) among His people. Jesus dwelling with His people should be seen as "nothing else than a claim by the Johannine community to be the true, eschatological heirs of the experience of Israel in the past."[42] The fulfillment of this promise continues on in 1 John in the language of abiding (μένω ἐν and εἰμί ἐν).[43] Here John asserts that the people are to abide in God as He abides in His people (2:24c; 3:24; 4:12–13,15–16). This abiding is important because it demonstrates that God is not only dwelling with His people but has also taken up residence *in* His people through His Holy Spirit (2:27; 3:9). Pryor notes that a contrast has been set up between the old covenant (Exod 33:7) where Yahweh dwells outside the camp of Israel with the new covenant in which Jesus tabernacles "among us."[44] This, however, does not go far enough in the contrast because God not only dwells among His people but also dwells in them and they in Him.[45]

Forgiveness and Cleansing of Sin

Another promise of the new covenant is the forgiveness and cleansing of sins. In Ezekiel 36:25,33, God promises to cleanse His people from all their filth, idols, and iniquities (cp. Jer 31:34). A fulfillment of this promise can be found throughout the first letter of John (1:7,9,2:1–2,12; 3:5; 4:10). Here the writer makes abundantly clear that one of the primary reasons Jesus came was that sin might be forgiven (3:5), and his readers who confess their sins are the benefi-

[41] Exod 25:8; 29:43–46; Lev 26:11–12; Deut 12:11.

[42] J. W. Pryor, *John: Evangelist of the Covenant People: The Narrative and Themes of the Fourth Gospel* (Downers Grove, IL: InterVarsity, 1992), 158.

[43] See Malatesta, *Interiority and Covenant*.

[44] Pryor, *John*, 158.

[45] Cp. E. S. J. Malatesta, "Covenant and Indwelling," *The Way* 17 (1977): 28.

ciaries of this gracious work and can have confidence that their sins are truly cleansed (1:7,9; 2:12).[46]

I Will Be Their God and They Will Be My People

In the new covenant Yahweh makes the promise, "I will be their God and they will be My people" (Jer 31:33; Ezek 36:28). This promise is fulfilled in at least two ways in 1 John. First, John regularly refers to his readers as "children of God" or those who have been "born of God" (2:29; 3:1; 3:9 [2x]; 4:7; 5:1 [3x], 4,18 [2x]).[47] In the Gospel two fundamental passages aid our understanding of what the writer means in his description of his readers as "born of God" or "children of God" (John 1:12–13; 3:1–8). To begin with, in 1:12 John asserts that those who "receive" Jesus and "believe in His name" are given the "right to become children of God." Moreover, this is further explained in verse 13 when he speaks of those "who were born not of blood nor the will of the flesh nor the will of man, but of God." This passage demonstrates that being children of God/born of God is completely different from being born of natural human procreation. It is something that occurs only by God's own doing. Moreover, this divine begetting is said to be a birth by means of the Holy Spirit (John 3:1–8). Therefore, being born of God is something done by God's own initiative (cp. 1 John 4:10,19) and is effected through His own Spirit coming to dwell in His people.[48] Perhaps this is why John pauses in his letter at the first mention of the divine birth (2:29) in order to bask in amazement (3:1–2) at the wonder of God setting His affections on His people and making them His own children. Such a relationship would fulfill the new covenant promise where God says, "I will be their God and they will be My people."

Second, John's readers are said to have fellowship with God (1:3,6,7). The four uses of this word in 1 John demonstrate that while it is true that "fellowship" involves "a close association involving

[46] See Brown, *Epistles of John*, 415.

[47] See also Pryor, *John: Evangelist of the Covenant People*, 173–79, for a detailed argument in favor of the motif of being "born of God" as a new covenant motif.

[48] Against Vellanickal who argues that the divine sonship is not a gift received at the time of believing in Jesus but something that is progressively realized through human cooperation with the work of God that is completed in glory (*Divine Sonship*, 105–52).

mutual interests," this "close association" is with God and other believers and the "mutual interests" in which one shares revolve around the eternal life (Jesus) that was with God and revealed to the apostles (1:2).[49] This fellowship with God is a close relationship that includes the ideas of "knowing" and "abiding" in Him as well. Thus, this motif would appear as another confirmation that John sees the fulfillment of the new covenant promise where Yahweh vows "to be their God and they will be My people."

Knowledge of God

As noted above, the knowledge of God is one of the key components of the new covenant. Such a knowledge is referred to throughout John's letter (2:3–4,13–14; 3:1,6; 4:6–8), and this knowledge should certainly be viewed as yet another fulfillment of the promises of the new covenant.[50] Marshall is correct in his observation that "in the Old Testament it is comparatively rare to find the thought that men know God, although this was something for which prophets hoped (Jer 31:34; cp. Heb 8:11)."[51] What is clear, however, is that the people of Israel are at times exhorted to know God (1 Chr 28:9; Jer 9:24) and the prophets are often found rebuking them for their failure to do so (Job 36:12; Jer 9:6; Isa 1:3; 5:13; 1 Sam 2:12). The evidence that they do not know God was their lack of knowing the Torah and their resulting disobedience to His commands and statutes for living. Such is seen in 1 Samuel when the sons of Eli were spoken of as those who "did not know the Lord" (1 Sam 2:12), or again in Hosea when he associates the moral failures of the people with there being no "knowledge of God in the land" (Hos 4:1–2). While John places more emphasis on the evidence of knowing God (i.e., the moral obligations

[49] See chap. 2.

[50] So also M. E. Boismard, "La Connaissance de l'alliance nouvelle, d'apres la premiere letter de saint Jean," *RB* 56 (1949): 366–71, 388–91; Brown, *Epistles of John*, 279.

[51] Marshall, *Epistles of John*, 122. Cp. J. M. Lieu, *The Theology of the Johannine Epistles* (Cambridge: Cambridge University Press, 1991), 32: "As in the Fourth Gospel, where knowing God is equally important and is the goal of the coming of the son (compare 1 John 5:20 with John 17:3), knowledge denotes relationship rather than factual knowledge or a perception of reality. This is equally true in the Old Testament, where knowledge of God involves acknowledgement, confession and obedience (Jer. 31:33–34); it belongs to the covenant relationship with God."

of knowing God),[52] it is nevertheless apparent that he assumes his readers do in fact know Him; otherwise, there would be no point to the "testing" of such knowledge that is seen throughout this epistle.

One Heart

Another promise of the new covenant is that God would give His people "one heart" (Ezek 11:19; cf. Jer 32:39). This is a promise that in the coming day, God's people would experience unity.[53] It is quite plausible that such a promise finds fulfillment in the unity that John insists upon in his emphasis on loving the brethren (2:9–11; 3:10b-24; 4:7–13,16–21; 5:1–2). The children of God are to love one another because they have one heart and share one Spirit. John expects this heart of unity as demonstrated in his insistence that they love one another, and he is therefore able to say that the one who does not love the brethren is in the darkness (2:9,11), has not been born of God (3:10), abides in death (3:14–15), is a murderer (3:15), does not know God (4:8), and is a liar (4:20).

Interiority and the Holy Spirit in the New Covenant

The idea of interiority and the Holy Spirit is a fundamental element of the new covenant. This is seen most clearly in Ezekiel 11:19–20 and 36:26–27. Here we see that God will place His own Spirit within His people for the purpose of enabling them to walk in all His statutes and observe all His ordinances. This kind of language is fulfilled in several ways in 1 John but perhaps most clearly in the passages that speak of the Holy Spirit. Such passages set forth the idea that

[52] So also Kruse, *Letters of John*, 78.

[53] So C. F. Keil and F. Delitzsch, *Ezekiel*, trans. J. Martin, vol. 9 of *Commentary on the Old Testament* (Grand Rapids: Eerdmans, 1982), 152: "I give them *one* heart. לֵב אֶחָד, which Hitzig is wrong in proposing to alter into לֵב אַחֵר, *another* heart, after the LXX, is supported and explained by Jer. xxxii. 39, 'I give them *one* heart and *one* way to fear me continually' (cf. Zeph. iii. 9 and Acts iv. 32). *One* heart is not an upright, undivided heart (לֵב שָׁלֵם), but a harmonious, united heart, in contrast to the division or plurality of hearts which prevails in the natural state, in which every one follows his own heart and his own mind, turning 'every one to his own way' (Isa. liii. 6). God gives *one* heart, when He causes all hearts and minds to become one. This can only be effected by His giving a 'new spirit,' taking away the stone heart, and giving a heart of flesh instead."

the Spirit brings about new birth and therefore enables people to live righteously (3:9,24; 4:13).

Above I argued that the Holy Spirit is referred to metaphorically as "the anointing" (τὸ χρῖσμα), who enables all believers to "know all things" so as not to be deceived or led astray by the false teachers (2:19–28).[54] In 3:9 it would appear that John again speaks of the Holy Spirit metaphorically, referring to Him as the "seed" (σπέρμα) who is the agent of new birth.[55] The structure of this verse is helpful for its interpretation.[56]

(a) Everyone who has been born of God
 (b) does not do sin
  (c) because His seed abides in him
 (b2) and he is not able to sin
(a2) because he has been born of God.

First, the divine birth (a, a2) should be understood as the controlling idea of the verse. Second, those born of God are not able to sin (b, b2). Third, the *reason* they are not able to sin is because God's "seed" abides in them (c). Throughout this letter we have seen three things abiding in the believer: (1) the message that was heard from the beginning (2:24), (2) the Holy Spirit/anointing (2:20,27), and (3) God Himself (3:24; 4:12–13,15–16). Within the context of the Johannine literature, the best choice among these three as the identity of the "seed" is the Holy Spirit. One would think that John's readers were familiar with the

[54] The interiority of the Spirit is evident in this passage in that the text says that the "anointing" abides in the believer and teaches them about all things. Cp. 5:20 ("understanding") and 4:4 ("greater is He who is in you than he who is in the world").

[55] So also Burge, *Anointed Community*, 176; Brown, *Epistles of John*, 411; Schnackenburg, *Johannine Epistles*, 175; Mills, "The Holy Spirit in 1 John," 36–37; Kruse, *Letters of John*, 125; Brooke, *Johannine Epistles*, 89. Of course, there have been several other interpretations of this passage. J. de Waal Dryden ("The Sense of ΣΠΕΡΜΑ in 1 JOHN 3:9: In Light of Lexical Evidence," *Filologia Neotestamentaria* 11 [1999]: 85–100) argues on lexical grounds for a corporate understanding and thus "the children of God" (cp. P. Perkins, *The Johannine Epistles*, New Testament Message [Wilmington, DE: Michael Glazier, 1979], 41–42; T. Griffith, *Keep Yourselves from Idols: A New Look at 1 John*, JSNTSup 233 [Sheffield: Sheffield Academic Press, 2002], 139). J. du Preez actually lists six different interpretations for σπέρμα αὐτοῦ ("'Sperma autou' in 1 John 3:9," *Neot* 9 [1975]: 105–06). These include (1) children of God, (2) the proclaimed word of God, (3) Christ, (4) the Holy Spirit, (5) new life from God, and (6) the new nature.

[56] This chiasm is also seen by Vellanickal, *Divine Sonship of Christians in the Johannine Writings*, 268; Kruse, *Letters of John*, 125; Mills, "The Holy Spirit in 1 John," 37.

passages of divine begetting in the Fourth Gospel (1:12–13; 3:3–6), where it is clear that new birth is from God by means of the Holy Spirit.[57] Burge is almost certainly correct in his assertion:

> The immediate context suggests that the σπέρμα . . . is simply a part of John's now familiar divine birth terminology: γεννᾶν ἐκ θεοῦ (2 times in 3:9). Divine birth employing σπέρμα echoes John 3:3ff., where such birth is also discussed in terms of the Spirit. Therefore σπέρμα in 1 John 3:9 is a symbol of the Spirit in a crude though legitimate application of the regeneration metaphor.[58]

Moreover, this work of the Spirit produces clear evidences that are observable in the public arena and enables people to see that one is a child of God as opposed to a child of the Devil. Those born of God through the work of the "seed"/Holy Spirit will live like their Father as manifested in their "doing righteousness" and "loving the brethren" (3:10).

Another instance where the interior work of the Spirit is present is His role in producing assurance of mutual abiding with God (3:24; 4:13).[59] There is some debate, however, as to how the Spirit produces such assurance. Some assert that these verses refer to the inner witness of the Holy Spirit that serves as an additional support to their assurance (cp. Rom 8:16).[60] While such an interpretation is possible, the context of each of these verses points toward the idea that the internal work of the Spirit produces particular observable manifestations such as a proper confession of Christ (3:24) or loving the brethren (4:13), whereby the believer is able to observe such behavior and draw assurance that he is abiding in God and He in him.[61]

The above interpretation can be supported by an examination of these two verses in their respective contexts. John begins 3:24 with

[57] So Brown, *Epistles of John*, 410–11; Mills, "The Holy Spirit in 1 John," 38.

[58] Burge, *Anointed Community*, 176.

[59] These two passages are clearly parallel: 1 John 3:24b: καὶ ἐν τούτῳ γινώσκομεν ὅτι μένει ἐν ἡμῖν, ἐκ τοῦ πνεύματος οὗ ἡμῖν ἔδωκεν. 1 John 4:13: Ἐν τούτῳ γινώσκομεν ὅτι ἐν αὐτῷ μένομεν καὶ αὐτὸς ἐν ἡμῖν, ὅτι ἐκ τοῦ πνεύματος αὐτοῦ δέδωκεν ἡμῖν.

[60] So Marshall, *Epistles of John*, 202; Schnackenburg, *Johannine Epistles*, 219; Akin, *1, 2, 3 John*, 169.

[61] See D. A. Carson, "Johannine Perspectives on the Doctrine of Assurance," in *Explorations: Justification and Christian Assurance*, ed. R. J. Gibson (Adelaide, South Australia: Openbook Publishers, 1996), 72. This is not to say that this role of the Spirit is not present in the New Testament (e.g., Rom 8). I simply do not think that it is the best understanding of 3:24 and 4:13 in their context.

a test, asserting that the one who keeps the commands is the one who experiences mutual abiding with God.[62] The parallelism between 3:24a and 3:24b should not go unnoticed. In both, the motif of testing (3:24a—"the one who keeps His commands" / 3:24b—"by this we know") and abiding (3:24a—"he abides in Him and He in him" / 3:24b—"He abides in us") are present. Given that the test in 3:24a has to do with observable behavior, it is certainly plausible that the test in 3:24b is dealing with the same thing. Moreover, there is the question in 3:24b of whether "by this" points forward to what John is about to say or back to what has just been said. If it points forward, then it is asserting that the Spirit helps the believer to know God abides in him because the believer has accepted the testimony of the Spirit about the person of Jesus and therefore has a right confession of Him (4:1–6).[63] If it points back to what has just been asserted,[64] then the Spirit's work of empowering believers to keep the commands, which includes loving the brethren, enables them to know that God is abiding in them. Regardless as to whether it is pointing forward, backward, or perhaps both,[65] the point of this verse seems to be that the internal work of the Spirit that bolsters assurance is His production of the objective manifestations of obedience to the commands and/or a right confession of Christ in the life of the believer.[66]

[62] 1 John 3:24a: ἐν αὐτῷ μένει καὶ αὐτὸς ἐν αὐτῷ.

[63] So R. Law, *The Tests of Life: A Study of The First Epistle of St. John*, 3rd ed. (Edinburgh: T. & T. Clark, 1914; repr., Grand Rapids: Baker, 1968), 263–64; Smalley, *1, 2, 3 John*, 211; Kruse, 144; J. C. Coetzee, "The Holy Spirit in 1 John," *Neot* 13 (1979): 52–53; Carson, "Johannine Perspectives on the Doctrine of Assurance," 73; Malatesta, *Interiority and Covenant*, 276.

[64] So B. F. Westcott, *The Epistles of St. John: The Greek Text with Notes and Essays* (Grand Rapids: Eerdmans, 1955), 121; D. W. Burdick, *The Letters of John the Apostle* (Chicago: Moody, 1985), 65–66.

[65] A good case can be made that it is pointing both forward and backward (so Mills, "The Holy Spirit in 1 John," 40). It seems that the strongest argument in favor of this reading is the fact that this statement is transitional. In 3:24 John introduces the Spirit, which is a subject continued in the first few verses of chap. 4 (4:1–6). So it seems best to see 3:24b as a transition sentence from one section to the next (cp. 3:10, where John transitions in one sentence from the test of obedience to the test of love; moreover, while there is much disagreement as to whether "by this" points forward, backward, or both in 3:24, many will admit that it probably goes both ways in 3:10). Cp. Kruse, *Letters of John*, 144, who refers to 3:24 as transitional even though he does not agree that it points both ways. If it is correct to understand 3:24 as transitional, then "by this" should probably be understood as pointing both backwards and forwards.

[66] J. R. W. Stott, *The Letters of John: An Introduction and Commentary*, TNTC, rev. ed. (Grand Rapids: Eerdmans, 2000), 155.

Likewise, the parallel 4:13 should also be understood as connected to either what precedes,[67] follows,[68] or both.[69] Again, for our purposes, it makes little difference which of these one believes, for each leads to the idea that the internal work of the Spirit in assurance is not simply an internal witness that is distinct from its observable manifestations. Quite the contrary, here as in 3:24, the believer's assurance that God is abiding in him is bolstered by the internal work of the Spirit, who leads the believer to love the brethren and have a right confession of Jesus.

Finally, I have already noted in chapter 3 of this study that one of the key roles of the Spirit is to testify to the truth of Jesus' work on the cross (5:6–8). The man Jesus was the Son of God all the way through both the water of His baptism and the blood He shed on the cross.[70] Here the role of the Spirit is to testify to this truth. Nevertheless, even in this passage it would appear that the work of the Spirit is not simply to produce an internal confidence regarding the person and work of Jesus but that this testimony of the Spirit also leads the believer into right belief regarding the person of Jesus. Such is seen in the context of this passage where the writer goes on to assert that one should receive the Spirit's testimony about Jesus because it is God's own testimony, and the testimony of God is greater than any testimony of man (5:9). Moreover, the one who believes in this testimony regarding the historic Son of God actually has this testimony in himself (5:10). This belief would appear to be yet another external criterion by which to observe the internal work of the Spirit.

Therefore, the writer's teaching on the Holy Spirit seems to mirror the promises of new covenant interiority, where God's own Spirit would dwell within His people and the Spirit's internal work would be that of enabling them to live holy lives (Ezek 36:27). Here it appears that each of the passages in this letter that refers to the Spirit focuses

[67] Westcott, *Epistles of St. John*, 152. Cp. Smalley, *1, 2, 3 John*, 249. While arguing strongly that "by this" pointed forward at 3:24, he does not seem as certain in this text. After stating that it probably points forward, he adds, "but ἐν τούτῳ can also look back to vv 7–12, and especially 12."

[68] So Brown, *Epistles of John*, 521; Kruse, *Letters of John*, 163.

[69] So Mills, "Holy Spirit in 1 John," 40–41; Carson, "Johannine Perspectives on the Doctrine of Assurance," 73.

[70] See chap. 5 for a defense of this reading.

not on the subjective internal witness but on the objective observable work that the Spirit produces in the life of the believer.[71]

Interiority and Abiding in 1 John

John's use of μένειν ἐν ("to abide in") and εἶναι ἐν ("to be in") in this letter also appears to fulfill some of the new covenant promises.[72] Here John says that believers abide in God and God abides in them (3:24; 4:13,15–16), the message they have heard from the beginning abides in them (2:24), and the Holy Spirit/anointing/seed abides in them and empowers them to live holy lives, know all things, and not be deceived by false teachers (2:20,27; 3:9). Consequently, believers who make up this new covenant community will have the words of Christ internalized in their hearts and have God's own Spirit dwelling in them, leading and enabling them to live for Him. They will therefore mutually abide in the closest possible relationship where "they will be made and kept holy by his indwelling, sanctifying presence."[73]

Obligations of Interior Renewal

Finally, the obligations that come with interior renewal are perhaps the clearest aspect of the new covenant motif in the Johannine literature.[74] Such obligations were evident in Deuteronomy when Moses foretold that the Israelites would not keep the commands he was giving because they were not able. What was wrong with the law was not the law itself but the ability to keep it (Deut 29:3[4]).[75] Thankfully, Moses also prophesied that a day would come when God would circumcise the hearts of His own for the very purpose that they might be able to love Him with all their heart and soul and be able to obey Him (Deut 30:6–7). The promise of this divine enabling was seen in the prophets as well where it is said that God's people would receive a new heart and a new spirit for the very purpose that they might walk

[71] So also Carson, "Johannine Perspectives on the Doctrine of Assurance," 73–74.

[72] See especially the work of Malatesta, *Interiority and Covenant*; idem, "Covenant and Indwelling," 27–32.

[73] Malatesta, "Covenant and Indwelling," 28–29.

[74] So Pryor, *John: Evangelist of the Covenant People*, 160.

[75] So also T. R. Schreiner, *The Law and Its Fulfillment: A Pauline Theology of the Law* (Grand Rapids: Baker, 1993), 83.

in His statutes and keep His ordinances (Ezek 11:20; 36:27; 37:24). The fulfillment of these promises is found in John's expectation of his readers to live righteously (2:29), which is seen in the various tests that spiral throughout the letter. It is precisely because God's Spirit now dwells in them that he expects them to have a right belief in Jesus, keep the commands,[76] and love one another. Thus, it is unequivocally the fulfillment of the new covenant promises such as God's dwelling with and in His people, their total renewal, and the divine enablement for their obedience that stands behind these obligations to abide, to love the brethren, to believe in the historic person of Jesus Christ, and to keep His commandments.

Conclusion

Therefore, there seems to be ample evidence to substantiate the thesis that John viewed his readers as members of a new covenant community. Support for this view is found in John's apparent allusion to the new covenant passage in Jeremiah 31. Moreover, it would also appear that John believed that the promises of the new covenant were fulfilled in the work of Christ, which is why he expected his readers to live in a manner that validated their divine birth. John's readers now had God's own Spirit dwelling within them so that they would live righteously. This then would appear to be the ground for the cycles of tests that make up the body of his letter and are the focus of the next chapter. It is precisely because the new covenant has been fulfilled in Christ that he expected his readers to have the Spirit dwelling in them and enabling them to pass the various tests of righteousness, love, and belief.

[76] We have already discussed John's use of μένω as new covenant language. Likewise, his use of τηρέω should not be missed. The idea of "keeping the commandments" is no doubt important covenant language in the Old Testament. Though φυλάσσω is the word used throughout the LXX to translate the Hebrew שָׁמַר, John's use of τηρέω comes as no surprise, for it seems that by the time of NT writing, τηρέω was preferred for the idea of keeping the commands (see S. Pancaro, *The Law in the Fourth Gospel: The Torah and the Gospel, Moses and Jesus, Judaism and Christianity According to John,* NovTSup [Leiden: E. J. Brill, 1975], 403–51, for a good overview of John's use of "keeping the commands").

Chapter 5

ASSURANCE SUPPORTED BY THE LIFESTYLE OF THE BELIEVER

Introduction

The first letter of John is laden with various sets of criteria by which its readers can evaluate their religious claims in light of the way they conduct their lives. The believer's lifestyle therefore serves as either a vital support to one's assurance or as evidence that he has never really passed over from death to life. In the previous chapter I argued that John viewed his readers as a new covenant community and thus expected God's own Spirit to be dwelling in them and empowering them to walk in the light. The emphasis on the various criteria or tests naturally follows from such an understanding, for the Holy Spirit should produce a changed life in the new covenant believer that is observable in the public arena and thus able to be tested and validated. Therefore, this chapter will focus on the nature of John's tests of life and seek to understand how they serve his overarching purpose for writing this letter.

Definition of "Tests"

It is widely accepted among Johannine scholars that the first letter of John is filled with a series of "tests" or "criteria" by which its readers might assess their lives and find added confirmation that they have been born of God, know Him, and abide in Him.[1] Accordingly, the

[1] While earlier writers spoke of or alluded to the idea of "criteria" or "testing" in 1 John (see the survey of Luther in the history of research), the label of testing appears to have received its popularity from R. Law's influential work, *The Tests of Life: A Study of the First Epistle of St. John*, 3rd ed. (Edinburgh: T&T Clark, 1914; repr., Grand Rapids: Baker, 1968). In this book Law asserts that there are three tests ("righteousness," "love," and "belief") that cycle throughout the letter, bidding its readers to "try themselves" in order that they might recognize whether they have been born of God (208). A perusal of the literature since Law's book demonstrates that the vast majority of commentators have followed this nomenclature of "tests." This is not to say that all interpreters who speak of tests in 1 John follow Law across the board. To be sure, each writer is nuanced in his or her interpretation of the tests. For example, some have added a fourth test in that they believe that perseverance should be understood as a separate test in this letter (so F. F. Bruce, *The Epistles of John: Introduction, Exposition, and Notes* [Grand Rapids: Eerdmans,

way in which one lives functions as either a support to one's assurance or perhaps a contradiction implying a false claim. Before examining the tests themselves, a few observations and points of clarification are in order.

Structural Definition of Tests

Structurally, these tests take on a variety of forms. First, there are several "we know" (ἡμεῖς οἴδαμεν) or "by this we know" (ἐν τούτῳ γινώσκομεν) statements given to support the reader's confidence in such things as "knowing God" (2:3), "being in Him" (2:5), "passing from life to death" (3:14), and "being of the truth" (3:19). A second form of testing language begins with a substantival participle. These could be either a claim made and demonstrated as false ("the one who says I have come to know Him . . . is a liar") or a statement about one's lifestyle and the corresponding interpretation ("the one who does righteousness is righteous"). Moreover, these participial phrases are often modified by πᾶς ("all"/"everyone") and therefore speak of people categorically ("everyone who has been born of God does not do sin"). A third type of test can be found in the form of a conditional sentence ("if we say that we do not have sin"), which is occasionally stated in the form of a question ("Who is the liar except [εἰ μὴ] the one who denies that the Christ is Jesus?"). Of course there is some overlap here since some of the "by this we know" statements are conditional (see 2:3). I include this third group, however, because there are some conditional sentences that do not fall into the first two categories but should also be understood as tests. Nevertheless, one must be cautious here because not every conditional sentence in 1 John should be viewed as a test (e.g., 5:14). Moreover, with the risk of convoluting the discussion, it is probably best to say that there are several individual statements of testing within a particular test

1979], 69; D. L. Akin, *1, 2, 3 John*, NAC, vol. 38 [Nashville: Broadman & Holman, 2001], 116–17). Others see only two tests, arguing that the test of righteousness is fulfilled in love and, thus, these two tests are one and the same (T. Häring, "Gedankengang und Grundgedanke des ersten Johannesbriefs," in *Theologische Abhandlungen Carl von Weizsäcker zu seinem siebzigsten Geburtstage*, ed. Adolf Harnack [Freiburg: J.C.B. Mohr, 1892], 173–200; Brooke, *Johannine Epistles*, xxxvii; J. Painter, *1, 2, and 3 John*, Sacra Pagina, vol. 18 [Collegeville, MN: Liturgical, 2002], 231). Nevertheless, regardless of various idiosyncrasies, most contemporary commentators speak of "tests" in this letter.

of life. For example, 2:3,4,5, and 6 are each statements of testing in and of themselves, and yet together they make up one of the tests of righteousness.

Debate over the Nature of the Tests

There is some debate over the precise nature of the tests. Some, who argue against the prevailing thought that there is a polemical aspect in 1 John, assert that these tests are not for the purpose of excluding the secessionists but for the assurance of those left in the community.[2] Such an understanding, however, is reductionistic. There is no doubt that the letter was written to believers (5:13); thus it is written with the purpose of bolstering their assurance. Nevertheless, the false teaching of the secessionists, complete with probable claims of having advanced beyond the basic gospel they had from the beginning (2 John 9), were some of the reasons John's readers were in need of assurance. Therefore, the demonstration that the secessionists have failed the tests is part and parcel of what brings assurance to those who have remained faithful.[3] The tests, then, do primarily serve to strengthen the community since they were written to believers. Nevertheless, one of the ways the tests fulfill their purpose is by exposing the false claims of the secessionists and demonstrating that they are actually children of the Devil.

Another recent debate over the nature of John's tests is worthy of note since it offers a rather innovative approach to reading 1 John. This dissension originates from a group known as the "Grace Movement," who strongly assert that assurance of salvation in the New Testament comes *only* from the finished work of Christ on the cross and to see any kind of secondary support by the way one lives his life is works righteousness.[4] This overarching theological construct is applied to

[2] See J. M. Lieu, *The Theology of the Johannine Epistles* (Cambridge: Cambridge University Press, 1991), 13–16, 22, 50–51.

[3] So also D. A. Carson, "Johannine Perspectives on the Doctrine of Assurance," in *Explorations: Justification and Christian Assurance*, ed. R. J. Gibson (Adelaide, South Australia: Openbook Publishers, 1996), 75–76: "One can no more choose between the strengthening of the orthodox and the exclusion of the heretics than between the left wing of an airplane and the right." See also Painter, *1, 2, and 3 John*, 86.

[4] Z. Hodges, *The Gospel Under Siege: A Study on Faith and Works*, 2nd ed. (Dallas: Rendencion Viva, 1991), 143: "Basically we insist that *the New Testament Gospel offers the assurance of eternal*

1 John by arguing that the series of tests should not be understood as "tests of life" or even "tests of assurance" but "tests of fellowship."[5] Support for this view comes from the assertion that 1:3 should be understood as the overarching purpose statement of the letter, and therefore John is not giving "tests of life" but "tests of fellowship."[6] Accordingly, some of the difficult tests that employ absolute language (e.g., 3:4–10) pose no problem, for such tests simply enable readers to comprehend whether they are currently living in fellowship with God.[7] Such an interpretation, however, completely ignores the background issues of this letter and therefore misses the whole point of the epistle. The issue in 1 John is not that those who fail the various tests simply demonstrate that their fellowship is momentarily broken, temporarily concealing the fact that they are really believers.[8] On the contrary, John makes every effort to demonstrate that those who fail the tests were neither presently nor previously in fellowship with God because they were liars, antichrists, and sons of the Devil as exhibited by their lifestyle.[9]

Inherent Problems in "Tests of Life" Nomenclature

While the "tests of fellowship" view misses the point of the author, it also provides a reminder that the terminology of "tests of life" or "tests of assurance" can be misleading in the interpretation of assurance in 1 John. This is because any discussion of the various "tests" has often led to a dialogue regarding the different "grounds" or "bases" of the believers' assurance.[10] Such discussions could lead

life to all who believe in Christ for that life. The assurance of the believer rests squarely on the Biblical promises in which this offer is made, and on nothing else" (emphasis his).

[5] See chap. 1 for a bibliographic reference for this view.

[6] Z. Hodges, *The Epistles of John: Walking in the Light of God's Love* (Irving, TX: Grace Evangelical Society, 1999), 50–52, 226–29. He argues that the only "test of salvation" occurs in 5:1 (144).

[7] For an excellent critique of this view, see T. R. Schreiner and A. B. Caneday, *The Race Set before Us: A Biblical Theology of Perseverance and Assurance* (Downers Grove, IL: InterVarsity, 2001).

[8] This is the argument of Hodges, *Epistles of John*, 139–46; idem, *The Gospel Under Siege*, 67–68.

[9] See Hodges' special pleading in his interpretation of 3:4–10 (*Gospel Under Siege*, 63–68; *Epistles of John*, 131–46).

[10] See J. R. W. Stott, *The Letters of John: An Introduction and Commentary*, TNTC, rev. ed. (Grand Rapids: Eerdmans, 2000), 60: "A fresh certainty about Christ and about eternal life,

one to believe that each of the tests serves as a separate "ground" or "basis" to assurance. This, however, is not the case in 1 John. I have already argued in the third chapter of this study that John begins his letter by grounding his readers' assurance on the person and work of Jesus Christ (1:1–2:2; 4:9–10). Here Jesus is clearly displayed as the believers' "advocate" with the Father and the "propitiation" of their sins. Given that sin is inevitable in the life of the believer (1:8,10; 2:1; 5:16–17), nothing other than the work of Christ can be viewed as the foundation of assurance, for it is the only effective remedy for their sins and thus the only ground for the believer's confidence of right standing with God. Nevertheless, we have seen in our fourth chapter that the work of Christ has ushered in the new covenant and all its promises. These tests thus provide vital corroborating evidence for assurance because the believer's new birth and subsequent divine enabling of the Spirit are manifested in righteous behavior that is observable in the public arena and can be tested. In light of this, Calvin's distinction between the "sure foundation" of assurance, which is the promises of God as fulfilled in the work of Christ, and the "evidence" or "accessory or inferior aid" that stems from their lifestyle, is helpful as we examine the various tests of life.[11]

Therefore, as we move into the exegesis of the various tests of life, remember John has fundamentally grounded his readers' assurance on the work of Christ (1:1–2:2; 3:5,8; 4:9–10; 5:5–6). This can

based upon the *grounds* which John gives, can lead Christian people into that boldness of approach to God and of testimony to the world which is sorely needed as it is sadly missing in the church today" (emphasis mine). See also I. H. Marshall, *The Epistles of John*, NICNT (Grand Rapids: Eerdmans, 1978), 55; C. G. Kruse, *The Letters of John*, PNTC (Grand Rapids: Eerdmans, 2000), 198–200.

[11] J. Calvin, *The First Epistle of John*, trans. John Owen, vol. 22 of *Calvin's Commentaries*, ed. D. W. Torrance and T. F. Torrance (Edinburgh: Oliver and Boyd, 1960; repr., Grand Rapids: Baker Books, 1999), 165–66, 173–75, 182, 218, 222. So also D. A. Carson, "Johannine Perspectives on the Doctrine of Assurance," 82: "In the thought of 1 John, the ultimate ground of assurance that our sins have been dealt with and that we are acceptable to the Father is the Advocate with the Father who is also the ἱλασμός for our sins (2:1–2). This 'ground' serves as ground because the death of the Son is the efficient solution to the problem. The so-called 'tests of life' constitute 'grounds' for assurance, but never because they are the efficient solutions to the problem, but because they provide corroborating evidence. The evidence is corroborating because the work of Christ, worked out in divine begetting, promises necessary change. But it is not a 'ground' of assurance in the same sense that Christ's death is." See also Schreiner and Caneday, *The Race Set before Us*, 298–300.

sometimes be lost as a result of John's pastoral emphasis on the necessity of right belief, love for the brethren, and fundamental obedience. So here the focus will be on the tests of life, which serve as a vital support to assurance.

The Test of Righteousness

The first test that will be examined is that of righteousness.[12] This test occurs in several different contexts (1:6–10; 2:3–6; 2:15–16; 3:3–10; 5:2) and bids readers to confirm that they know God and have been born of Him by examining the way they live their lives. Due to significant overlap between ideas in the various "tests of righteousness," I have chosen to focus here on 2:3–6 and 3:4–10, which are the two examples that best exemplify this particular test and raise the most questions for interpretators.

By This We Know We Have Come to Know Him (2:3–6)

Perhaps the clearest test of righteousness comes in 2:3–6. Here the writer sets forth the basic premise that one's assurance of knowing and abiding in God is either strengthened or possibly eradicated by his obedience or lack thereof. Verse 3 begins with one of John's basic statements of testing: "by this we know" (cp. 2:5; 3:16,19,24; 4:2,13; 5:2). The context of 2:3 makes clear that "by this" should be understood as pointing forward to what follows.[13] In other words, people can know[14] they have come to know God as they examine their life and see that they are keeping His commandments.

[12] For simplicity of recognition, I have followed Law's well-known nomenclature on each of the various tests (*Tests of Life*, 208, 231, 258). Other possible names for this test include "moral test" or "test of obedience."

[13] See R. E. Brown, *The Epistles of John: Translated with Introduction, Notes, and Commentary*, The Anchor Bible, vol. 30 (New York: Doubleday, 1982), 248–49, for an attempt in establishing criteria regarding decisions as to whether ἐν τούτῳ ("by this") goes with what precedes, follows or perhaps both in each particular instance. At the end of the day, however, context ultimately drives every instance, which unfortunately leaves these decisions to be somewhat subjective as seen in the wide difference of opinion in the commentaries.

[14] Some of the older commentators have argued that a different meaning should be ascribed to οἶδα and γινώσκω. This line of thought asserts that γινώσκω refers to experiential knowledge that one learns by experience while οἶδα refers to the immediate certitude that stems from intuitive knowledge of what God is (so Brooke, *Johannine Epistles*, 67–68; Law, *Tests of Life* 364–67; Stott, *Letters of John*, 122; B. F. Westcott, *The Epistles of St. John: The Greek Text with*

Above it was asserted that John's use of "knowing God" language does not refer to an intellectual or mystical knowledge of God but is covenantal language that refers to an experiential knowledge, which manifests itself in acknowledging God in all one's ways and obeying His commands.[15] Thus, with a new covenant background in mind, it is perfectly natural that the test for knowing God is keeping the commands. There is, however, some debate as to the precise meaning of the author's use of "His commands" (τὰς ἐντολὰς αὐτοῦ). To begin with, there is the question of whose commands are to be kept. In proposing an answer, it is important to look back to the first instance of αὐτός in this verse. Here the writer says, "We know we have come to know Him" (γινώσκομεν ὅτι ἐγνώκαμεν αὐτόν). The context of the letter indicates that the pronoun αὐτόν almost certainly refers to God the Father. Given the secessionists' heretical views of Christ and their claims to fellowship with God (1:6), John is likely interacting with a false claim of knowing God.[16] With this in mind, it is probably best to understand the writer's use of αὐτοῦ ("his") to modify τὰς ἐντολὰς ("commands") as again referring to God,

Notes and Essays [Grand Rapids: Eerdmans, 1955], 82; B. A. du Toit, "The Role and Meaning of Statements of 'Certainty' in the Structural Composition of 1 John," *Neot* 13 [1979]: 86–87). Such a reading, however, probably falters given the actual overlap between the two words and John's proclivity to vary his vocabulary for stylistic purposes (cp. John's use of "love" and "see"). It would seem that in 1 John, experiential knowledge is actually spoken in terms of both οἶδα (3:2,14,15; 5:13) and γινώσκω (2:3,5,29; 3:18–19,24; 4:13; 5:2). Moreover, although John always refers to knowing God/Christ in this epistle with γινώσκω, in the Gospel he employs οἶδα for the same thing (8:19; 14:7). Therefore, the majority of recent commentators have moved away from this distinction (see M. M. Thompson, *1–3 John*, The IVP New Testament Commentary Series (Downers Grove, IL: InterVarsity, 1992), 52; K. Grayston, *The Johannine Epistles*, New Century Bible Commentary [Grand Rapids: Eerdmans, 1984], 63; Brown, *Epistles of John*, 250; Marshall, *Epistles of John*, 167 n. 10).

[15] For helpful discussions on "knowledge" in 1 John, see M. E. Boismard, "La connaissance dans l'alliance nouvelle d'après la première letter de Saint Jean" *RB* 56 (1949): 365–91; Marshall, *Epistles of John*, 121–22; R. Bultmann, "Γινώσκω," in *Theological Dictionary of the New Testament*, ed. G. Kittle, trans. G. W. Bromiley (Grand Rapids: Eerdmans, 1965, 1999), 689–714; Schnackenburg, *Johannine Epistles*, 95–101; G. Strecker, *The Johannine Letters: A Commentary on 1, 2, and 3 John*, trans. L. M. Maloney, Hermenia (Minneapolis: Fortress, 1996), 222–26.

[16] So also R. Schnackenburg, *The Johannine Epistles: Introduction and Commentary*, trans. Reginald and I. Fuller (New York: Crossroad, 1992), 82; J. Chaine, *Les épîtres Catholiques* (Paris: Gabalda, 1939), 154; R. Bultmann, *The Johannine Epistles*, trans. R. P. O'Hara, L. C. McGaughy, R. W. Funk, Hermenia (Philadelphia: Fortress, 1973), 24; Brown, *Epistles of John*, 90; Akin, *1, 2, 3 John*, 90).

so "His commands" are the commands of the Father.[17] Moreover, it would appear that each instance where the command(s) is modified by αὐτοῦ ("his") is in reference to the command(s) of God.[18] If this is correct, then it is possible that "His commands" could be a reference to the teaching of the Torah, or even more specifically, the Ten Commandments.[19] To be sure, new covenant texts such as Jeremiah 31:33–34 linked knowing Yahweh with internalizing and obeying the Torah (cp. Hos 4:1–6). Nevertheless, such an understanding must be tempered by both the consistent New Testament teaching where Jesus sums up the whole law by asserting that one must love God and love one another (Mark 12:28–31; Matt 22:36–40; Rom 13:8; 1 Cor 9:21; Gal 5:14; 6:2; Jas 2:8) as well as the Johannine emphasis of the love command (John 13:34–35; 15:12,17; 1 John 2:7–11; 3:11–18,23; 4:7–12). Perhaps the most helpful clue as to what the writer means here in 2:3 when he speaks of God's commands comes at the end of chapter 3 (3:23), where all of the commands are summed up under one bipartite command, namely, believing in Jesus and loving one another (3:22–23).[20] Therefore, it seems best to say that John's use of

[17] So also Brown, *Epistles of John*, 251–52. Against Kruse, *Letters of John*, 78–79, who argues that every usage of the noun ἐντολή refers to the commands or command of Christ in this letter.

[18] Of course it is important that one does not press this distinction between the commands of God and the commands of Jesus, since the Fourth Gospel makes clear that the teaching and commands of Jesus are directly from God the Father (3:34; 7:16; 10:18; 12:49,50; 14:24,31). Thus it is certainly possible that John can say the command of Jesus or the command of God and be referring to the same thing.

[19] So Strecker, *Johannine Letters*, 40; Law, *Tests of Life*, 211; Brown, *Epistles of John*, 280–81. Cp. S. S. Smalley, *1, 2, 3 John*, WBC, vol. 51 (Waco: Word Books, 1984), 45, who says it is a reference to the "moral law of God."

[20] John employs the plural of ἐντολή eight times in this letter and the singular ten times. There does not seem to be a distinction between the singular and the plural except to say that the singular is the summing up of the plural as seen in 3:23. Here, similar to Jesus' summing up of the commands into loving God and loving one another, John seems to sum up all the "commands" into one "command," which has the two parts of believing in Jesus and loving one another (so also Marshall, *Epistles of John*, 200–1; Akin, *1, 2, 3 John*, 166–67 Kruse, *Letters of John*, 79. Against U. C. von Wahlde, *The Johannine Commandments: 1 John and the Struggle for the Johannine Tradition*, Theological Inquiries: Studies in Contemporary Biblical and Theological Problems, ed. Lawrence Boadt [New York: Paulist, 1990], 53–54, 69, who argues that "believing in Jesus" is another way of saying, "keeping the words of Jesus." In light of this, he argues that the commandments in 1 John are [1] to keep the words of Jesus [1 John 2:5,7] and [2] to love one another).

"His commands" refers to God's law as found in the Torah, which can be summed up as believing in Jesus and loving the brethren.[21]

In 2:4, the writer's test of righteousness intensifies in its specificity in that it appears to interact with another specific claim of the secessionists, namely, their claim to "know God."[22] The author counters such a claim with a negative test contending that any who say they know God but fail to keep His commands are liars and the truth is not in them (cp. 1:6,8). The writer's argument here should probably not be understood as a warning to his readers, but another instance where his readers are offered assurance by the elucidation of the secessionists' failure to support their claims with their lifestyle. Here, therefore, John's readers find comfort in understanding that the false claims of those who are trying to deceive them have no value because they do not keep the commands of God.

The next verse returns to a positive application of the test where the writer again reassures his readers that whoever "keeps His word"[23] finds that "the love of God is made complete in them" (2:5a). There is some ambiguity in the phrase "the love of God" (ἡ ἀγάπη τοῦ θεοῦ). Should τοῦ θεοῦ ("of God") be taken as an objective genitive or subjective genitive? In other words, is John referring to our love for God (objective) or God's love for us (subjective)? To be sure, both are possible. This is especially true in a book that clearly demonstrates

[21] See T. R. Schreiner, *The Law and Its Fulfillment: A Pauline Theology of the Law* (Grand Rapids: Baker, 1993), 220: "John can summarize the keeping of the commandments under love because love accurately describes what the commandments intend. The connection between *commandments* with *word* suggests that this love is not separate from the ten commandments but fulfills them. . . . John insists, however, that to fulfill the commandments one must believe that Jesus is the Messiah. . . . John recognizes an indissoluble connection between keeping the commandments, loving the brothers and sisters, and believing in Jesus as the Messiah (1 John 5:1–2). These things are possible only for those who 'have been born of God' (1 John 5:1)."

[22] The ὅτι clause could be understood as indirect discourse and thus indicate a direct quotation of the secessionists (ὁ λέγων ὅτι ἔγνωκα αὐτόν). Law asserts that John's phrase ὁ λέγων ὅτι ἔγνωκα αὐτόν "is not an arrow shot at a venture, but has a definite mark in the Antinomian intellectualist for whom his self-assured knowledge of Divine things superseded all requirements of commonplace morality" (*Tests of Life*, 210).

[23] The oscillation between λόγος and ἐντολή would seem to indicate that these two words are virtually synonymous and should be seen as another Johannine instance of saying the same thing in different ways for stylistic purposes (so Brown, *Epistles of John*, 252, 254, 265). Marshall, however, sees some nuance between the two noting that John's use of αὐτοῦ τὸν λόγον "moves beyond the thought of obeying God's commands and includes the thought of receiving and believing his promises" (*Epistles of John*, 124).

that our love for God comes from His love for us (4:19). Nevertheless, the context of this verse and the Johannine idea that the one who loves God obeys His commands (John 14:15) indicate that our love for God may be at the forefront (cp. 1 John 5:3). Of course it is possible that modern grammarians are forcing a distinction that John never had in mind, so perhaps it is best to see both aspects in view here.[24] If this is correct, then our love for God, which flows from His love for us, is perfected when we keep His word.[25]

This test of righteousness is completed in 2:5c–6, where the reader once again comes across another "by this we know" statement. Unlike the test of 2:3, there are no grammatical indicators as to whether "by this" (ἐν τούτῳ) points forward or backward here.[26] Since "being in Him" is parallel to "abiding in Him," it is probably best to view "by this" as pointing forward and introducing the test of abiding found in verse 6.[27] Abiding in God (μένω ἐν) is another Johannine statement of interiority that is important to this letter (2:5,6,27–28; 3:6,24; 4:13,15–16; 5:20).[28] At times this abiding is described as mutual indwelling (3:24; 4:13,15–16), while other times only one side of the equation is noted. While the precise nature of this relationship is somewhat difficult to define, it does seem that it refers to the closest possible union between God and His people, where God's own Spirit has actually taken up residence in them and enables them to live in a manner pleasing to God (cp. Ezek 11:19–20; 36:26–27). The test of

[24] See D. B. Wallace, *Greek Grammar Beyond the Basics: An Exegetical Syntax of the New Testament* (Grand Rapids: Zondervan, 1996), 119–20, who labels the genitive where the objective and subjective aspects are both in view as a "plenary genitive."

[25] So also Brown, *Epistles of John*, 93.

[26] For some who find a reference backward, see Westcott, *Epistles of St. John*, 50; Bultmann, *Johannine Epistles*, 26; Schnackenburg, *Epistles of John*, 104; C. Haas, M. de Jonge, and J. L. Swellengrebel, *A Translator's Handbook on the Letters of John*, UBS Handbook Series (New York: United Bible Societies, 1972), 47. For some who find a reference forward, see Marshall, *Epistles of John*, 126; C. H. Dodd, *The Johannine Epistles*, The Moffat New Testament Commentary (New York: Harper & Brothers, 1946), 32; Bruce, *Epistles of John*, 52; J. L. Houlden, *A Commentary on the Johnannine Epistles*, BNTC, 2nd ed. (London: A & C Black, 1994), 55; Stott, *Letters of John*, 91.

[27] See chap. 2 where it is argued that "knowing" and "abiding" in God are parallel in describing intimate fellowship with God.

[28] See E. S. J. Malatesta, *Interiority and Covenant: A Study of* εἶναι ἐν *and* μένειν ἐν *in the First Letter of Saint John*, Analecta Biblica 69 (Rome: Biblical Institute, 1978); J. W. Pryor, *John: Evangelist of the Covenant People: The Narrative and Themes of the Fourth Gospel* (Downers Grove, IL: InterVarsity, 1992), 157–80.

abiding therefore comes as no surprise, for the one who abides in God ought to walk as Jesus walked (2:6). Such a test is parallel with that of 2:3–5a in that Jesus is depicted as having kept all of the Father's commands as He lived on earth.

Therefore, the sum and substance of 1 John 2:3–6 is that the test of whether one knows and abides in God is whether he keeps the commandments (i.e., walks as Jesus walked). On the one hand, the person who keeps the commands can have confidence that he knows and abides in God. On the other hand, the one who claims to know God but does not keep the commands proves himself to be a liar. John does not envisage the possibility where one can know God and not live in a manner pleasing to Him. Of course one would be remiss in interpreting this emphasis on keeping the commands as the means to knowing and abiding in God. On the contrary, such should be understood as the sign or confirmation of knowing God. This sign or confirmation is testable precisely because knowing God and obeying Him are inextricably tied together.

No One Born of God Sins (3:4–10)

Another important test of obedience is found in 1 John 3. Here the writer sets forth clear demarcations between those born of God and those born of the Devil. The idea of divine birth is introduced in 2:29, where John asserts that everyone who does righteousness has been born of God. Like 2:29, the focus in this test is not on the nature of being born of God but on the evidences of divine birth. So the author's purpose behind distinguishing between those born of God and those born of the Devil may be to enable his readers to evaluate the false claims of the heretics by examining their lifestyle.[29]

Following a brief parenthesis focusing on the greatness of God's love and the believer's present standing as a child of God (3:1–3), the writer returns to the theme introduced in 2:29 that those born of God live like the One who begat them. Here he emphasizes the importance of living righteously and avoiding "sin" (ἁμαρτία), as seen in the repetitive usage of ἁμαρτία and the introduction of ἀνομία. It is

[29] See Kruse, *Letters of John*, 114.

plausible that this emphasis stems from the secessionists' attempt to deceive John's readers into thinking that sin was not an issue for the Christian (cp. 3:7; 1:6,8,10).[30] John therefore responds with a test, where he demonstrates that the manner in which people conduct their lives distinguishes whether they are children of God or children of the Devil (3:10).

Beginning in 3:4, John contends that everyone who does[31] sin also does ἀνομία. It is important, then, to understand what John meant in his use of ἀνομία. It is possible to interpret ἀνομία in its root meaning of "lawlessness" and see it as a further definition of "sin."[32] Such a reading can be supported in the LXX in Psalms 31 [32] and 50 [51], where these two words are used interchangeably (cp. Rom 4:7–8 [quotation of Ps 31 (32)]; Heb 10:17). This understands sin as the breaking of God's Law and therefore the sinner as one who lives without the Law (i.e., lawless). Moreover, such an interpretation fits the context in that it focuses on the moral responsibilities of the Christian.[33] Nevertheless, this interpretation of ἀνομία fails to take into consideration the fact that νόμος ("law") is not used at all in this letter, which makes it difficult to see why John would introduce the whole concept of law and lawbreaking here. Moreover, de la Potterie has pointed out that ἀνομία as "lawbreaking" is completely absent in the New Testament.[34]

A more fitting interpretation of ἀνομία in this context is probably to understand it as something "associated with the final outbreak of evil against Christ and that it signifies rebellion against the will of

[30] See Marshall, *Epistles of John*, 176.

[31] Akin asserts, "The word *poion* is used frequently in this section (vv. 3,4,7,8,9,10) to imply a continual practice of sin as well as a realization of sin's completeness. In other words, it is a willful, habitual action" (*1, 2, 3 John*, 140; see also K. Inman, "Distinctive Johannine Vocabulary and the Interpretation of 1 John 3:9," *WTJ* 40 [1977–78]: 136–44). Such an understanding fails to take into account the parallel statements that do not include the verb ποιέω (3:6,9c; 5:18). It would seem that this is one more instance of John varying his language for stylistic purposes.

[32] So A. Plummer, *The Epistles of St. John*, Pineapple Commentaries (Cambridge: Cambridge University Press, 1886; repr., Grand Rapids: Baker, 1980), 75; Law, *Tests of Life*, 133–34; Stott, *Letters of John*, 122; Bonsirven, *Epitres de Saint Jean*, 153–54; Brooke *Johannine Epistles*, 85; Bruce, *Epistles of John*, 89; Houlden, *Johannine Epistles*, 92; Westcott, *Epistles of St. John*, 102.

[33] So Law, *Tests of Life*, 133.

[34] I. de la Potterie, "'Sin Is Iniquity' (I Jn 3,4)," in *The Christian Lives by the Spirit*, ed. I. de la Potterie and S. Lyonnet (New York: Alba House, 1971), 40–46.

God."[35] This reading not only fits the context of the letter (2:18,22; 4:3) but is also supported by the common Hebrew and New Testament understanding of the word. In the LXX ἀνομία is used to translate several Hebrew words including עָוֹן which was a common DSS term used to describe the realm of iniquity that stood opposed to God's justice and truth.[36] Moreover, the word ἀνομία was also employed in the LXX on two occasions to translate the word בְּלִיַּעַל (2 Sam 22:5; Ps 18:5 [17:4]), which refers to "destruction" (2 Sam 22:5) or "ungodliness" (Ps 18:5 [17:4]) and would later become a technical name for the Devil and his spirits in the intertestamental literature and New Testament.[37] This can be seen in various texts where the people's sin is said to derive from the powers of wickedness or Satan and his spirits (*T. Dan* 5:4–6; 6:1–6; *T. Naph* 4:1; 1QS 3:18–21; 4:9,19–20,23). Those who sin are then referred to as "children of iniquity" or "men of iniquity" (1 QS 3:20; 5:2; 10:10:20).[38]

Likewise, in the New Testament, ἀνομία is consistently used in reference to those who are aligned with the Devil and opposed to the kingdom of God. This is evident in the Gospel of Matthew, where ἀνομία is used "consistently in association with false prophets or others who oppose God's kingdom, and always with some association in the context with the last days or the final judgment (Matt 7:23; 13:41; 23:28; 24:21)."[39] Such a teaching reaches its climax in the New Testament in Paul's discussion of the final day of the Lord that will not come about until the revealing of final eschatological evil, which

[35] Marshall, *Epistles of John*, 176. See also Schnackenburg, *Johannine Epistles*, 185–87; de la Potterie, "'Sin Is Iniquity' (I Jn 3,4)," 37–55; Haas, *A Translator's Handbook on the Letters of John*, 81; S. Lyonnet, "The Notion of Sin in the Johannine Writings," in *Sin, Redemption, and Sacrifice: A Biblical and Patristic Study*, ed. S. Lyonnet and L. Sabourin (Rome: Biblical Institute, 1970), 42–43; Smalley, *1, 2, 3 John*, 154–55; Kruse, *Letters of John*, 117–19; Brown, *Epistles of John*, 399–400. Cp. F. Manns, "'Le péché, c'est Bélial' 1 Jn 3,4 à la lumière du Judaïsme," *RevScRel* 62 (1988): 1–9.

[36] Brown, *Epistles of John*, 400. See 1 QS 3:17–21: "God has appointed for human beings two spirits in which to walk until the time of His visitation: the spirits of truth and iniquity. The generations of truth spring from a fountain of light, but the generations of iniquity from a source of darkness. All the sons of righteousness are under the rule of the prince of light and walk in the ways of light, but all the sons of iniquity are under the rule of the angel of darkness and walk in the ways of darkness."

[37] Ibid.

[38] Kruse, *Letters of John*, 117.

[39] Ibid.

he refers to as "the man of lawlessness" (2 Thess 2:3–8). In light of such a background, John's parallel assertions in 3:4 that "everyone who does sin also does lawlessness" and 3:8, where he says "everyone who does sin is of the Devil," are apparently descriptions of his opponents and their fulfillment of apocalyptic expectations of the coming antichrists, who are children of the Devil and oppose God and reject the Christ (cp. 2:18,22; 4:3).[40] Such a statement is therefore best understood as a polemic aimed directly at the secessionists and their rejection of Jesus as the Christ and their view that sin is not important for the Christian.[41]

The exposure of the secessionists' failures continues in 3:5–6 upon the idea that avoidance of sin is vitally important for the believer because Jesus appeared for the purpose of taking away sin (3:5). Such a statement is another allusion back to the work of Christ. This is the only instance in the letter where the verb αἴρω is used, and it has the meaning of "taking away" sins (cp. John 1:29), which refers to His atoning death on the cross (2:2; 4:10) where sins were cleansed and forgiven (1:7,9). In this context, however, the primary thrust is not to reassure his readers that their sins have been dealt with on the cross but to point out that if Jesus came for the purpose of taking away sins and there is no sin in Him, then those who are indifferent to sin obviously do not abide in Him (3:6).[42] Precisely because there is no sin in Jesus, everyone who abides in Him does not sin. Moreover, the language of this test is heightened in the following verses when John says that the one who does sin is of the Devil (3:8) and those born of God

[40] Brown, *Epistles of John*, 400: "When 1 John 3:4 says that everyone who acts sinfully is making manifest the Iniquity, and when 3:8 says that everyone who acts sinfully belongs to the devil, the author is again appropriating the apocalyptic expectations of the final time to describe his opponents. Not only in their belief about the Christ but also in their ethical stance of ignoring sin are they manifestations of the Antichrist and sons of diabolic Iniquity." See also Smalley, *1, 2, 3 John*, 155: "The act of sin (John seems to be saying) involves a rebellious alignment with the devil, rather than with God in Christ (cf. vv. 8–10). It implies not merely breaking God's law, but flagrantly opposing him (in Satanic fashion) by so doing."

[41] So Smalley, *1, 2, 3 John, 153;* Brown, *Epistles of John,* 398: "Here in my judgment . . . it is not a general observation but refers to the secessionists, corresponding to the secessionist-inspired boasts of 1:8,10, . . . This is confirmed by 3:4b which identifies with the apocalyptic Iniquity the sin of those who act sinfully, just as the secessionists were identified with the Antichrist in 2:18-19."

[42] See Marshall, *Epistles of John*, 177; Kruse, *Letters of John*, 120.

do not sin because God's seed abides in them (3:9). Verse 10 goes on to explain that this test is for the purpose of distinguishing between the children of God and the children of the Devil.

Does John Expect Sinless Perfection?

To be sure, the absolute statements that believers do not sin (3:6,9; 5:18) are difficult to understand, especially when compared to his teaching elsewhere that readers should confess their sins and trust in the cross-work of Christ for the forgiveness and cleansing thereof (1:6–2:2) as well as praying for other brothers who sin (5:16–17). This tension has given rise to much debate, and the complexity of this discussion can be seen in the number and diversity of solutions that have been proposed in an effort to reconcile this apparent contradiction. Therefore, before proposing a solution, it is important to overview six common views regarding the apparent contradiction of 1:6–2:2 and 3:1–10 (cp. 5:18).[43]

Narrow the definition of "sin." Some have argued that the best way to resolve this tension is to interpret sin narrowly. One such proposal comes from David Scholer, who asserts that the distinction between the "sins that lead to death" and the "sins that do not lead to death" (5:16–17) supplies the most adequate solution to this tension.[44] He contends that the sin believers cannot commit is the "sin unto death," while the sin believers can and do commit is the "sin not unto death."[45] Smalley rightly dismisses this view, however, when he says, "In 3:6,9 and 5:18 John is evidently describing sin as an entity, rather than particular expressions of it; moreover, it is doubtful if he would have

[43] For other lists of interpretations see Stott, *Letters of John*, 134–40; Brown, *Epistles of John*, 413–16; Kruse, *Letters of John*, 126–32; Smalley, *1, 2, 3 John*, 159–63.

[44] D. M. Scholer, "Sins Within and Sins Without: An Interpretation of 1 John 5:16–17," in *Current Issues in Biblical and Patristic Interpretation: Studies in Honor of Merrill C. Tenney Presented by His Former Students*, ed. G. F. Hawthorne (Grand Rapids: Eerdmans, 1975), 244–46.

[45] Ibid., 244: "It is at this point that the meaning of the terms 'sin not unto death' and 'sin unto death' in 1 John 5:16–17 applies to the solution of the larger problematic in 1 John in which it is stated that believers both sin (1:5–2:2) and do not (and cannot) sin (3:4–10). For the author to say that believers do not sin (5:18) immediately after a discussion of believer's sins (5:14–17) can mean only that two different concepts of sin are in view. The believer does 'sin not unto death' but does not and cannot 'sin unto death.'"

expected the present passage to have been interpreted in the light of a definition which was to occur much later in his letter."[46]

Colin Kruse also attempts to resolve the tension between sin and perfection by limiting the definition of sin.[47] He asserts that "we might say that the sin which distinguishes the children of the devil is the sin of the devil, rebellion or *anomia*, and it is this sin that is impossible for believers to commit because God's 'seed' remains in them and they cannot commit it."[48] He goes on to assert that this sin (ἀνομία) "involves opposition to and rebellion against God, and so is similar to the opposition and rebellion of Satan."[49] "The children of God do sometimes commit sins (2:1), but the one thing they do not do is commit *anomia*, the sin of rebellion, the sin of the devil."[50]

Against Kruse, however, stands an argument similar to that leveled against Scholer. It seems evident that John is referring to sin in general throughout this passage and not simply this one particular expression of it. While Kruse's argument would provide a tidy solution, it fails to take into consideration the overall comparison between doing righteousness and doing sin. If we limit the doing of sin to the sin of rebellion (ἀνομία) throughout this whole passage, then what are we to suppose John means when he refers to doing righteousness? Is the doing of righteousness fulfilled so long as his readers do not fall into all-out rebellion (ἀνομία)? Such an argument would appear to destroy John's emphasis throughout this letter on obedience (2:3–6). In other words, limiting doing sin to ἀνομία would weaken John's point in contrasting the doing of righteousness and the doing of sin. Moreover, this passage is introduced with the exhortation to purify oneself (3:3). Such a statement certainly indicates more than steering clear of the ultimate rebellion (ἀνομία), it refers to the actual purification of oneself against sin in general. In point of fact, the one who says, "I know Him," must keep the commands and walk as Jesus walked.

[46] Smalley, *1, 2, 3 John*, 160. Cp. Marshall, *Epistles of John*, 179.

[47] C. G. Kruse, "Sin and Perfection in 1 John," *AusBR* 51 (2003): 60–70; idem, *Letters of John*, 131–32.

[48] Kruse, *Letters of John*, 132. Cp. de la Potterie, "'Sin Is Iniquity' I Jn 3,4," 50; T. Griffith, *Keep Yourselves from Idols: A New Look at 1 John*, JSNTSup 233 (Sheffield: Sheffield Academic Press, 2002), 138.

[49] Kruse, "Sin and Perfection in 1 John," 70.

[50] Ibid.

Present tense solution. Another attempt at solving the tension between sin and perfection is grammatical. This solution is actually closely related to those above in that it attempts to resolve the tension by narrowing the definition of sin down to "habitual sin" as a result of one's interpretation of the present tense verbs found throughout this passage.[51] According to this argument, "John is not suggesting that the child of God will not commit a single act of sin. Instead, John is describing a way of life, a character, a prevailing lifestyle."[52]

While there is truth in the theology of this view, it fails as the explanation of the tension for a variety of reasons. First, it is doubtful that the writer would place so much theological weight on a specific interpretation of a verb tense.[53] While the present tense verb often has a durative aspect, the context must ultimately dictate how one interprets the tense, which leads to the second problem with this view. Taking the present tense verbs in 3:4–10 as habitual would appear to contradict John's usage of the present tense verbs in 1:8 and 5:16, which are actually similar in context. Taking the present as ongoing in 5:16, for example, would contradict the present tense solution, for it would assert that a habitual sin does not lead to death.[54] To be sure, the present tense is flexible and the argument could be made that John could use it differently in each passage. Nevertheless, the similarity of contexts in 3:4–10 and 5:16–18 only serves to strengthen our first criticism that it is hard to believe that John would put so much theological weight on the subtlety of the present tense verb. Third, it is actually more plausible that the present-tense verbs used in these verses should be considered timeless statements of fact (i.e., gnomic). This is due to the fact that John is making statements that are true *any* time, and the subjects of these verbs are generic, which

[51] Some who argue for this view include Stott, *Letters of John*, 139–40; Westcott, *Epistles of St. John*, 104; Akin, *1, 2, 3 John*, 143–44.

[52] Akin, *1, 2, 3 John*, 143.

[53] So also Dodd, *Johannine Epistles*, 79; Wallace, *Greek Grammar Beyond the Basics*, 525; Smalley, *1, 2, 3 John*, 160; Marshall, *Epistles of John*, 180; S. Kubo, "I John 3:9: Absolute or Habitual," AUSS 7 (1969): 47; B. M. Fanning, *Verbal Aspect in New Testament Greek* (Oxford: Clarendon, 1990), 217.

[54] See also Wallace, *Greek Grammar Beyond the Basics*, 525; Smalley, *1, 2, 3 John*, 159–60; Griffith, *Keep Yourselves from Idols*, 128–29.

can be seen as a possible indicator that a gnomic is in view.[55] If this is the case, then the present tense argument would actually soften the point the author is trying to make with the absolute statements found here. This leads to the fourth problem with the present tense view in that it does not appear to pay enough attention to the situation behind the writing of this letter, where the writer is combating the secessionists' indifference to sin.[56] In that context John's absolute statements should probably be viewed as an intentional attempt to draw a sharp contrast between those who sin and are of the Devil and those who do not sin and are of God.[57] In summary, while there is theological truth in the present tense solution that will be explored below, the attempt to solve this tension on the rendering of the present tense verb ultimately fails.

Already but not yet. Still another proposal to resolve the sin/perfection tension is found in the writer's eschatological understanding that the children of God live between the already and the not yet.[58] This argument is laid out in an article by P. P. A. Kotzé, who asserts that "the believer is 'born of God' but he is 'not yet' what he will

[55] See Wallace, *Greek Grammar Beyond the Basics*, 523, who states that the gnomic present is most often seen in "*generic* statements to describe something that is true *any* time. . . . Pragmatically, it is helpful to note a particular grammatical intrusion: *A gnomic verb typically takes a generic subject or object*. Most generics will be subjects. . . . Further, the present participle, especially in such formulaic expression as πᾶς ὁ + *present participle* and the like, routinely belong here" (italics his). So also Fanning, *Verbal Aspect*, 217, who says that the "sense of a generic utterance is usually an *absolute* statement of what each one does once, and not a statement of the individual's customary or habitual activity." Cp. J. P. Louw, "Verbal Aspect in the First Letter of John," *Neot* 9 (1975): 103, who asserts that "expository discourse of which the First Letter of John is an example, employs the present predominately for it is a zero tense of factual actuality."

[56] So Kubo, "1 John 3:9: Absolute or Habitual?" 49–50.

[57] Ibid., 50: "The verse needs to be understood in this sharp contrast. There are only two sides, and for the moment there are no gradations or intermediate stages between or within them. Either you sin and are a heretic, a member of the forces of darkness and of the devil, or you do not sin and are a Christian and a member of the forces of right and of God. To say in this context that the author means only that the Christian does not habitually sin is appreciably to weaken his point. He cannot and does not sin because he is a child of God. . . . The sharp antithesis is intentional and any qualifications or reservations at this point would undermine the argument. The sharp antithesis must stand. The absoluteness of the statement must remain."

[58] Schnackenburg, *Johannine Epistles*, 257–58; P. P. A. Kotzé, "The Meaning of 1 John 3:9 with Reference to 1 John 1:8 and 10," *Neot* 13 (1979): 68–83; Marshall, *Epistles of John*, 182; Smalley, *1, 2, 3 John*, 164.

be when Christ comes again."[59] Christians are children of God now and have the "anointing" and God's "seed" dwelling in them and empowering them, and yet they are not what they will be. He concludes by asserting that "with respect to life one can say that the believer already has it but in a sense he does 'not yet' have it. In a negative sense the same must also be true with respect to sin."[60] As will be seen, this view has much to commend it and must be kept in mind in working through this text. However, without qualification it appears that it fails to understand John's purpose of distinguishing between the children of God and children of the Devil (3:10).[61]

Idealistic. A fourth proposal can be found in the article by Kubo, who argues the statements throughout 3:6–10 about sin must not be interpreted habitually but absolutely.[62] He is actually quite helpful in the fact that his view fits into several of the categories listed here. While he appeals to the "already but not yet tension" as well as the "situation" behind the church as part of the solution, he also emphasizes that 3:6–9 should be understood not as what is real for the believer but what is the ideal. In interacting with the tension between 1:6–2:2 and 3:4–10, Kubo argues that John's "purpose in 1:8 is not to indicate that Christians cannot make these assertions. Rather it is to point out the falsity of such statements made by those who were walking in the darkness, who were living in sin."[63] Moreover, 2:1 should not be seen as a contradiction to such a view because "it is realistic while the other idealistic."[64] To be sure, Kubo's article has much to commend it, as will be seen below. Nevertheless, if left unqualified, his view that those born of God do not sin ideally but realistically do sin would appear to invalidate the author's point of 3:4–10 in that it again fails to help the readers distinguish between the children of God and the children of the Devil, which was clearly John's focus in this passage (3:10a).

[59] Kotzé, "The Meaning of 1 John 3:9 with Reference to 1 John 1:8 and 10," 81.
[60] Ibid.
[61] See Kruse, *Letters of John*, 132, for the same critique of this view.
[62] Kubo, "1 John 3:9: Absolute or Habitual?" 47–56.
[63] Ibid., 55.
[64] Ibid., 56.

Exhortation. Another proposal seeks to resolve the tension by asserting that John is urging his readers to become what they already are. On this reading, John's emphasis is on the phrase "no one who abides in Him sins" in 3:6. Here it is argued that to the degree that the believer abides, he does not sin.[65] Nevertheless, while verse 6 might be taken in this manner, verses 9–10 serve to provide criteria by which to distinguish those who are born of God and those born of the Devil.[66]

Situational. The situational argument is yet another proposed solution to the tension. While it is vitally important to keep the situation in mind in interpreting this passage, the problem with this view is seen in the fact that there appear to be as many situational solutions as there are proponents.[67] Law alluded to such an argument when he said that John's absolute declarations throughout this section were "the language not of calm and measured statement, but of vehement polemic."[68] Dodd's situational approach argues that John was interacting with two groups of heretics in this letter. Those who were complacent and assumed that they had already reached perfection (1:6–2:2) and those who were morally indifferent (3:4–10).[69] While Kubo agrees with Dodd that the situation behind the writing is vital to explaining these verses, he disagrees with his understanding of two groups.[70] Still another proposal comes from Swadling, who argues that 3:6,9 and 5:18 should be seen as quotations of the actual

[65] So Brooke, *Johannine Epistles*, 86–87, who cites Augustine's dictum, "in quantum in ipso manet, in tatum non peccat" ("to the extent that the Christian remains in Christ, to that extent he does not sin"). Cp. Houlden, *Johannine Epistles*, 94; Bultmann, *Johannine Epistles*, 51–53.

[66] So also Schnackenburg, *Johannine Epistles*, 255–56.

[67] See, for example, Dodd, *Johannine Epistles*, 78–81; Kubo, "1 John 3:9," 49–56; H. C. Swadling, "Sin and Sinlessness in I John," *SJT* 35 (1982): 205–11; J. Bogart, *Orthodox and Heretical Perfectionism in the Johannine Community as Evident in the First Epistle of John*, SBLDS 33 (Missoula, MT: Scholars, 1977), 25–39; R. E. Brown, *The Community of the Beloved Disciple: The Life, Loves, and Hates of an Individual Church in the New Testament Times* (New York: Paulist, 1979), 124–27.

[68] Law, *Tests of Life*, 162.

[69] Dodd, *Johannine Epistles*, 78–81.

[70] Kubo, "1 John 3:9," 56: "They are the same people making the same claims on the same basis. In 1:8 they claim to be sinless; in 3:9 they claim to be born of God. Both claims arise from a common ineffable experience and one implies the other. In 1:8 the reason their claims are denied is that they continue to walk in darkness; in 3:9 because they sin. Both claims are denied on the same grounds, their sinfulness. . . . There is no difference between those dealt with in 1:8 and those in 3:9. They are the same people. The author in his circular method is approaching the same subject again and again but from different angles."

slogans of his opponents so his readers could assess their claims with the criteria that those who do right are righteous and those who do not are of the Devil.[71] Finally, Brown and Bogart, though not agreeing on every point,[72] attempt to resolve the tension by asserting that the writer is interacting with two different types of perfectionism in this letter: orthodox perfectionism and heretical perfectionism.[73]

Conclusion: An Eclectic Approach. The above survey demonstrates the difficulty of resolving the tension between 3:4–10 and 1:6–2:2. While no one solution will probably ever be proposed that is generally accepted by all, the previous attempts have provided helpful insights for future interpreters. Therefore, this present proposal takes an eclectic approach that begins with the overarching purpose of the letter and incorporates some of the more helpful aspects from some of the previous solutions described above.

Any proposed solution must take into account the writer's own statement of purpose for which he composed the entire letter (5:13). In other words, if John has truly written this letter to assure his readers that they have eternal life, then one must seek to understand how absolute statements like those found in 3:4–10 do not eradicate such a goal but actually serve to bolster his reader's confidence, even though it is clear that no one lives a perfectly righteous life (1:6–10).[74] So the most appropriate place to begin is with the situation behind the letter. I have already argued that the heretics had presumably made claims regarding their spiritual experiences such as knowing God, abiding in God, and probably being born of God, even though they were apparently indifferent toward sin. In the midst of this, John's readers were probably suffering from doubts due to the inability to distinguish

[71] Swadling, "Sin and Sinlessness in I John," 206–9.

[72] The key difference between these two is that Brown understands both forms of perfectionism to have come from interpretations of the Gospel of John (Brown, *Epistles of John*, 413–16, 30), whereas Bogart sees orthodox perfectionism coming from an interpretation of the Gospel of John but heretical perfectionism as being influenced by gnosticism (Bogart, *Orthodox and Heretical Perfectionism*, 25–39).

[73] Brown, *Epistles of John*, 413–16, 30; idem, *Community of the Beloved Disciple*, 124–27; Bogart, 25–39.

[74] This is of course assuming that the writer would not contradict himself in such a short amount of space. In the Nestle 27th, the statements found in 1:6–2:2 are less than three full pages from those in 3:4–10. If the writer is granted the benefit of the doubt, then it would seem that 3:4–10 must be read in light of 1:6–2:2.

between true and false claims regarding a spiritual experience with a God who is invisible. Hence, John moves his readers to evaluate all spiritual claims, which can be highly subjective, through the objective lens of examining one's lifestyle.[75] The absolute statements therefore serve as a polemic aimed directly at the secessionists, in order to expose their indifference to sin and demonstrate the falsehood of their claims and the reality that they are actually children of the Devil. So in some sense the demonstration that the heretics' claims are false brings comfort to those who have remained in the community. This interpretation finds support right in the middle of this section where John exhorts his readers to let no one deceive them (3:7). The children of God must not be deceived by false claims but must instead test them, by examining whether the lifestyle matches the claim. Therefore, it appears that John counters the false teachers with antithetical black-and-white language. Those born of God live like God (i.e., walk as Jesus walked). Those born of the Devil live like the Devil, who has sinned from the beginning.

Nevertheless, even if the above interpretation is correct, those born of God are still confronted with the positive side of the absolute statements that children of God do not sin. Yet it would appear that any lessening of these statements—by asserting that he is only speaking about habitual sin or the like—would undermine the writer's purpose.[76] So it seems there is an exhortative aspect to the absolute statements similar to that of a father telling his child, "In this family, children do not hit each other." Like this father the writer is not saying that such sin is an ontological impossibility. It is instead a statement that sin is not the norm for the child of God. Here, then, the "already but not yet" tension in this letter provides help, for he has just reminded his readers that they are children of God now (3:1), but they are not yet what they will be (3:2; cf. 2:8,17).[77] Thus, the children of God do not sin because they live like the One who begat them. Nevertheless, children of God are not yet what they will be, so there

[75] So also Marshall, *Epistles of John*, 123.

[76] To be sure, the writer certainly does not seem to be saying that it is tolerable for the believer to sin so long as he does not live in sin, which is often argued by those purporting a present tense view.

[77] Thompson, *1–3 John*, 91.

will be sin, and such sin is a deviation of what is the norm for a child of God. In this sense there is validity to the theological construct of the present tense argument. Fundamentally, those who are now children of God will live like the One who begat them. John insists on this truth. Nevertheless, since they are not yet what they will be, there will be the sin. The thrust of 3:3 lends support to such an idea in that everyone who has the hope of what is to come "purifies himself." So it appears that there is somewhat of a progression involved. If those born of God were ontologically incapable of sin, they would not need to purify themselves. John does not specify what it means to purify oneself, but the immediate context implies that the emphasis here is on striving to live free from sin.[78] Moreover, given the statements in 1:7–2:2, we might add that purifying oneself includes the confession and forgiveness of sins.

Therefore, there is a clear distinction between the children of God and the children of the Devil. On the one hand, the children of God are those who strive to live without sin. Nevertheless, they are not what they will be (3:2–3) and therefore do sin. Those born of God, however, understand that each sin runs contrary to their new nature as children of God, and they must take sin with utmost seriousness and confess it and trust in the atoning sacrifice of Jesus for the forgiveness thereof. As such, they are truly changed people and are clearly distinguishable from the children of the Devil. On the other hand, the children of the Devil make claims to have fellowship with God but are nevertheless indifferent to sin. They have rejected the atoning sacrifice of Christ because they have no need for it. Thus, there is a marked distinction in the way the two conduct their lives.

The Tests of Love

Closely related to the tests of righteousness are the tests of love. This relationship can be seen in the way the author moves almost seamlessly from the tests of righteousness to the tests of love in chapters 2 and 3. Nevertheless, it does appear that John deals with them separately in his letter, and therefore they will be treated separately

[78] See Marshall, *Epistles of John*, 174.

here. The tests of love are found in 2:7–11; 3:10b-24; 4:7–13,15–21; 5:1–2. As with the tests of righteousness, there is much overlap within the various love tests, so I have chosen to focus on the first two while making periodic comments on the others when appropriate.

The One Who Loves His Brother Abides in the Light (2:7–11)

In this section John draws a clear line of demarcation between those who love the brethren and abide in the light (2:10) and those who hate the brethren and walk in the darkness (2:11). The actual test does not come until 2:9, but the preceding verses provide helpful background information for the love command in 2:7–8. These verses appear to be transitional as the writer moves from the more general topic of obedience to the commands (2:3–6) to the more specific command of brotherly love (2:7–11).[79] He begins the section on brotherly love by referring to his readers as "beloved" (ἀγαπητοί).[80] Here John contends that he is not giving them a new command they have never heard before, which might be construed as the author defending himself against the complaint that he is introducing new commands to the tradition.[81] On the contrary, the old command that John is referring to is the message they have had from the very beginning (ἀπ' ἀρχῆς). The ἀρχή ("beginning") in this context, therefore, is probably the beginning of the community or the time when John's readers first heard the gospel.[82] The old command is the message of the gospel, which almost certainly included Jesus' command to love one another.

In 2:8, the writer appears to contradict his previous teaching in that he now says that it is a new commandment. The resolution to this apparent contradiction should probably be seen as coming from John's Gospel where Jesus is found giving His disciples the "new commandment" to love one another (13:34). Hence, it is a new commandment

[79] See Painter, *1, 2, and 3 John*, 178; Kruse, *Letters of John*, 82; Akin, *1, 2, 3 John*, 95; Stott, *Letters of John*, 97.

[80] ἀγαπητοί is replaced by ἀδελφοί in K, L, 049, 69, and M. Both the external evidence and the context of this section which focuses on brotherly love support ἀγαπητοί as original (so B. M. Metzger, *A Textual Commentary on the Greek New Testament*, 2nd ed. [Stuttgart: Biblia-Druck, 1998], 709; Brooke, *Johannine Epistles*, 34).

[81] So Brown, *Epistles of John*, 264; Kruse, *Letters of John*, 82.

[82] Kruse, *Letters of John*, 82.

because it was described by Jesus as such.[83] Nevertheless, many years have now passed since the ministry of Jesus and even the beginning of the community. Therefore, the new commandment of Jesus is now an old commandment for those in John's church, for it is something they were taught a long time ago. Kruse is probably correct in his assertion, "The striking juxtaposition of what appear to be contradictory statements, then, is the author's way of saying that he is not imposing some novel obligation upon his readers, but only recalling them to what they have known from the very beginning of their Christian walk."[84]

The argument is moved forward by the assertion that this new commandment is true in Jesus and in the community (2:8b). This phrase is best understood as parenthetical in apposition to the previous clause.[85] Hence, the new commandment was true or realized in Jesus as He demonstrated His love for His own ultimately in the cross (John 13:14–17,34–35; 15:12–17) and in the disciples when they follow His example (1 John 3:16).[86] John then explains why this new command is realized in Jesus and his readers (2:8c). It is because the darkness is passing away and the true light is already shining. In other words, the true light has broken in through Christ and is already shining (John 1:9). Jesus came as the light of the world and has demonstrated what love should look like and commanded His disciples to do the same (John 13:34–35). Those who live in the light love the brethren. Nevertheless, the passage also makes clear that believers live between the already and the not yet.[87] Even though the true light is already shining, the darkness is still in the process of passing away, so there are still those who dwell in the darkness. Therefore, the following verses demonstrate that one's behavior toward the children of God is a clear indicator of the realm in which one dwells.

[83] See Brown, *Epistles of John*, 266–67, for a helpful discussion on why Jesus was able to refer to His commandment as a new commandment in the Gospel of John even though it was present in the Old Testament.

[84] Kruse, *Letters of John*, 83. See also Law, *Tests of Life*, 232–33.

[85] So also Law, *Tests of Life*, 376; Smalley, *1, 2, 3 John*, 56.

[86] It is probably best to interpret ἀληθής here as "verified," "realized," or "truly expressed" (see Marshall, *Epistles of John*, 129; Kruse, *Letters of John*, 83; Smalley, *1, 2, 3 John*, 56–57; Brown, *Epistles of John*, 267).

[87] See also Smalley, *1, 2, 3 John*, 58; Akin, *1, 2, 3 John*, 97.

In 2:9–11, John once again focuses on those who make empty claims (2:9) to intimacy with God while actually walking in the darkness (cp. 1:6).[88] In this context, the test for whether one walks in the light is the love for the brethren. First in 2:9, the test is stated negatively. The one who makes a claim to be in the light yet hates his brother is actually in the darkness until now. Stated positively, the one who loves his brother not only abides in the light, but there is no "cause for stumbling in him" (2:10).

There are two related exegetical difficulties with this statement. First, does ἐν αὐτῷ refer to the believer ("in him") or the light ("in it")? Second, is the σκάνδαλον a "stumbling block" in the life of the believer, or does the believer cause others to stumble?[89] To be sure, a decision is difficult for either option. With regard to the phrase ἐν αὐτῷ, it seems best to see it as a reference to the light.[90] This reading best fits the context since this verse is set in contrast with verse 11, where the individual is said to walk in the darkness and does not know where he is going. Moreover, a parallel thought is found in John 11:9, where we read that the man who walks in the day (i.e., the light) will not stumble. Likewise, the context indicates that σκάνδαλον is best understood as a stumbling block for the believer himself.[91] In contradistinction to verse 11, which focuses on the fate of the man who hates his brother, this verse focuses on the one who walks in the light and encounters no stumbling block as he loves the brethren. Verse 10 is therefore the converse of verse 11, where the one who

[88] The phrase, ὁ λέγων, would again seem to point to one of the claims made by the secessionists.

[89] The word σκάνδαλον means "trap," but is also used figuratively to refer to "temptation to sin," "enticement to apostasy" and is therefore often translated "cause of stumbling" or "stumbling block" (so BDAG, s.v. "σκάνδαλον"). "Cause of stumbling" or "stumbling block" makes the most sense in this context, given the parallel with 2:11 (so also Brown, *Epistles of John*, 274; Smalley, *1, 2, 3 John*, 62. Against Bultmann, *Johannine Epistles*, 28; BDAG, s.v. "σκάνδαλον"; G. Stählin, "σκάνδαλον," in *TDNT*, ed. Gerhard Kittle, trans. G. W. Bromiley [Grand Rapids: Eerdmans, 1965, 1999, 356–57], who prefer "blemish" or "stain").

[90] So J. C. O'Neill, *The Puzzle of 1 John: A New Examination of Origins* (London: SPCK, 1966), 16 n. 1; Schnackenburg, *Johannine Epistles*, 108; Smalley, *1, 2, 3 John*, 62; Akin, *1, 2, 3 John*, 99. Against Malatesta, *Interiority and Covenant*, 156; Marshall, *Epistles of John*, 132; Brooke, *Johannine Epistles*, 40; Plummer, *Epistles of St. John*, 43–44.

[91] So Malatesta, *Interiority and Covenant*, 157; Kruse, *Letters of John*, 86; Marshall, *Epistles of John*, 132.

hates his brother is said to walk in the darkness and does not even know where he is going, because darkness has blinded his eyes.[92]

Therefore, this passage demonstrates that one of the clearest criteria for whether one walks in the light is the love for the brethren. The strong dualistic language in this passage should not be missed. One either loves or hates his brother. There is no middle ground with John. Such language would once again appear to have as its purpose the differentiation between John's readers and the secessionists, reassuring those born of God. While the secessionists have made claims to be in the light, their hatred for John's readers demonstrates that they not only walk in the darkness, but their eyes have actually been blinded.

Brotherly Love Produces Assurance of Passing from Death to Life (3:10b-20)

Another test of love is found in 3:10b-20.[93] This test begins in the second half of 3:10, which is another one of the author's transition verses from one theme to the next.[94] The transition from the test of righteousness (3:4–10a) to the test of love (3:10b–20) again demonstrates the close relationship between these two. Here the one born of God not only does righteousness but also loves his brother.[95] Verse

[92] This verse seems to recall John 12:40, where John refers to Isa 6:10 in order to demonstrate that the Jews' rejection of Jesus was a fulfillment of prophecy. See J. Lieu, "What Was from the Beginning: Scripture and Tradition in the Johannine Epistles," *NTS* 39 (1993): 472–74.

[93] The actual division of this unit is difficult as seen in the various divisions offered by commentators. Some do not see a break until 3:24 (so Smalley, *1, 2, 3 John*, 176–213; Houlden, *Johannine Epistles*, 24; Kruse, *Letters of John*, 132–44). Others break the text after v. 18, noting that v. 19 leads to vv. 20–22 (so Bonsirven, *Épitres de Saint Jean*, 172; Stott, *Letters of John*, 148; Dodd, *Johannine Epistles*, 87; Bruce, *Epistles of John*, 97). Still others break the text between vv. 17–18 on the grounds that 3:18 begins with τεκνία, which is a title of address (So Thompson, *1–3 John*, 31; Brown, *Epistles of John*, 467). I have chosen to break the text here at v. 20, for it seems that even though one could break the text between 3:17 and 3:18 with the transitional τεκνία, vv. 18–20 seem to provide the conclusion for John's love test here as will be seen in the exegesis below. Moreover, I have broken the text at v. 20 instead of v. 24 due to the fact that the writer seems to move away from the love test at this point, employing the transitional ἀγαπητοί and moving into a new teaching on assurance in prayer (so also Schnackenburg, *Johannine Epistles*, 187).

[94] See Strecker, *Johannine Letters*, 105; Smalley, *1, 2, 3 John*, 178–79; Kruse, *Letters of John*, 126; Akin, *1, 2, 3 John*, 150.

[95] ἐκ τοῦ θεοῦ should be viewed here as a shortened form of ὁ γεγεννημένος ἐκ τοῦ θεοῦ.

11 thus moves to the reason one's origin of birth can be tested by his love for the brethren, namely, because this is a message they have had from the beginning of their Christian experience (cp. 2:7). Therefore, just as one's righteousness or lack thereof displays whether he is a child of God or a child of the Devil, so too one's love for the brethren demonstrates that he is a child of God and one's hatred of the brethren demonstrates that he is a child of the Devil.

The comparison of the children of God and the children of the Devil continues into 3:12–15, where the writer begins with the juxtaposition of Cain and Abel. This stark contrast should no doubt be viewed with the situation in the community as the backdrop.[96] Here John's readers are told to love one another. This love, however, is the antithesis of Cain's actions, who was from the evil one (i.e., born of the Devil) and slew his brother because Abel's deeds were righteous and his were evil. John's use of the Cain and Abel imagery is therefore employed as a graphic description of the deeds of the secessionists.[97] Just as Cain slew Abel (3:12) because his deeds were righteous, so too the secessionists hate John and his readers. For this reason, John tells his readers not to marvel when the world, in which the secessionists belong, hates them (3:13).[98] The comparison between Cain and the secessionists reaches its climax in 3:15 when John links their hatred with murder and reminds his readers that no murderer has eternal life abiding in him. In contrast, John's readers have already been assured that they have passed from death to life precisely because they love the brethren (3:14).[99] So here the lines are clearly drawn. The test of whether one is of the Devil or of God is whether he loves the brethren. The secessionists hate the brethren, are murderers, have failed to pass from death to life, and therefore do not have eternal life abiding in them. On the other hand, John's readers do love one another and demonstrate that they have passed from death to life and have eternal

[96] So also Thompson, *1–3 John*, 101–2; Smalley, *1, 2, 3 John*, 185.

[97] Brown, *Epistles of John*, 468.

[98] The word κόσμος has the meaning here of the unbelieving human race that is hostile to both God and believers and in this context would seem to be another reference to the secessionists (cp. 4:5).

[99] This phrase is a link back to John 5:24 and should be understood as a clear reference to salvation.

life abiding in them. Therefore, these verses serve to reinforce further the assurance of John's readers by both demonstrating their passing of the love test and once again exposing the failure of the heretics, who are depicted in the light of the original murderer.

In the following verses we find both the ground for the love command (3:16) and a practical application (3:17–18). The ground is the love Jesus displayed for His own as demonstrated on the cross (cp. 4:7–11; John 13:15,34; 15:12–13). Here John tells his readers that they know what true love is because of Jesus' work on the cross. John's purpose here is not to recount again how the cross-work of Christ brings sinners into right relationship with God but as an injunction for them to love one another in like manner. To be sure, the love demanded here includes the willingness to lay down one's life to the point of death.[100] Nevertheless, the writer understands that one is not often put in a situation to sacrifice one's life in this way, so in the next two verses he gives a practical application regarding ways in which they can lay down their lives for others in the warp and woof of everyday life. He begins this with a rhetorical question: How does the love of God[101] abide in a person who has the goods of the world but does not use them to help a brother in need? The obvious answer is that it does not. This is because those who have truly passed over from death to life will love the brethren and such love is demonstrated in tangible ways. Hence, John exhorts his readers to love not with mere lip service but in deed and in truth.[102] Such love is one of the most fundamental signs that one has truly passed over from death to life and is now a child of God.

God is greater than our hearts. Following his brief exhortation to love in tangible ways (3:17–18), John returns to the idea that his readers can bolster their assurance by way of examining their love for

[100] The language of laying down one's life (ἐκεῖνος ὑπὲρ ἡμῶν τὴν ψυχὴν αὐτοῦ ἔθηκεν) recalls John 15:13, where Jesus tells them that there is no greater love than to lay down their lives for their friends. Cp. John 10:11,15,17–18; 13:37–38.

[101] See above for a discussion of the phrase the "love of God." It would seem that the same thing could be said here in that it probably refers to God's love for us that produces our love for Him.

[102] It is possible that loving in truth refers to "a love which is in accord with the divine revelation of reality in the love shown by Jesus" (Marshall, *Epistles of John*, 196. See the discussion on truth in chap. 3).

the brethren (3:19). Moreover, an intriguing addition is tagged on to this test that is not found in any of the other testing passages. Here John adds that when his readers examine their love for the brethren and their own hearts condemn them, they must trust in God, who knows all things and is greater than their hearts. These verses (3:19–20), however, are probably the most difficult to interpret in the entire epistle. Scholars have referred to them as the *crux interpretum*,[103] or more negatively "gibberish,"[104] or even the "worst" of John's already "inept" grammar.[105] Nevertheless, one need not pose such a negative outlook on these verses. To be sure, the grammar is difficult, but the overall meaning seems clear.

The link between verses 18 and 19 appears to be the word *truth* (ἀλήθεια). Having just exhorted his readers to love one another in deed and in truth, John reminds them that such brotherly love is a test of whether they are of the truth. We have seen throughout this letter that while the phrase "by this" usually points forward, context must ultimately decide. Here the writer's overall argument, including the aforementioned word link of ἀλήθεια, implies that it is referring back to what has just been said.[106] Hence, by loving the brethren in deed and in truth, John's readers can have confidence that they are of the truth (cf. 3:14), and will also reassure[107] their hearts before

[103] Schnackenburg, *Johannine Epistles*, 184.

[104] A. F. Loisy, *Les Epîtres dites de Jean*, in *Le Quatrième Evangile*, 2nd ed. (Paris: Émile Nourry, 1921), 559, ("*un galimatias*").

[105] See Brown, *Epistles of John*, 453: "We have already seen that the epistolary author is singularly inept in constructing clear sentences, but in these verses he is at his worst."

[106] So also R. A. Culpepper, *1 John, 2 John, 3 John*, Knox Preaching Guides (Atlanta: John Knox, 1985), 72; R. Kysar, *I, II, III John*, Augsburg Commentary on the New Testament (Minneapolis: Augsburg, 1986), 86; Dodd, *Johannine Epistles*, 90; Houlden, *Johannine Epistles*, 101; Smalley, *1, 2, 3 John*, 200; Schnackenburg, *Johannine Epistles*, 201; Stott, *Letters of John*, 148–49; Bruce, *Epistles of John*, 98; Marshall, *Epistles of John*, 197.

[107] There is much debate over the meaning of the word πείθω in this verse. The regular meaning of this word is "to persuade" or "to convince." This reading is accepted by Kruse, *Letters of John*, 140; Akin, *1, 2, 3 John*, 163; Plummer, *Epistles of St. John*, 87. On the other hand, πείθω can also mean "to reassure" or "to set at rest" (cp. 2 Macc 4:15; Matt 28:14), which seems to better fit the context of this passage (so also BDAG, s.v. "πείθω"; Marshall, *Epistles of John*, 197 n. 197; Thompson, *1–3 John*, 106; Strecker, *Johannine Letters*, 121; Smalley, *1, 2, 3 John*, 201). Perhaps Thompson is correct in her assertion that the difference between these two options "is not very great, since the point of 'persuading' our hearts is to reassure ourselves in the presence of God" (*1–3 John*, 106). Cp. Strecker, *Johannine Letters*, 121, who argues that "no matter how

God (ἔμπροσθεν αὐτοῦ) whenever[108] their hearts[109] condemn them, because God is greater than their hearts.

Quite a bit of theology in this one long sentence must be unpacked in order to comprehend what the writer is saying here. To begin with, in 3:19 the verbs γινώσκω and πείθω are in the future tense (γνωσό μεθα, πείσομεν). So John is probably not only referring to one's continued assurance but perhaps to a time in the future when the believer will struggle with doubt that he is truly a child of God.[110] In such an instance, John has encouraged his readers to test themselves by looking at their love for the brethren. Nevertheless, he also understands that there will be times when the children of God test themselves and are condemned by their own hearts. Perhaps they consider the fact that they do not love perfectly or they ponder passages like 3:4–10 and struggle with the reality that they still sin. John therefore explains that his readers can reassure their hearts whenever they condemn them because God is greater than their hearts and knows all things.

While John's teaching here has been taken by some as an exhortation or even a warning,[111] such an interpretation would appear to fall

πείσομεν is translated, in any case it implies the idea that the human conscience is disturbed and suffering doubts. Therefore, it requires 'consolation' legitimated by God."

[108] This translation comes from the second of three uses of ὅτι found in 3:19–20. The three uses of this word pose problems for interpretation. The first ὅτι signals a content clause giving the content of what "we know" and is best translated as "that." The second ὅτι, however, is more difficult to interpret. If it is taken as content or causal ("that" or "because"), then it renders the third ὅτι redundant. This difficulty is avoided, however, if the second ὅτι is taken as a neuter of the relative pronoun ὅστις (ὅ τι) and understood to be linked with the word ἐὰν, which is equivalent to ἄν. On this reading the second ὅτι would mean "whenever," which makes good sense of the text and does not make the final ὅτι redundant. On this reading, the final ὅτι clause would be causal and translated "because" (so Marshall, *Epistles of John*, 197 n. 4; Smalley, *1, 2, 3 John*, 200; Schnackenburg, *Johannine Epistles*, 202).

[109] Most commentators interpret the word καρδία as a reference to what is typically understood as our conscience (so Brooke, *Johannine Epistles*, 99–100; Marshall, *Epistles of John*, 198; Stott, *Letters of John*, 149–50; Westcott, *Epistles of St. John*, 117), but Brown notes that it is also possible that it refers to the "emotional element in human life and can refer to the affections, feelings, and impulses" (Brown, *Epistles of John*, 456). Strecker is probably correct in seeing both aspects involved here (*Johannine Letters*, 121 n. 11; cp. Akin, *1, 2, 3 John*, 164).

[110] So also Marshall, *Epistles of John*, 197; Smalley, *1, 2, 3 John*, 201.

[111] Some view this not as an encouragement but as a warning to the believer. Commenting on these verses, J. M. Court asserts, "The demand for sacrificial charity has been made towards 'a poor man, one of your brethren' (Deut xv.7, cf. 1 John iii.17); but a base thought arises in the heart of the Christian which condemns the sacrifice demanded as unnecessary, and suggests that it can be avoided and that love can be maintained apart from a definite surrender of life or

well short of the writer's intention of assuring his readers of eternal life both in this specific context through the love test (3:10b-20) and in the overall thrust of the letter (5:13).[112] Here John is asserting that his readers can find assurance even when their hearts condemn them because God is greater than their hearts and knows all things. These two affirmations are an encouraging reminder that our hearts are not the final judge (cp. 1 Cor 4:3–5).[113] God is the One who knows and loves His children (4:10,19). Moreover, He knows there will be shortcomings among His children and has therefore provided His Son as their παράκλητος and ἱλασμός (2:1–2).[114] Therefore, similar to 2:1–2, the message here is that the believer must strive to live righteously by loving the brethren in tangible ways. Nevertheless, there will be failures along the way, and the believer's heart may condemn him as a result. When this occurs, the child of God must entrust himself to the mercy of God, who knows all things and is greater than his heart.[115]

The Tests of Belief

The last group of tests to be examined are John's tests of belief. Like the others, these tests point toward the false teaching of the secessionists. Here the various tests of belief will be examined (2:18–27; 4:1–4; 14–15; 5:1,5–6),[116] which will demonstrate that these tests

goods. The writer of the letter insists that this impulse, however natural, must be eradicated. The heart must be reasoned with and persuaded in the presence of God to make the sacrifice willingly. The demand of God is greater than the base and ignorant impulse of the human heart (cf. iv.4). Moreover, His knowledge is infinite, and no motion of the heart escapes His notice" ("Blessed Assurance?" *JTS* 33 [1982]: 512; so also Kruse, *Epistles of* John, 140; Akin, *1, 2, 3* John, 163–65). Another view where these verses are seen as a warning can be found in Calvin where it is argued that "God is greater than our heart" is in reference "to judgment, that is, because he sees much more keenly than we do, and searches more minutely and judges more severely" (*1 John*, 222; cp. Grayston, *Johannine Epistles*, 115).

[112] So also Schnackenburg, *Johannine Epistles*, 184–86; Thompson, *1–3 John*, 107–8; Stott, *Letters of John*, 148–50.

[113] See Thompson, *1–3 John*, 107–8; Marshall, *Epistles of John*, 198.

[114] See also M. Luther, *Lectures on the First Epistle of John*, ed. Jaroslav Pelikan, trans. Walter A. Hansen, vol. 30 of *Luther's Works* (St. Louis: Concordia, 1967), 280; Schnackenburg, *Johannine Epistles*, 186.

[115] So also Brown, *Epistles of John*, 477.

[116] I do not focus in detail on 4:15 and 5:1 due to their overlap with 5:5 and 2:22 respectively.

were written to reassure John's readers by clearly distinguishing the liars (2:22), the antichrists (2:22), those who do not have the Father or the Son (2:23), and who are not from God (4:3) from those who truly have the Father and the Son (2:23), are from God (4:2), enjoy an abiding relationship with God (4:15), have been born of God (5:1), and overcome the world (5:5). Once again, it is clear there are no gray areas for the author. What people believe about Jesus demonstrates whether they are from God or are antichrists.

The Liar Denies that the Christ Is Jesus (2:18–27)[117]

After an exhortation not to love the world (2:15–17), the writer turns and reveals the true identity of the secessionists and exposes their false teaching regarding the person of Jesus Christ. Here he begins by referring to the false teachers as "antichrists" (ἀντίχριστοι)[118] and contends that their arrival on the scene and departure from the fellowship demonstrate that the last hour has come (2:18–19). They were able to depart from the fellowship because they were never really part of it. Such an exodus of presumed brethren inevitably caused doubts in the minds of those who remained. Therefore, John seeks to bolster his readers' confidence by reminding them that they all have an anointing from the Holy One (2:20) and goes on to reassure them further by elucidating that he has not written these warnings because they do not know the truth about Jesus[119] but because they do know it (2:21). He then issues his test in order clearly to distinguish the "antichrists" from the faithful. The "antichrists" are those who deny that the Christ is Jesus (2:22–23). This test is accompanied by an exhortation to continue in the teaching they heard from the beginning about Jesus instead of following this novel teaching being espoused by the secessionists (2:24).[120] Those who abide in the historic message also abide in the Father and the Son and therefore have the promise of

[117] The context of this test has been treated in some detail in chap. 4. Rather than repeat what was said elsewhere, I will simply overview the flow of thought of this section before interacting on the specific test found in 2:22–23.

[118] This linking of the secessionists with the antichrists is made clear in 2:22 and 4:3.

[119] See my treatment of ἀλήθεια in chap. 3. Cp. Smalley, *1, 2, 3 John*, 109–10.

[120] This is implied in his exhortation to abide in the message that they heard from the beginning.

eternal life (2:24b-25). However, John is concerned about the possibility of further inroads by the false teachers. Hence, he again reminds them that these things he has been saying are a warning regarding the secessionists and their teaching. Nevertheless, he concludes with a note of reassurance in that he asserts his confidence that his readers will not abandon the teaching they have had from the beginning because they have received the anointing that teaches them all things (2:27).

Who is the liar? (2:22–23). The above flow of thought demonstrates that this particular test of belief (2:22–23) is located in the context of both a warning about the secessionists and a word of encouragement that John's readers would ultimately not be lured into this heresy. It would seem, then, that the test is aimed at reassuring his readers since the particular heresy "is so obviously a falsehood that John expects his readers to recognize it as such, and hence to draw the conclusion that the people who hold to it cannot possibly have any share in God the Father (v. 23)."[121] He begins by asking the rhetorical question: "Who is the liar?" (v. 22). This question flows from the previous verse where John told his readers that he wrote them because they know the truth and every lie is not from the truth. He therefore progresses from the lie to the liar. The liar is none other than the one who denies that "the Christ is Jesus" (Ἰησοῦς οὐκ ἔστιν ὁ χριστός).

Here we come across the first instance where John refers to the Christ or the Son of God as Jesus (4:15; 5:1,5). Such phrases pose problems for interpretation in that it is somewhat difficult to decipher between the subject and the predicate nominative. It is typically understood that in a sentence with a verb of being (εἰμί), the nominative with the article (where there is no other nominative with an article or an expressed or implied pronoun) is the subject of the sentence.[122] McGaughy, however, argues that this verse as well as 4:15; 5:1,5 and John 20:31 should be viewed as the only five exceptions to this rule in

[121] Marshall, *Epistles of John*, 157.

[122] See E. C. Colwell, "A Definite Rule for the Use of the Article in the Greek NT," *JBL* 52 (1933): 12–21; L. C. McGaughy, *A Descriptive Analysis of* Εἶναι *as a Linking Verb in New Testament Greek*, SBLDSup 6 (Missoula, MT: SBL, 1972), 51–52. See also S. E. Porter, *Idioms of the New Testament*, 2nd ed. (Sheffield: Sheffield Academic Press, 2004), 109.

the entire New Testament.[123] It seems more likely, however, that his argument stems more from the traditional translation of these texts than actual exceptions to the rule that is otherwise universal.[124] In fact, given the proposed background of the letter, it is probably best to understand these texts not as exceptions but as examples that further demonstrate the rule. Therefore, the question at stake for John is not "Who is Jesus?" but "Who is the Christ/Son of God?"[125] The answer, of course, is that the Christ or Son of God is the man Jesus.

The specific denial of the liar therefore appears to be his rejection of the unity between the divine Christ and the man Jesus (cp. 4:15; 5:1,5).[126] Such a denial finds its closest parallel in the aforementioned Cerinthian form of proto-gnosticism that believed that the divine Christ came upon the human Jesus at His baptism but left Him sometime before His death.[127] If this is correct, then the secessionists were denying the reality of the incarnation and therefore, by implication, the importance of the atoning sacrifice of Jesus the Christ.[128] Such a denial, John says, is that which is made by the antichrists and is nothing short of a denial of the Father and the Son.[129] John contends that

[123] McGaughy, *A Descriptive Analysis of* Εἶναι, 51–52.

[124] So E. V. N. Goetchius, "Review of *A Descriptive Analysis of* Εἶναι *as a Linking Verb in New Testament Greek*, by L. C. McGaughy," *JBL* 95 (1976): 148; Porter, *Idioms*, 110.

[125] See D. A. Carson, "The Purpose of the Fourth Gospel: John 20:30–31 Reconsidered," *JBL* 108 (1987): 643, for a convincing argument in support of the view espoused above (so also Porter, *Idioms*, 109–10; Akin, *1, 2, 3 John*, 54–55).

[126] The negative particle οὐκ after the verb of negation ὁ ἀρνούμενος is dropped from the statement, Τίς ἐστιν ὁ ψεύστης εἰ μὴ ὁ ἀρνούμενος ὅτι Ἰησοῦς οὐκ ἔστιν ὁ Χριστός, in English translations. This is a classical Greek construction that is often used to deny direct speech. In other words, the secessionists said that "Jesus is not the Christ" (so also Smalley, *1, 2, 3 John*, 111; Brown, *Epistles of John*, 352; F. Blass and A. Debrunner, *A Greek Grammar of the New Testament and Other Early Christian Literature*, trans. and rev. Robert W. Funk [Chicago: University of Chicago Press, 1961], 429).

[127] This understanding of the background was espoused in the second chapter and will be argued further in the synthesis below. Therefore, I will reserve further elaboration until then.

[128] This implication is made clear in John's truth test in 5:5–6, which will be covered below.

[129] To deny that the Christ is Jesus is parallel with the denial that the Son of God is Jesus. Thus this test is a virtual equivalent with that of 4:15. The shift from Christ to Son of God is also found in the parallel passages of 5:1 and 5:5. Smalley notes that it might be "that for John both titles indicated the exalted status of Jesus, with little basic difference in meaning between them. As the Son of God and Messiah, Jesus is intimately related to the Father" (Smalley, *1, 2, 3 John*, 276). Likewise Marshall, *Epistles of John*, 157, says, "It is likely that he regarded 'Christ' and 'Son' as virtually equivalent terms." Cp. M. de Jonge, "The Use of the Word ΧΡΙΣΤΟΣ in the Johannine Epistles," in *Studies in John, Presented to Professor Dr. J. N. Sevenster* (Leiden: Brill,

the heretics were critically mistaken if they thought that they could have fellowship with God while denying Jesus. This truth was clearly set forth in 2:1–2, for Jesus is the One who serves as the "advocate" between man and God and it is only through His atoning death that men have fellowship with God the Father. Hence, those who confess the Son have relationship with the Father, while those who reject the Son do not (2:23).

Those from God Confess that Jesus Christ Has Come in the Flesh (3:24b-4:6)

The next test of belief is found in 3:24b–4:6. Following the transition sentence in 3:24b,[130] John exhorts his readers not to believe every spirit[131] but to test them in order to see if they are from God (4:1). Such a warning implies that John is combating yet another false claim of the secessionists; namely, that they have received the Spirit and are claiming to speak in His name.[132] He, therefore, offers a clear test to enable his readers to distinguish between the spirits that have come from God and the many that are not from God (i.e., false prophets).[133]

Jesus Christ come in the flesh. The specific test in this passage is found in 4:2–3, where the writer emphasizes the importance of the incarnation, which again points toward the secessionists' rejection of

1970), 66–74; W. Grundmann, "Χριστός," in *Theological Dictionary of the New Testament*, ed. G. Kittle, trans. G. W. Bromiley (Grand Rapids: Eerdmans, 1965, 1999), 570–71.

[130] As noted in our discussion of the Holy Spirit above, 3:24b should probably be viewed as a transition sentence that moves the discussion from a test of love to another test of belief. This sentence introduces the πνεῦμα, which leads into the discussion about testing the spirits found in 4:1–6. Thus, I noted above that one's Spirit-led confession of Christ as found in 4:1–6 helps a person to know that God is abiding in them.

[131] The context of testing in this passage indicates that the uses of the word "spirit" (πνεῦμα) are all probably referring to something like an "utterance of the Spirit" or a "person inspired by the spirit" (see Marshall, *Epistles of John*, 204). This is probably the case even in 4:2 when John refers to the "spirit of God" (τὸ πνεῦμα τοῦ θεοῦ). If this is correct, then τοῦ θεοῦ is best understood as a genitive of source and thus, John is speaking of a spirit that has its origin from God as opposed to the Spirit of God.

[132] So also Kruse, *Letters of John*, 144; Smalley, *1, 2, 3 John*, 217–18; Marshall, *Epistles of John*, 203–04.

[133] The statement in 4:1, "many false prophets have gone out into the world," is a parallel passage to 2:19 that points the departure of the secessionists from the community and their going out into the world (i.e., "they went out from us").

the union between the divine Christ and the man Jesus. John therefore specifies that only those who confess Jesus Christ, who has come in the flesh, are from God (4:2).[134] The participial modifier ἐληλυθό τα is in the perfect tense, which was plausibly employed to emphasize Christ's ongoing status as divinity come in the flesh (cf. 2 John 7). "Far from coming upon Jesus at the baptism and leaving him before the cross, the Christ actually came in the flesh and has never laid it aside."[135] The one who is from God will confess Jesus Christ, who has come in the flesh, while those who do not confess[136] Jesus are not from God.

Two key points should be noted with regards to this test of belief. First, it looks as though this test is a different way of interacting with the same issue found in 2:22–23. The issue in both passages appears to be a Cerinthian flavored proto-gnosticism that denies the union between the divine Christ and the human Jesus. Hence, John goes at the one issue in two different ways. In 2:22 he asserts that the liar is the one who denies that the divine Christ is the human Jesus (i.e., union between God and flesh). In 4:2–3, the one who confesses Jesus Christ, who has come in the flesh (i.e., union between God and flesh), is the one from God.

Second, like the test of 2:22–23, this test would likely give comfort to his readers since a clear distinction is drawn between the message

[134] The most straightforward reading of the confession is to understand the whole phrase Ἰησοῦν Χριστὸν ἐν σαρκὶ ἐληλυθότα as the object of the confession as seen in my translation above (so also Schnackenburg, *Johannine Epistles*, 200–1; Brown, *Epistles of John*, 493; Smalley, *1, 2, 3 John*, 222–23; Marshall, *Epistles of John*, 205; O'Neill, *Puzzle*, 46–48; Brooke, *Johannine Epistles*, 109).

[135] Stott, *Letters of John*, 158.

[136] A textual variant that places λύει in place of μὴ ὁμολογεῖ has found the support of several recent commentators (so Brown, *Epistles of John*, 494–96; Schnackenburg, *Johannine Epistles*, 201; Bultmann, *Johannine Epistles*, 62). It is interesting that such a reading has found such support, given its poor external evidence (vg; Ir1739mg, Cl1739mg, Or1739mg, Lcf). Nevertheless, against the overwhelming external evidence, these commentators have argued for the originality of this reading along similar lines of Schnackenburg, who asserts that it is "so strange that it must surely be regarded as original" (Schnackenburg, *Johannine Epistles*, 201). On the contrary, this should probably be viewed as a good illustration of an abuse of the general rule of textual criticism that the more difficult reading is to be preferred. Instead, given the overwhelming textual evidence, it is best to understand this reading as a "second century polemic against Gnostics who made a distinction between the earthly Jesus and the heavenly Christ" (Metzger, *Textual Commentary*, 644–45; see also B. E. Ehrman, "1 Joh 4.3 and the Orthodox Corruption of Scripture," *ZNW* 79 [1988]: 242).

that was heard from the beginning and the aberrant message of the heretics. Assuming John's readers were under pressure from the "spirit-inspired" heretics regarding this new teaching, the clear lines of demarcation would again serve to reassure his readers that they were the ones holding to the historic teaching of Jesus. Moreover, John seems confident that his readers will not succumb to such a teaching, for they are from God and have overcome the false teachers, because the One in them is greater than the one in the world (4:4).[137] A similar idea to that of 3:1–10, where a person lives like their progenitor, is presented here, but this time in reference to their belief. Those from the world listen and believe the things of the world, while those from God listen and believe the things of God (4:5–6).

The One Who Overcomes (5:5–11)

John begins chapter five with yet another test of belief (5:1).[138] Here he asserts that the one who believes that the Christ is Jesus has been born of God (cp. 2:22).[139] This test is followed by John's demonstration of the link between the three tests, of which I will reserve comment until later. He returns to the test of belief in 5:5 where he contends that the one who overcomes is the one who believes the Son of God is Jesus (cp. 4:15). This description of Jesus continues on into verses 6–10, which adds further support to his earlier tests of belief (2:22–23; 4:1–6; 4:15; 5:1,4) and is perhaps the clearest indicator of the actual heresy that John has been debunking throughout these tests.[140]

[137] "The One who is in you" (ὁ ἐν ὑμῖν) is probably another reference to the Holy Spirit. In support of this reading is the fact that this passage is parallel in substance to the first test of belief (2:19–27), where John told his readers that they had an "anointing" (i.e., the Holy Spirit) "abiding in them" who would enable them to not be misled by the false teaching of the secessionists (see also Stott, *Letters of John*, 160; Brown, *Epistles of John*, 497–98; against Strecker, *Johannine Letters*, 137).

[138] Note the repetition of these belief tests. 5:1 is parallel to 2:22 in that both assert that the Christ is Jesus. Moreover, 5:5 is parallel to 4:15 in that both assert that the Son of God is Jesus. The parallelism between 5:1 and 2:22 with 5:5 and 4:15 is also worthy of note.

[139] Above it was the one who passed the righteousness test who was said to be born of God. Here the criterion for being born of God is one's proper belief in Jesus.

[140] See Bruce, *Epistles of John*, 118–19; Akin, *1, 2, 3 John*, 195; Stott, *Letters of John*, 180–81; Marshall, *Epistles of John*, 231–33; D. A. Carson, "The Three Witnesses and the Eschatology of 1 John," in *To Tell the Mystery: Essays on New Testament Eschatology in Honor of Robert*

In 5:6a, John asserts that Jesus Christ is the One "who came through water and blood" (οὗτός ἐστιν ὁ ἐλθὼν δι' ὕδατος καὶ αἵματος, Ἰησοῦς Χριστός).[141] Moreover, to avoid misunderstandings, he further asserts in 5:6b that He came "not by water alone, but by water and by blood" (οὐκ ἐν τῷ ὕδατι μόνον ἀλλ' ἐν τῷ ὕδατι καὶ ἐν τῷ αἵματι). Several grammatical issues are important to one's understanding of this verse.[142] To begin, John's use of the preposition διά ("through") in 5:6a should not be missed. This preposition clearly modifies both of the anarthrous nouns ὕδατος ("water") and αἵματος ("blood") and therefore constitutes one composite unit.[143] Moreover, it seems best to understand διά with the genitive in its typical spatial meaning, denoting Jesus as coming *through* both the water and the blood.[144] Hence, if we take this with the test of 5:1 and 5:5, it would appear that John's point is that the man Jesus was the Son of God/Christ all the way through both His baptism and His death on the cross. In other words, he is again counteracting what appears to be a Cerinthian type of proto-gnosticism that argued something along the lines of the divine Christ coming upon the man Jesus at the time of His baptism but departing sometime before His death on the cross. Against such a heresy, John insists that Jesus the Christ came through both.

If this were not clear enough, the point is sharpened in 5:6b. Here the writer appears to go directly at this false teaching and asserts that Jesus did not come by water alone (οὐκ ἐν τῷ ὕδατι μόνον) but by water and by blood (ἐν τῷ ὕδατι καὶ ἐν τῷ αἵματι). The phrase "not by water alone" indicates that the secessionists did not have a problem agreeing that He came by water. Their point of contention

H. Gundry, JSNTSup100, ed. T. E. Schmidt and M. Silva (Sheffield: Sheffield Academic Press, 1994), 219, 226–30. Against Griffith, *Keep Yourselves from Idols*, 153.

[141] See also chap. 3, where I have already discussed this passage at some length. I have tried to avoid significant overlap on issues where I went into detail on this passage in chap. 3. With this text being important both to the discussion of the centrality of the cross and the test of belief, some overlap is an unavoidable result.

[142] For a helpful discussion of the various grammatical issues in these verses, readers should consult Carson, "The Three Witnesses," 226–30.

[143] See also Brown, *Epistles of John*, 573.

[144] Against Marshall, *Epistles of John*, 232, n. 6, who contends that "no good sense can be attached to the phrase 'through blood.'" Carson, however, is correct in his assertion that such an objection is to confuse "the symbol with the thing symbolized" ("Three Witnesses," 226).

was the cross. Hence, John tackles this issue head on. Jesus Christ did not come by water alone but by water and by blood. The author makes his point by shifting to the preposition ἐν, distributing the preposition over each of the nouns (ἐν τῷ ὕδατι and ἐν τῷ αἵματι), as well as employing the article with each of them.[145] Both the articles and the individual prepositions draw attention to each specific event. Therefore, between the two statements of 5:6a and 5:6b, the writer leaves no doubt that the Christ was Jesus all the way through the baptism and the cross. Against the proto-gnostic heretics he was combating, the Christ did not come by water alone but by water and by blood.

In 5:6c, the author says that the Spirit is the One who testifies because the Spirit is truth. If the above interpretation is correct, then it is plausible that John's reference to the Spirit at the end of the verse is a reference to the Spirit's testimony in John 1:32–34 that Jesus is the Son of God. In this instance the Baptist bears witness (μαρτυρέω) that the Spirit enabled him to comprehend that Jesus was the Son of God (John 1:33–34; cp. 1 John 4:15; 5:5). Therefore, in the Gospel as well as here, the Spirit bears witness to the truth that Jesus is divine. Moreover, Carson is correct when he asserts,

> The Baptist's witness is cast in such a way that the text makes clear that the descent of the Spirit does not *constitute* Jesus as the Son of God, but *identifies* him as the Son of God. That is entirely in line with the point derived from the force of διά with a form of ἔρχομαι: against Cerinthus, Jesus the Son of God, one person, existed before the baptism, came *through* the baptism, and was (according to the Baptist) identified to others by the experience of the Spirit's descent.[146]

The Gospel account also makes clear that God was the One who sent the Spirit (John 1:33), so it was ultimately God's own testimony regarding His Son. This too is consistent with the account in 1 John where the three witnesses of 5:7–8 are shown to be the one unified

[145] Carson, "The Three Witnesses," 227. Against Akin, *1, 2, 3 John*, 195; Bultmann, *Johannine Epistles*, 79; Smalley, *1, 2, 3 John*, 280, who argue that the change is merely stylistic. While this is certainly possible and does not really weaken the point, it does seem that the change in preposition strengthens the author's point.

[146] Ibid., 228.

testimony of God concerning His Son in 5:9 that is greater than any testimony of man.

So this test is perhaps the clearest description of the heresy of the secessionists. The one who is born of God (5:1) and overcomes the world (5:5) is the one who believes that the Christ/Son of God is Jesus, who came all the way through the water and the blood.[147] As in the other tests of belief, the conclusion of this section (5:13), which is also the formal conclusion of the epistle, implies that he has great confidence that his readers are those who do believe in Jesus as laid out throughout this letter.

Summary of John's Tests of Life

Above I examined the individual tests of life and saw that the tests of righteousness, love, and belief were written in order to strengthen the assurance of his readers. By way of summary, it is important to look at these tests holistically and make a few concluding observations.

Tests Fit the Situation in the Church

Interpreters of 1 John must not miss the fact that John's series of tests are given as a result of the situation in the community to which it was written. The truth test serves to reveal the identity of the secessionists as liars and antichrists (2:22) who are not from God (4:3), for they have denied the incarnation and the importance of Jesus' atoning sacrifice. Moreover, the test of righteousness demonstrates that the false teachers are liars (2:4) and children of the Devil (3:10), for they are the ones who are indifferent to the importance of righteous living. Finally, the test of love serves to expose the heretics as those who

[147] While there is nuance in each of these tests of belief, it seems best to view each of them as different ways of saying the same thing (cp. Kruse, *Letters of John*, 146 n. 161; Schnackenburg, *Johannine Epistles*, 201; against, Smalley, *1, 2, 3 John*, xxii, 338–39; idem, "What About 1 John?" 338–39. Smalley argues that John is combating two groups in this letter: [1] Jewish Christians and [2] Hellenistic Christians. Thus he argues that some of John's tests of belief are directed at the Jewish Christians who found it difficult to accept that Jesus was the Messiah, while others were focused on the Hellenistic Christians who found it difficult to embrace the full humanity of the Christ). In other words, the focus of each of John's tests of belief is the secessionists' denial of the union between the man Jesus and the divine Christ and therefore, their denial of the incarnation and the importance of His atoning sacrifice.

remain in darkness (2:9) and in death (3:14), for they not only fail to love the brethren but actually hate them (2:9,11).

Tests Are Grounded in the Message Heard from the Beginning

These tests, however, are not simply the result of the current situation in which John's readers find themselves. Quite the contrary, they are also grounded in the message they had heard from the beginning. Take for example the test of belief. Here the writer insists that the one who is born of God believes that the Christ/Son of God is Jesus, who came in the flesh. Such a teaching is nothing short of the apostolic gospel they heard when they first believed. Moreover, the test of love is nothing new. It is grounded in Jesus' teaching that they must love one another and by such love all men would know that they were truly His disciples (John 13:34–35; 15:12–14). Finally, the test of obedience comes directly from Jesus' own insistence that living for Him and obeying His commands are part and parcel of believing in Him (John 8:30–31; 14:15,21,23).

Overlap Within the Tests

These tests also combine to form one overarching test of life. There are indicators throughout this letter that there is genuine overlap among the three tests. This was seen above in the way in which the test of righteousness (3:4–10b) flowed right into the test of love (3:10c-20). Moreover, in 4:7–11 it is clear that the truth of the work of Christ is the impetus for believers loving one another. However, in the first five verses of chapter five this linking of the tests is most apparent. To begin with, in 5:1 John says that everyone who believes that the Christ is Jesus is born of God, and everyone who loves the Father loves the one born of Him. Here there is a clear link between the test of belief and the test of love. Then in verse 2, he asserts that it is by our love for God and the keeping of His commands that we know that we love the children of God; thus the test of love and the test of obedience are linked. Finally, in 5:3–5 it is clear that the one who obeys the commands overcomes the world (3–4) and the one who overcomes the world is none other than the one who believes that the Son of God is Jesus. Here then the tests of obedience and truth are linked together. Hence, in these five short verses, the love test is linked to the tests of truth and obedience (5:1,2), the truth test is linked to the tests of love and obedience (5:1,3–5), and the obedience test is linked to the tests of love and truth (5:2–5). Therefore, these tests should not be viewed as mutually exclusive but as one composite description of the one who is born of God.

Introspective Aspect of the Tests: Tests Written to Assure

The overarching purpose statement of this letter indicates that the writer's primary objective behind his series of tests was to bolster his readers' assurance of eternal life (5:13). As noted above, this is accomplished by the demonstration that they are the ones who know God, have fellowship with Him, and abide in Him, while the secessionists are displayed as children of the Devil. To be sure, as John's readers come across the truth tests and evaluate their own lives, they are reassured because they see that they are the ones who hold to the Christology described by John. Moreover, the tests of righteousness also serve to bolster his reader's confidence, in that they ascertain that they are the ones who keep the commands, purify themselves, and trust in the atoning sacrifice of Christ. Finally, the love test supports their assurance as they look at their lives and see that they have a genuine love for one another that is demonstrated in practical ways.

Retrospective Aspect: Written to Enable Readers to Discern Those Who Have Fallen Away

The retrospective and introspective aspects of these tests are inextricably tied together. As with any true test, some pass and some fail. Thus, the tests not only enable John's readers to ascertain that they pass them; they also enable them to understand why others have departed from the fellowship. They have departed because they were never genuinely part of the children of God as demonstrated in their ability to reject the person and work of Jesus Christ, to disregard the importance of how they live their lives, and to hate the children of God. While the primary purpose of the tests is the assurance of the children of God, the revealing of the children of the Devil is a compatible result. To be sure, when John says such things as "the one who says I have come to know Him and does not keep His commands is a liar" (2:4), his readers cannot help but look back at those who have departed and see that such a teaching applies to them. Therefore, the byproduct of John's tests of life is this retrospective aspect that allows those who walk in the light to reflect upon those who have departed and see that they have done so because they were never genuinely born of God.

Prospective Aspect: Written to Spur Readers on to Persevere in Righteousness, Love, and Right Belief

Finally, one more aspect is at least implicit within the various tests of life: a prospective or exhortative element. While this is not the primary purpose of the tests, any child of God who comes across a test like "the one who says I have come to know Him and does not keep His commands is a liar" (2:4) would likely take such a passage seriously and find added impetus to strive to keep the commands so as not to become a liar. The same could certainly be said for John's absolute statements found in chapter 3 as well. To be sure, statements such as "no one born of God sins" (3:9) were penned with the primary purpose of distinguishing between those who were indifferent to sin and those who were striving to live righteously. Nevertheless, a byproduct of such a passage is that it motivates those who are born of God to continue to strive to live without sin.

If this is true, one could also say that these tests are prospective in that they ultimately lead believers to look to the cross of Christ. Any honest children of God who come across passages like 3:9 and 5:18 struggle because they know that while they might strive to live without sin, there will be sin (2:1). In that sense they are forced to look beyond themselves to the atoning work of Christ (2:2). This is analogous with John's statement in 2:1, where he says that he is writing so that his readers might not sin and if/when they do sin, they can rest assured that they have Jesus as their "advocate" and "propitiation." It is therefore in looking to Jesus—who intercedes for believers (2:1), is the propitiation for their sins (2:2; 4:10), forgives and cleanses them of their sins (1:7,9), enables them to overcome the evil one (2:12–14), and keeps them in the faith (5:18)—that ultimately gives his readers assurance and enables them to persevere in righteousness.

Perseverance and Apostasy in 1 John

The retrospective and prospective aspects of the tests discussed above lead to the difficult issue of perseverance and apostasy in 1 John and how these themes relate to the believer's assurance of eternal life.[148] To be sure, John insists that his readers persevere in the message/word they have heard from the beginning (2:14,24), in God/Christ (2:27–28; 3:6,24; 4:13,15–16), in love (4:16), and in fellowship with the community of believers (2:19). So what are we to think of those who fail to persevere and abandon the community of believers? Does John believe that those who have been born of God and have eternal life abiding in them can abandon their divine begetting and pass back over from life to death? Is the "sin that leads to death" to be interpreted as a sin that one who is born of God is able to commit? Such questions are vital to one's conception of assurance in this letter. Hence, it is important to probe two key texts regarding perseverance and apostasy (2:19; 5:16–18) as well as examining some of John's exhortations in order to see how they relate to his overarching purpose of assuring his readers of eternal life.

They Went Out from Us Because They Were Never Really of Us (2:19)

Perhaps no other passage speaks as clearly about the identity of those who fail to persevere than 1 John 2:19. This verse occurs within

[148] In his comment on 2:19, F. F. Bruce contends that perseverance should actually be viewed as the fourth test in this letter. Here he says, "To the tests already laid down—the test of obedience and the test of love—another, the test of perseverance or continuance, is now introduced" (*Epistles of John*, 69; so also Akin, *1, 2, 3 John*, 116). There is certainly some validity to this idea in that perseverance is an important theme in this letter. Those who have genuinely been born of God cannot walk away from the faith but will no doubt persevere to the end (2:19; 5:18). Nevertheless, it is probably incorrect to view this as a separate test. To begin with, perseverance is nowhere tied to one of John's many "by this we know" statements. Moreover, as John ties each of his tests together in chap. 5, perseverance is not one of the tests involved. On the other hand, it does seem that John expects his readers to persevere in each of the three tests. Hence, it is probably best to view perseverance not as a separate test but that the writer expects his readers to persevere in righteousness living, love for the brethren, and right belief.

the context of John's description of the "antichrists," whose coming made evident the arrival of the last hour (2:18). Moreover, the writer goes on to say that these individuals have gone out from us (ἐξ ἡμῶν ἐξῆλθαν).[149] The use of the phrase "from us" (ἐξ ἡμῶν) demonstrates that those he now refers to as "antichrists" were once a part of the community to which he is writing. Those who departed had probably made a Christological confession, been baptized, and taken on every appearance of one who was born of God. Nevertheless, the writer makes clear that these individuals were never genuinely part of the fellowship ("but they were not of us"), and thus never genuinely part of the Father and the Son (cp. 1:3).[150] In other words, the secessionists had never been born of God (3:9–10), did not know God (3:6), and were in the darkness even until now (2:9). The following clause gives the reason[151] John is able to make such a bold pronouncement regarding those who departed. Here, in the form of a conditional sentence, he insists that if they were actually "of us" (ἐξ ἡμῶν) they would have remained (μεμενήκεισαν)[152] "with us" (μεθ' ἡμῶν). Hence, those who are genuinely "of us," will persevere in the fellowship of the children of God.

The author's use of μένω ("abide") here should not be missed, for the motif of "abiding" is significant in his teaching on perseverance.[153] Elsewhere it is clear that those who have been born of God are to abide in the message/word they have heard from the beginning (2:14,24), in God/Christ (2:27–28; 3:6,24; 4:13,15–16), and in their love for the brethren (4:16). Here John insists that those who are genuinely "of us" will abide "with us." There is no place in the author's mind for

[149] If John's readers knew the Fourth Gospel, then it is plausible that his use of ἐξῆλθαν here would have recalled the departure of Judas, the quintessential secessionist (John 13:30–31—λαβὼν οὖν τὸ ψωμίον ἐκεῖνος ἐξῆλθεν εὐθύς. ἦν δὲ νύξ. Ὅτε οὖν ἐξῆλθεν, λέγει Ἰησοῦς· νῦν ἐδοξάσθη ὁ υἱὸς τοῦ ἀνθρώπου καὶ ὁ θεὸς ἐδοξάσθη ἐν αὐτῷ). Such would add weight to the seriousness of the departure.

[150] Against Smalley, *1, 2, 3 John*, 103, who argues that the schismatics "were in the first place believers with a genuine, if uninformed, faith in Jesus."

[151] I take the γὰρ as the ground for the statement ἀλλ' οὐκ ἦσαν ἐξ ἡμῶν.

[152] The word μένω naturally carries an ongoing aspect.

[153] See C. D. Bass, "A Johannine Perspective of the Human Responsibility to Persevere in the Faith through the Use of Μένω and Other Related Motifs," *WTJ* 69 (2007): 305–25, where I argue that John's purpose for his motif of abiding in the Fourth Gospel is to incite his readers to persevere in their faith.

an individual to be born of God and not remain vitally connected to the community of brethren. Therefore, there can be no doubt that for John a crucial mark of one who is born of God and has passed over from death to life is that he abides in the fellowship, which is part and parcel of abiding in the Father and the Son (1:3).

Finally, the verse concludes with a declaration regarding the purpose of the departure of the secessionists. John's statement, "but in order that it might be shown" (ἀλλ᾽ ἵνα φανερωθῶσιν), is elliptical, so the reader must supply the verb ἐξῆλθαν ("they went out") from earlier (cp. John 1:8; 9:3). Hence, following the strong disjunction (ἀλλά), John contends that their departure was for the purpose[154] of illustrating the fact that they were all imposters.[155]

This verse perspicuously illustrates that those who are genuinely part of the fellowship will no doubt persevere. Failure to remain in the community of the children of God demonstrates that one was never a bona fide member. In other words, they prove that they have never passed from death to life but actually abide in death even until now. So John apparently has a clear category for spurious faith (cp. John 2:23–25; 8:30–59; 13:21–30). Even though a person might make some form of Christological confession and perhaps appear as a part of the fellowship of believers for a time, his ability to depart and abandon previously held beliefs exposes the truth that his faith was spurious. Moreover, the converse is also made evident in this verse. Here the writer demonstrates that a vital mark of a child of God is that he will in fact persevere. Those who are truly "of us" will no doubt "remain with us."

The Sin That Leads to Death (5:16–17)

What then are we to say of the sin that leads to death? Do these verses contradict the writer's teaching in 2:19? To be sure, this passage

[154] I take ἵνα plus the subjunctive φανερωθῶσιν as denoting purpose. Moreover, the passive φανερωθῶσιν is best understood as a divine passive (cp. John 1:31; 9:3). Brown also notes that John's use of ἀλλ᾽ ἵνα "often pertains to a general aspect of God's plan (John 1:8,31; 9:3; 14:31; 15:25)" (*Epistles of John*, 340).

[155] The meaning of ὅτι οὐκ εἰσὶν πάντες ἐξ ἡμῶν is somewhat disputed. It is best to understand πάντες as a reference to the secessionists as opposed to the Johannine congregation. The latter would force an unexpected shift in subject as well as requiring different word order (see Smalley, *1, 2, 3 John*, 104; Brown, *Epistles of John*, 340–41).

is vital to one's understanding of perseverance and assurance in this letter. Hence, it will be helpful to analyze this text and interact with some of the pertinent questions.

Before exploring some of the specific questions that arise from this text, it is important to look briefly at the context around these two verses. Here it becomes evident that 5:16–17 is surrounded by passages of assurance. Beginning in 5:13 John assures those who believe in Jesus that they have eternal life. This is followed with an assurance that prayers prayed in the will of God will be answered (5:14–15). He then continues his general message of assurance in prayer by moving to a specific application,[156] asserting that their prayers for fellow brothers who sin will be answered and will serve as one of the means of their preservation. In the flow of thought, the comment on the sin that leads to death seems to be a parenthetical reminder[157] that they need not pray for those who commit this sin. Nevertheless, all sin is unrighteousness, and the children of God are to pray for their brothers and sisters who commit sins not leading to death. Therefore, 5:16–17 actually appears to continue John's reassurances by offering a reminder that their prayers for sinning brethren will be answered even though they need not pray for those who commit a sin unto death.[158] This teaching transitions seamlessly into the subsequent assurance that those born of God do not sin because Jesus Himself protects them from sin and the evil one will not touch them (5:18; cp. 5:19–20). Thus, with this context in mind, there are several important questions regarding the two types of sins that are pertinent to the discussion of assurance and perseverance that must be addressed.

Who is the "brother"? In 5:16, John says that if someone sees his brother (τὸν ἀδελφὸν αὐτοῦ) sinning a sin that is not unto death, he

[156] See R. K. J. Tan, "Should We Pray for Straying Brethren? John's Confidence in 1 John 5:16–17," *JETS* 45 (2002): 599; Strecker, *Johannine Letters*, 202–3; Thompson, *1–3 John*, 141; Brooke, *Johannine Epistles*, 145; Schnackenburg, *Johannine Epistles*, 248; Akin, *1, 2, 3 John*, 207; Smalley, *1, 2, 3 John*, 297.

[157] So also Thompson, *1–3 John*, 141–42; T. Ward, "Sin 'Not unto Death' and Sin 'Unto Death' in 1 John 5:16," *Churchman* 109 (1995): 228; Smalley, *1, 2, 3 John*, 299. Cp. Brown, *Epistles of John*, 636, who says that the sin unto death is mentioned by the author "in passing." Against Tan, "Should We Pray for Straying Brethren?" 607.

[158] See Brown, *Epistles of John*, 636: "The main purpose of 5:16–17, then, is positive: through prayer, sin need not be deadly for the believer."

will ask and will give life to the one who sins not unto death (5:16a). An initial question that surfaces at this point has to do with John's meaning of the term *brother* in this verse. Stott has argued that in this context, this word should not be understood in its usual sense but in a "broader sense either of a 'neighbour' or of a nominal Christian, a church member who professes to be a 'brother.'"[159] This interpretation, however, fails, for in this context John is reassuring his readers of the efficacy of their prayers for one another. Moreover, with the exception of 3:12, where he refers specifically to Abel as the ἀδελφός of Cain, John's consistent use of the term ἀδελφός is a reference to those who are part of the Johannine community and are therefore Christians.[160]

Why does a "brother" need life? Such an interpretation leads to a second question: What does John mean when he says that through prayer a brother who sins a sin that is not unto death will be given "life"? This question is especially difficult given that the writer has elsewhere asserted that readers already have eternal life (3:14; 5:11–13).[161] There are at least four plausible answers. First, Thompson has posited that God grants forgiveness to the believer who repents of his sin, and receiving this forgiveness means having life with God.[162] This interpretation falls short in that it equates life with forgiveness, which is not done elsewhere in the letter.[163] Second, Scholer asserts that God will give believers who repent of their sins reconfirmation of their transition from death to life.[164] The idea of "reconfirmation," however, does not fit the general tenor of the letter, for that would assume that each time a person sinned he would experience doubt of his present status with God and need his life to be reconfirmed. So the idea of reconfirmation fails in that it does not take into account the writer's continued assurances of his readers' present status with

[159] Stott, *Letters of John*, 192.

[160] So also Marshall, *Epistles of John*, 246 n. 15; Westcott, *Epistles of St. John*, 191; Smalley, *1, 2, 3 John*, 299.

[161] Any attempt to answer this question, however, must admit that John himself does not answer it, so any proposal is at best speculative (so Marshall, *Epistles of John*, 248).

[162] M. M. Thompson, "Intercession in the Johannine Community: 1 John 5:16 in the Context of the Gospel and Epistles of John," in *Worship, Theology and Ministry in the Early Church: Essays in Honor of Ralph P. Martin*, JSNTSup 87, ed. M. J. Wilkins and T. Paige (Sheffield: Sheffield Academic Press, 1992), 244.

[163] So also Kruse, *Letters of John*, 191.

[164] Scholer, "Sins Within and Sins Without," 246.

God (2:12–14; 3:1–2; 5:13,19–20). Third, Marshall argues that verse 17 helps supply the answer in that it reminds the reader that all sin is unrighteousness and therefore dangerous since it is characteristic of a life apart from God. Moreover, he asserts that the sins of believers and the sins of unbelievers are essentially the same: disbelief in Jesus, failure to keep the commands, and lack of love for the brethren. So for Marshall, "there is always the danger that a person who sins unconsciously or unwittingly may move to the point of sinning deliberately and then turning his back completely on God and the way of forgiveness."[165] This interpretation also falls short since it not only fails to take into account the present context of assurance but also denies the letter's own evidence that the "brother" will not ultimately turn his back on God (2:19; 3:9; 5:18). Finally, Kruse offers the most plausible suggestion when he contends that this passage is forward-looking in that God will give the promised resurrection life to sinning believers who repent.[166] This fits the writer's already-but-not- yet tension that is found throughout the letter (2:8,28; 3:2–3). While eternal life is the present possession of those born of God (5:13), it is also described as something that is still to come (2:25). In light of this, the future tense δώσει is best understood as prospective and the intercessory prayers of the brethren as one of the means God[167] uses to preserve His children, who still commit sins that do not lead to death. Hence, for the brother who sins not unto death, intercessory prayers can be offered, which are presumably within the will of God (5:15).

[165] Marshall, *Epistles of John*, 248–49.

[166] Kruse, *Letters of John*, 191. Against Tan, "Should We Pray for Straying Brethren?" 601, n. 9, who argues that options 1, 2, and 4 "provide complementary explanations from different perspectives."

[167] Two main interpretations are given for the phrase αἰτήσει καὶ δώσει αὐτῷ ζωήν. The issue is who is the subject of the verb δώσει. Given that the subject of the verb αἰτήσει is the one who sees the person sinning, then the simplest answer grammatically speaking is to say that the petitioner is the subject of δώσει as well (so Brooke, *Johannine Epistles*, 146; Stott, *Letters of John*, 189; Strecker, *Johannine Letters*, 202; Dodd, *Johannine Epistles*, 135; Plummer, *Epistles of St. John*, 122). Of course, this translation runs into problems theologically, which has led other interpreters to see a change in subject from the first verb to the second and, hence, God is the subject of δώσει (so Scholer, "Sins Within and Sins Without," 239–40; Schnackenburg, *Johannine Epistles*, 249; Akin, *1, 2, 3 John*, 207; Marshall, *Epistles of John*, 246). In the end there is actually little difference between the two, since God is the One who was said above to answer prayers (5:14–15) and thus is ultimately the One who gives life.

Therefore, these prayers will be answered, the brother will repent, and God will give eternal life on the last day.

The identity of the sin that leads to death. There is, however, a sin that leads to death (5:16b), and the author does not require prayer for those who commit such a sin. Since the writer does not tell us the precise identification of this sin, one must use the context in an attempt to understand what was meant here. The difficulty of identifying this sin can be seen in the numerous answers that have been posited. Here I will interact with five common views.[168]

1. One view of the sin that leads to death is that it is a sin so serious that "God could, and sometimes did, inflict [physical] *death* more or less immediately" upon the offender.[169] Proponents of this view cite both Old and New Testament examples of sins and sinners where the punishment was physical death (e.g., Num 18:22; Deut 22:25–26; Acts 5:1–11; 1 Cor 11:30). While there were cases of sins that led to physical death, this view is untenable, for it fails to understand the ideas of "life" and "death" in the Johannine literature. Within the confines of this letter, "life" (ζωή) occurs 13 times (1:1–2; 2:25; 3:14–15; 5:11–13,16,20). Each instance is in reference to spiritual life either as a reference to eternal life or Jesus as the embodiment of eternal life. Given that death here is contrasted with life, then life and death no doubt refer to spiritual life and spiritual death in 1 John.[170] The letter's only other occurrence of "death" (θάνατος) outside of 5:16–17 stands in support of this reading (3:14). Moreover, Brown is helpful when he says:

[168] I am well aware that other answers have been and continue to be proposed on this matter. I have avoided those that seem to have no plausibility, such as the medieval distinction between mortal and venial sins. For other helpful lists see especially Ward, "Sin 'Not unto Death' and Sin 'Unto Death'," 226–37; Brown, *Epistles of John*, 612–19; Kruse, *Letters of John*, 193–95; Stott, *Letters of John*, 190–93; Law, *Tests of Life*, 138–42.

[169] Hodges, *Epistles of John*, 233 (emphasis [bold in the original] his). So also S. M. Reynolds, "The Sin unto Death and Prayers for the Dead," *Reformation Review* 20 (1973): 130–39. Cp. Bruce, *Epistles of John*, 124, who proposes this view as one of several but does not seem to choose one in the commentary. Elsewhere, however, Bruce does seem to argue for this view (*Answers to Questions* [Grand Rapids: Zondervan, 1973], 134).

[170] This is the view of the majority of commentators (see, for example, Griffith, *Keep Yourselves from Idols*, 113; Tan, "Should We Pray for Straying Brethren?" 600–1; Scholer, "Sins Within and Sins Without," 235; Ward, "Sin 'Not unto Death' and Sin 'Unto Death'," 232; Stott, *Letters of John*, 189–90; Schnackenburg, *Johannine Epistles*, 249–50); Law, *Tests of Life*, 139.

> There is no reason to think a *Johannine* audience would have been taught to fear sin on the basis of whether or not it would lead to physical death. The Johannine Jesus says, "If a person keeps my word, he shall never see death" (John 8:51); and "Everyone who is alive and believes in me shall never die at all" (11:26). Indeed, in 12:24 Jesus speaks of physical death as fruit-bearing.[171]

2. Another view argues that the difference between the sin that leads to death and the sin that does not lead to death is best understood along the lines of the Old Testament and Qumran distinction between intentional and unintentional sins (Lev 4:1–3,13,22,27; 5:15,17–18; Num 15:22–25,27–31; Deut 17:12; 1QS 8:21–9:2).[172] Here sacrifices could be made for unintentional sins, but deliberate sins committed arrogantly with a "high hand" were punishable by death. While the sin that leads to death is certainly intentional, nothing in the context of 1 John would indicate that such a distinction is what the author has in mind here.

3. A third view argues that the sin leading to death is best understood as the unpardonable sin of blasphemy against the Holy Spirit (Mark 3:29; Matt 12:32).[173] Here Stott asserts that this sin, which was committed by the Pharisees, "was a deliberate, open-eyed rejection of known truth" where the works of Jesus were ascribed to Beelzebub.[174] Stott goes on to assert that

> it leads him inexorably into a state of incorrigible moral and spiritual obtuseness, because he has willfully sinned against his own conscience. In John's own language he has "loved the darkness instead of the light" (John 3:18–21), and in consequence he will "die in his sins" (John 8:24).[175]

While this view is correct in seeing the sin as "deliberate, open-eyed rejection of known truth," it does, however, fall short in that John nowhere gives the explanation given by Mark that this sin involves ascribing to the Devil the miraculous works of Jesus.

[171] Brown, *Epistles of John*, 614–15.

[172] W. Nauck, "Das Problem der Redaktion," in *Die Tradition und der Charakter des ersten Johanesbriefs* (Tübingen, 1957), 133–46; Marshall (*Epistles of John*, 247–48) mentions this as a profitable approach but goes on to describe the deliberate sin as apostasy.

[173] Stott, *Letters of John*, 191.

[174] Ibid.

[175] Ibid.

4. A similar interpretation of the sin that leads to death is that it is a deliberate rejection of Christ and apostasy from the true faith.[176] Plummer begins his description of this sin by asserting that one must remember that there is no sin that cannot be repented of and forgiveness granted.[177] However,

> it is possible to close the heart against the influences of God's Spirit so obstinately and persistently that repentance becomes a moral impossibility. . . . Such a condition is necessarily sin, and "sin unto death." "Sin unto death," therefore, is not any *act* of sin, however heinous, but a *state* or *habit* of sin wilfully [*sic*] chosen and persisted in: it is constant and consummate opposition to God.[178]

However, depending on one's definition of apostasy (i.e., theological apostasy or phenomenological apostasy),[179] this definition runs into a couple of different problems. On the one hand, if a proponent of this view argues for "theological apostasy," they would appear to be at odds with John's unambiguous teaching in 2:19, where those who are able to depart are able to do so only because they were "never really of us" (cf. 3:9; 5:18). On the other hand, an appeal that John is speaking here of "phenomenological apostasy" is indeed on the right track but left unqualified, does not say enough regarding how this view fits the overall context and argumentation of the letter.

5. A better solution would therefore begin with the situation behind the letter and the writer's line of argumentation that he has carried throughout. Readers of this letter cannot help but notice John's dualistic framework:

[176] So Plummer, *The Epistles of John*, 122–23; Dodd, *Johannine Epistles*, 136; Griffith, *Keep Yourselves from Idols*, 144–45; H. A. A. Kennedy, "The Covenant Conception in the First Epistle of John," *ExpTim* 28 (1916–17): 23–26; R. R. Williams, *The Letters of John and James*, Cambridge Bible Commentary (Cambridge: Cambridge University Press, 1965), 60.

[177] Plummer, *Epistles of John*, 122.

[178] Ibid., 122–23.

[179] By "theological apostasy," I am referring to the belief associated with Arminian theology where it is said that a person who has been genuinely born of God and has passed from death to life can walk away from the faith once held and pass from life back to death and become a child of the Devil. By "phenomenological apostasy," I am referring to the view associated with Calvinistic theology that asserts that anyone who joins himself to the church of God, tastes of the heavenly gift, and then falls away demonstrates that he has never genuinely been born of God (i.e., "they were never really of us" [2:19]).

light	darkness
sons of God	sons of the Devil
those who have gone out	those who have remained
sin that leads to death	sin that does not lead to death
etc.	

Here, too, there appears to be a distinction between the sin of the "brother" (i.e., a Christian in the community), which is not unto death, and the sin unto death that is not specified to be of a "brother."[180] Such a distinction is confirmed in the context in which the sin unto death is located. As noted above, these two verses are situated right in the middle of assurances of answered prayer (5:14–15) and of divine preservation of those born of God (5:18). Moreover, the first part of 5:16, is a continuation of his message of assurance in prayer that says a wayward brother can be brought back to repentance by means of prayer. In what appears to be a parenthesis in his assurances, he then reminds his readers that there is, however, a sin that leads to death in which they are not expected to pray. Given John's statements in 5:15 regarding praying in God's will, it is plausible that the readers need not pray for those who commit this sin because eternal life for them is outside of God's will (5:15).

Therefore, the context of this passage as well as the distinction between the sin of the brother and the sin of the nonbrother would seem to indicate that the sin that leads to death is the sin of the nonbrother, who in this letter is none other than the secessionist.[181] These are the ones already referred to by the writer as liars (1:6; 2:4), those who dwell in the dark (2:9,11), antichrists (2:18,22; 4:3), those who have departed from the fellowship (2:19), and children of the Devil (3:10). This interpretation finds further support when we consider that by the time we get to this passage John has already illustrated that

[180] So also Brown, *Epistles of John*, 617; Kruse, *Letters of John*, 194; Scholer, "Sins Within and Sins Without," 238.

[181] For others who link the sin that leads to death with the sin of the secessionists, see Brown, *Epistles of John*, 617–18; Grayston, *Johannine Epistles*, 144; Scholer, "Sins Within and Sins Without," 238; Painter, *1, 2, and 3 John*, 318–19; T. Ward, "Sin 'Not unto Death' and Sin 'Unto Death,'" 236; Akin, *1, 2, 3 John*, 210; Kruse, *Letters of John*, 194; Culpepper, *1 John, 2 John, 3 John*, 110.

the secessionists have failed each of his three crucial tests of life. They have refused to believe that the Christ is Jesus who came through water and blood, which is a denial of both the incarnation and necessity of the atoning sacrifice of Jesus. Moreover, they have failed to live righteously and love the brethren, whereby they have demonstrated that they are actually children of the Devil. Therefore, the secessionist's departure from the fellowship and rejection of the incarnation, cross work of Christ, and belief that it was necessary to live righteously and love the brethren is described here as "the sin that leads to death," and it is for those sinning such a sin that John's readers need not pray.[182]

Can a genuine believer commit the sin that leads to death? Another question is whether one who has actually passed over from death to life can commit the sin that leads to death, passing back over from life to death. Marshall, for one, answers in the affirmative.[183] He contends that while John was thinking primarily of those who had left the church, he nevertheless believed that his readers who had been born of God could also commit the sin that leads to death; otherwise there would have been no need to warn them against failing to remain in the truth.[184]

There are several things, however, within this letter, as well as in the broader Johannine writings, that stand against the idea that the one who is born of God can finally commit the sin that leads to death.[185] To begin with, we have already discussed John's teaching in 2:19, where it is made clear that the antichrists went out from the community because they were never really a part of it. This verse demonstrates that those who are part of the fellowship, which is part and

[182] See Ward, "Sin 'Not unto Death' and Sin 'Unto Death'," 236.

[183] Marshall, *Epistles of John*, 249–50; idem, *Kept by the Power of God*, 183–87. So also Brown, *Epistles of John*, 636; Painter, *1, 2, and 3 John*, 317–20; Smalley, *1, 2, 3 John*, 299.

[184] Marshall, *Epistles of John*, 250; idem, *Kept by the Power of God*, 184. In reference to the various warnings in the Johannine letters, he asserts that "these verses express the possibility that John's readers may go astray and lose their salvation. . . . Hence we must allow the possibility that believers might lapse from the true faith through following the false teachers, whether or not the group of teachers were themselves regarded as believers." Moreover, he asserts that "sin is a possibility among believers, even to the point of denial of Christ, and the teaching of the Epistle is not fully accounted for if sin is regarded as a possibility only among those who have never been truly converted" (*Kept by the Power of God*, 186–87).

[185] See Culpepper, *1 John, 2 John, 3 John*, 110; Akin, *1, 2, 3 John*, 210.

parcel of fellowship with the Father and the Son (i.e., a Christian), will persevere and not apostatize. Moreover, above we saw that 3:9 affirms that the one who is born of God does not sin because God's seed abides in him. There we argued that God's seed is best understood as the Holy Spirit. If this is correct, then we have an instance of divine preservation, making it impossible for one who has been born of God to have a life characterized by sin. Finally, within two sentences of John's mentioning the sin that leads to death, he asserts that the one born of God cannot live a life characterized by sin like the secessionists, because Jesus Himself protects them and the evil one is not able to touch them. Here again, John assures his readers by asserting that there is divine preservation for those born of God and they are therefore unable to apostatize.

This interpretation is corroborated in John's Gospel. By way of comparison, it might be helpful to examine at least two of the many promises elucidated by Jesus regarding believers being called and kept by the power of God.[186] For instance, in 6:37–44 Jesus unequivocally avows that those whom the Father has given Him will come to Him. Moreover, those who come will most assuredly not be cast out.[187] This same emphasis on God's sovereign control in the salvation and preservation of His people is repeated in 6:44. Here Jesus is direct and to the point. People are unable to come to the Father (i.e., for salvation) unless the Father Himself "draws" them. The use of ἑλκύσῃ is informative in that it carries a meaning of drawing or dragging by force[188] as seen in its other usages in the New Testament.[189]

[186] I have chosen only two of the many passages throughout John where the idea of God's sovereignty in salvation is undeniable. For a fuller examination, see R. W. Yarbrough, "Divine Election in the Gospel of John," in *Still Sovereign: Contemporary Perspectives on Election, Foreknowledge and Grace*, ed. T. R. Schreiner and B. A. Ware (Grand Rapids: Baker, 2000), 47–62.

[187] I get this strong wording from the οὐ μὴ plus the subjunctive in 6:37, which is of course the strongest way possible to negate something in Greek. Wallace (*Greek Grammar Beyond the Basics*, 468) notes that this construction denies even the *potentiality* of something.

[188] H. G. Liddell and R. Scott, *A Greek-English Lexicon*, 9th. ed., rev. H. S. Jones and P. G. W. Glare (Oxford: Clarendon, 1996), s.v. "ἕλκω"; BDAG, s.v. "ἕλκω."

[189] In 18:10 we see Peter forcefully drawing his sword from its sheath in order to cut off the ear of the high priest's servant. In 21:6 and 21:11 we see the same word employed to denote the forceful dragging of the fishing net trying to hoist in a miraculous catch. Moreover, outside of John, the only other place it is used in the New Testament is found in Acts 16:19 where Paul and Silas are seized and *dragged* into the marketplace. Though it is not the place to enter into a lengthy discussion of the use of this word in John 12:32, I would argue that it is being used in

This implies that ἑλκύσῃ carries in its meaning more than a simple wooing.[190] Moreover, for those who are drawn by Christ, there is the promise that He will raise them up on the last day. There is no hint of the idea that those who are His are able to depart and not ultimately be raised up to eternal life.

Again in the tenth chapter of John, there is more evidence that God is the One who is ultimately in control of preserving believers. In 10:26–29 Jesus makes clear that only those who are His sheep truly believe in Him (10:26). They hear His voice and follow Him, and this following is not in doubt. Moreover, Jesus and not their own meritorious works gives them eternal life, so they most assuredly will not perish.[191] This is because no one is able to snatch them away from either Jesus' or the Father's hands in which they dwell. The result of Jesus' divine preservation over the lives of believers is that they will certainly not apostatize and thus perish.

What about warnings and exhortations to persevere? Nevertheless, Marshall is correct in raising the question of the purpose of warnings and exhortations to persevere. There are several instances throughout this letter where the author appears to exhort his readers to persevere (2:15a,24,27–28; 3:7; 4:1; 5:21). In fact, he even chose to conclude his letter on a note of admonition (5:21). Understanding that there are many who will appear as believers for a time but by falling away prove they were never really believers to begin with (2:19), what are we to make of such passages that give exhortation or warnings to those who have been born of God?[192] The most cogent answer lies

the same sense as we have discussed for 6:44. In other words, Jesus is teaching that when He is lifted up there will be an intense drawing of all kinds of men to Himself. Of course there is a debate here that centers upon the meaning of "all," to which I would argue that John is speaking about "all" without distinction (i.e., both Jews and Gentiles) and not "all" without exception (i.e., every single person).

[190] See also Yarbrough, "Divine Election in the Gospel of John," 50: "It is hard to avoid the impression that John 6:44 refers to a 'forceful attraction' in bringing sinners to the Son."

[191] οὐ μὴ ἀπόλωνται.

[192] Here I make a distinction between John's "tests of life" and some of the warnings and exhortations to persevere. As argued above, I understand John's tests to have primarily an introspective aspect to them with a clear purpose of assurance. In other words, when John's readers read these "tests," they are able to look at their lives and see that they are walking in the light and therefore find support for their assurance. I have also argued, however, that inherent in such tests are both a retrospective aspect that helps them understand that those who have failed such tests were never truly part of the community and a prospective aspect that would spur

within the tension itself. On one end of the spectrum, there is no denying that God is in complete control of the salvation (4:9–10; 19) and preservation (3:9; 5:18) of His people.[193] Paradoxically, on the other end of the spectrum, it is also painfully obvious that those who do not abide in Jesus and His fellowship are antichrists, sons of the Devil, and destined for punishment. Both are simultaneously affirmed as true. The best solution therefore is to affirm that these exhortations and warnings are real in that the one who does not heed them and abide in Christ demonstrates that he was never really "of us" and faces spiritual death, which involves punishment. Likewise, we must also affirm that the promises that we are born of God and kept by divine preservation are real in that those who do heed the warning and abide in Christ are only able to do so because God's seed abides in them (3:9) and Jesus Himself keeps them from sin and the perils of the evil one (5:18; cp. John 6:44; 10:28–29). So those who have truly been born of God apparently will take such warnings and admonitions seriously and therefore persevere in striving to live righteously (3:3) and confessing sin along the way (1:7,9). Those who fail to do so demonstrate that they have never truly been born of God. In this vein we can say that John's exhortations and warnings are at least one of the means by which God preserves His children.[194]

Of course at this point those like Marshall might levy the complaint that functionally there is no difference here between this view and that of the Arminian since in both cases only the one who abides has eternal life.[195] The difference, however, is the question of who is

them on to continue in righteousness, love, and right doctrine. The warnings and exhortations to which I am referring here are those such as 2:15,24,27–28; 3:7; 4:1; and 5:21, which do not appear to have any kind of introspective or retrospective aspect to them but purely serve a prospective function to warn them of the perils of failure and exhort them to persevere.

[193] In 1 John it is clear that God has taken all of the initiative in bringing sinners into fellowship with Him (cp. 4:9–10,19). The notion of being "born of God" elucidates this truth.

[194] For a thorough explanation of this prospective aspect of admonitions and warnings, see Schreiner and Caneday, *The Race Set Before Us*, 142–213. It should be made clear at this point that I am not asserting that the warnings are "the" means of God's preserving His people; rather, they should be viewed as one of many means God uses in the preservation of His people. Other means we see in Scripture include, but are not limited to, the inner working of the Holy Spirit (Rom 8:16; 1 John 4:13), the encouragement and/or rebuke of another brother or sister in Christ (Gal 6:1–2) and the prayers of the saints (1 John 5:16; Jas 5:16–20).

[195] See Marshall, *Kept by the Power of God*, 313. "The Calvinist 'believer' cannot fall away from 'true' faith, but he can 'fall away' from what proves in the end to be only seeming faith. The

ultimately in control.[196] In the Johannine literature God is in control of every aspect of saving His people, all the while His people are responsible for abiding in Christ. Therefore, those born of God must strive to "let the message of the true gospel abide in them" and "keep themselves from idols," knowing that in the end, their perseverance is due to the divine preservation of God's seed abiding in them (3:8) and Christ Himself keeping them from falling away (5:18). In this sense John's teaching is analogous to that of Paul, who both exhorts and assures his readers when he tells them to work out their salvation with fear and trembling, knowing that, in the end, God is both willing and working in them for His good pleasure (Phil. 2:12b-13). Such an understanding no doubt fosters both assurance in the confidence of God's divine preservation and an impetus to persevere in righteousness.

Conclusion

This chapter has focused on the series of three tests of life that permeate this letter. It was argued that these tests not only address the situation in the church or group of churches to which he was writing but also are grounded in the gospel message they have heard from the beginning. Moreover, from the first five verses of 1 John 5 these tests are not mutually exclusive but make up one composite test of life. The tests were written primarily for the purpose of the recipients' introspection and subsequent reassurance as they comprehend

possibility of falling away remains. But in neither case [Calvinist or Arminian] does the person know for certain whether he is a true or seeming disciple. All that he knows is that Christ alone can save and that he must trust in Christ. . . . Whoever said, 'The Calvinist knows that he cannot fall from salvation but does not know whether he has got it,' had it summed up nicely. But this can be counterfeit and misleading. The non-Calvinist knows that he has salvation—because he trusts in the promises of God—but is aware that left to himself, he could lose it. So he holds Christ. It seems to me the *practical effect is the same*" (emphasis mine).

[196] See D. A. Carson, "Reflections on Assurance," in *Still Sovereign: Contemporary Perspectives on Election, Foreknowledge, and Grace*, ed. T. R. Schreiner and B. A. Ware (Grand Rapids: Baker, 1995, 2000), 268–69, for an excellent response to Marshall. Carson says Marshall's statements are correct only at a "mechanistic level." It is, however, the focus of the two systems that is diametrically opposed. "Despite Marshall's salutary emphasis on the promises of God, at the end of the day the security of the believer finally rests with the believer. For those from the opposite camp, the security of the believer finally rests with God—and that, I suggest, rightly taught and applied, draws the believer back to God himself, to trust in God, to renewed faith that is of a piece with trusting him in the first place."

that they hold to a right belief in Jesus, strive to live righteously, and love the brethren while the secessionists have rejected the true gospel message, are indifferent to sin, and actually hate God's offspring. In this vein I argued that these tests were also retrospective in that they enabled John's readers to comprehend that those who have departed have done so because they were never genuinely part of the community, as made obvious by their failure of each of the three tests. Moreover, I argued that an implicit byproduct of these tests was an exhortative element that serves as an impetus for continued perseverance in right belief, righteous living, and love for one another. This in turn led to a discussion on perseverance and apostasy in this letter. Here it was concluded that those who have truly been born of God will take John's warnings and admonitions seriously and therefore persevere in striving to live righteously (3:3) and confess their sins along the way (1:7,9). Those who fail to do so demonstrate that they have never truly been born of God.

Chapter 6
SUMMARY AND PASTORAL IMPLICATIONS

Introduction

Any pastor who diligently shepherds his flock will tell you that there is a high probability during the course of any given week that he will interact with at least one person who is struggling with assurance. Perhaps it is the phone call of a faithful young mom who is striving with all her might to live her life for Christ but has a weak conscience. Perhaps it's a discipline issue with a middle-aged man who claims he walked an aisle 25 years ago but you know well that he has lived like the Devil ever since. Maybe it is a four-page e-mail from a new convert who now has more questions than answers. Whatever the case may be, this study is loaded with practical implications for interacting with people on such issues of assurance. Therefore, I will begin this chapter by tying together the findings of chapters 2–5 and then move to an examination of how such findings affect our everyday lives and ministry to others.

Putting the Pieces Together

John makes clear at the end of his letter that he wrote so his readers might know they have eternal life (5:13). In other words, from the first words to the last, this letter was penned so that the children of God might have assurance that they have been born of God, have passed over from death to life, and have eternal life abiding in them.

The Need for Assurance in 1 John

The second chapter of this study proposed a working hypothesis regarding the historical setting of the letter. There I said that John wrote to a church or group of churches in which a schism had occurred (2:19). Those who had departed almost certainly denied the union between the man Jesus and the divine Christ. Closely tied to this faulty Christology was a denial of the necessity to live righteously (1:6–10; 2:3–6; 2:15–16; 3:3–10; 5:2). In fact, it is plausible that these folks were completely indifferent to sin (1:6,8,10). Moreover, the secessionists probably claimed to have a special knowledge of God, fellowship with God, and anointing of God, which seems to have led to an arrogant and unloving attitude toward those who had remained in the community. Thus, John wrote to a group of believers who found themselves in need of both reassurance and exhortation. They needed reassurance that they were the ones in fellowship with God, who knew God, had an anointing, and had eternal life abiding in them. And they needed exhortation to continue to hold on to the gospel that was proclaimed from the beginning, which would actually serve to bolster their confidence.

Assurance Grounded in Christ

The third chapter of this study focused on the person and work of Jesus Christ. On this point John began by assuring his readers that his words about Jesus could be trusted since he was an actual eyewitness (1:1–4). This was vital to the assurance of his readers because over and against the false teaching of the secessionists (who had never seen Jesus), John had personally heard, seen, and even touched Him. John's teaching, therefore, was not mere hearsay; rather, it was something he learned directly from Jesus.

John then pivoted off of his reassurance that his words could be trusted and focused on the ground of their assurance of eternal life. Here he told them that "God is light and in Him there is no darkness at all" (1:5). This statement about God's holiness was given to elucidate how sinners could have fellowship with a God who is perfect. On this point John offered three negative and three positive examples, illustrating what it looks like to walk in the darkness and what it looks like to walk in the light (1:6–2:2). The negative examples are parallel to one another and are found in 1:6,8, and 10. In 1:6, John wrote that those who make false claims to have fellowship with God, while walking in the darkness, lie and do not practice the truth. In 1:8, he said that those who deny they are sinners not only lie but actually deceive themselves and the truth is not in them. Finally, in 1:10, those who deny they have sinned not only deceive themselves but also make God a liar and His word is not in them. Hence, walking in the darkness is not only walking in the sphere where God does not dwell (1:5) but is also a complete denial that one is a sinner. In other words, walking in the darkness involves ambivalence to sin and thus a complete rejection of one's need for the atoning sacrifice of Jesus Christ. For such a person any confidence of fellowship with God should be completely eradicated.

On the other hand, the three positive examples were also parallel and had the cross-work of Christ as their common theme. The three positive examples of how one can be in fellowship with God (1:7,9; 2:1–2) are extremely enlightening in that they demonstrate the fact that walking in the light does not necessitate a sin-free life. Quite the contrary, it appears that walking in the light is to strive to live a righteous life (1:6a; 2:1a), which nevertheless includes sin (1:7c,9), confession (1:9), and trusting in the work of Christ on the cross as the propitiation of God's righteous wrath (2:2) and the cleansing of all sin and unrighteousness (1:7,9). Hence, John began his letter by making absolutely certain that fellowship with God and the assurance thereof is fundamentally grounded in the atoning sacrifice of Christ. Such assurance cannot ultimately stem from a claim to have fellowship with God, a false assertion of sinlessness, or even the discernment that one is passing the various tests of life that are found throughout the letter. Assurance of fellowship with God ultimately finds its foundation to be Jesus' atoning sacrifice, for this is the only effective remedy for sins and therefore the only way a sinner can have fellowship with a God who is light.

Moreover, John not only grounded his readers' assurance in the past work of Jesus on the cross but also pointed them toward the promise of His ongoing work of preserving those who have been born of God. Here it was clear that those born of God could have confidence they would persevere to eternal life because of the promise that Jesus keeps them from sin and the clutches of the Devil.

Assurance Supported by Lifestyle

Before one thinks, however, that all he must do is have a mental assent to the truths of the historic gospel and pray a sinner's prayer, we must remember that the first letter of John is laden with various sets of criteria or "tests" by which its readers are to evaluate their religious claims in light of the way they conduct their lives. The believer's lifestyle therefore serves as either a vital support to his or her assurance or as evidence that he has never really passed over from death to life. In chapter 4, I argued that John viewed his readers as a new covenant community and expected God's own Spirit to be dwelling in them and empowering them to walk in the light. John's emphasis on tests was a natural outflow of such an understanding, for the Holy Spirit should produce a changed life in the new covenant believer that is observable in the public arena and thus able to be tested and validated.

Therefore, the fifth chapter of this study focused on the nature of John's tests of life and sought to understand how such tests served the writer's overarching purpose of the letter. These tests were written primarily for the purpose of the recipients' introspection and subsequent reassurance as they came to understand that it was they who held to a right belief in Jesus, sought to live righteously, and loved the brethren, while the secessionists had rejected the true gospel message, were indifferent to sin, and actually hated the children of God. Thus John's tests were also retrospective in that they enabled his readers to comprehend that those who departed had done so because they were never genuinely part of the community, as made obvious by their failure on each of the three tests. Finally, I argued that an implicit byproduct of the tests was an exhortative or prospective element that serves as an impetus for continued perseverance in right belief, righteous living, and love for one another. While this is not the primary purpose of the tests, any child of God who comes across a test like "the one who says 'I have come to know Him' and does not keep His commands is a liar" (2:4) would take such a passage seriously and find added impetus to strive to keep the commands so as not to become a liar.

Likewise, we looked at some of John's warnings and exhortations to his readers to persevere in the faith. Here it was concluded that those who have truly been born of God will take John's warnings and admonitions seriously and therefore persevere in striving to live righteously (3:3) and confess their sins along the way (1:7,9). Those who fail to do so demonstrate that they have never truly been born of God (2:19).

Pastoral Implications

John's teaching on assurance is no doubt loaded with practical implications. While we are not able to delve deeply into all of them, it is helpful to press beyond a mere academic exercise, believing that the Scriptures were not written simply to study theology but because they apply directly to our lives. Here we will look at the implications of (1) assurance grounded in Christ, (2) assurance supported by lifestyle, and (3) spurious faith. We will then look at five case studies to see the variegated nature of the application of John's teaching.

Assurance Grounded in Christ

There are significant practical implications to the understanding that assurance of salvation is grounded in the person and work of Jesus Christ. Any honest Christian knows that while there is a fundamental change of life after coming to saving faith in Christ, believers nevertheless sin every day (1:8,10). Even though we have been transferred out of death and into life (3:14), there will always be sin in the camp (1:7–2:2; 5:16–17). No doubt, when we honestly examine our lives, we realize we could have believed more confidently, loved more purely, and obeyed more faithfully. At the end of the day, then, our assurance can never rest on ourselves but only on the solid foundation of the finished work of Christ.

That said, if and when believers struggle with assurance, they must continually look back to the atoning sacrifice of Jesus. This and this alone is where the believer's confidence before a holy God ultimately rests. It is the contemplation of John's teaching that Jesus stands as our advocate before God, who is light, that brings assurance. We find comfort not in looking to our own merit but when we ponder the truth that Jesus' death on the cross was the propitiation of the righteous wrath of God for every single sin of those who believe. Therefore, as we interact with those we think are genuinely born of God but have a weak conscience, we must encourage them continually to cast their eyes back to the finished work of Christ. They must be reminded that

Jesus died for all of our sins—not just those committed before coming to faith.[1]

No doubt, some readers might take issue at this point, thinking that such a teaching sounds like "easy believism." This, however, could not be further from the truth. We have already seen that the believer's confidence in the work of Christ does not serve as a deterrent to righteousness but should actually incite believers to strive to live a holy life. Take for example 3:1–3, where John seems to stand amazed that we could actually be called children of God (3:1) and have a glorious future to look forward to as a result (3:2). Of course the reason we can be called children of God is the work of Christ that he has already described. This truth, however, does not lead John to teach that we should sin so that grace may abound (see Rom 6:1–2). Quite the contrary, in verse 3, he asserts that "everyone who has this hope purifies himself as He is pure." In other words, the work of Christ and the understanding of what He has done for us should always serve to strengthen our desire to live for Him. Certainly, this is not a way of "paying Him back," for believers would never be able to do that.[2] The fact is, every Christian is in deeper need of His grace every single day. This notwithstanding, when a person truly has a proper understanding of who he is as a sinner and what the Lord Jesus has done for him in His work on the cross, he is never satisfied simply to rest on his laurels but desires nothing more than to live his life as a living sacrifice to the One who saved him.

Lifestyle of the Believer as a Vital Support to Assurance

The above truth leads to our second implication, which should actually be seen as the outworking of the first. John unambiguously teaches that while assurance is grounded in Christ, it is vitally supported by the way one lives his life. Therefore, a person's lifestyle serves as vital corroborating evidence as to whether he has truly placed his faith in Christ's finished work on the cross for his sins. John viewed his readers

[1] It is also true that such a mind-set guards the believer against any notion of a works-based righteousness.

[2] See J. Piper's helpful article on what he refers to as the "debtors ethic" (J. Piper, *Brothers, We Are Not Professionals: A Plea to Pastors for Radical Ministry* [Nashville: Broadman & Holman, 2002], 33–38.

as a new covenant community, expecting God's own Spirit to dwell in them and empower them to walk in the light. This is why he insists that those who have been born of God be obedient to the commands and love one another. Those who made spiritual claims (i.e., to have fellowship with God [1:6], to know God [2:4], to abide in God [2:6], to be in the light [2:9], to love God [4:20], etc.) and did not back them up with a lifestyle of believing the historic gospel, obeying the commands, and loving the brethren were said to be liars (1:6; 2:4; 4:20), self-deceived (1:8), and living in the darkness (2:9). So according to John, if someone comes to saving faith, there will be lasting change. To be sure, the change does not occur at the same rate for all people, but it will be present and it will last. Otherwise, this person is not a believer but is still dwelling in darkness.

There appears, however, to be a complete disconnect between John's teaching and what we find in so many of our evangelical churches today. In our right desire to see as many people as possible come to faith in Christ and join our churches, I am afraid that we have watered down John's teaching of salvation and assurance.[3] Instead, people are being invited to walk an aisle and repeat a prayer of salvation without any counsel to see whether they really understand the historic gospel, and without any teaching on what the Christian life looks like. If this were not enough, many churches then inundate these "new converts" with assurance and the pithy slogan "once saved always saved." The unfortunate result is that many believe that their lifestyle is irrelevant because they can never lose their salvation. Sadly, we are seeing the evidence of generations of church members who were called to make such a profession of faith, and now many of our churches are filled with those who are still deceived and living in the darkness, as made evident through their apathetic church involvement, their tipping of God rather than sacrificial giving, youth and young adult Bible studies where sexual

[3] I focus here on John's teaching of assurance since this book focuses on 1 John. I would argue, however, that John's teaching of assurance is corroborated throughout the rest of the New Testament. For a broader discussion of assurance throughout the New Testament, readers should consult T. R. Schreiner and A. B. Caneday, *The Race Set Before Us: A Biblical Theology of Perseverance and Assurance* (Downers Grove, IL: InterVarsity, 2001); D. A. Carson, "Reflections on Assurance," in *Still Sovereign: Contemporary Perspectives on Election, Foreknowledge, and Grace*, ed. T. R. Schreiner and B. A. Ware (Grand Rapids: Baker, 2000).

immorality runs rampant, a divorce rate in our churches that keeps pace with society at large, and a complete disinterest in loving and serving other brothers and sisters in Christ.

Some 70 years ago Dietrich Bonhoeffer described this sort of belief as "cheap grace," which he defined as "grace we bestow on ourselves."[4] Cheap grace, then, is a "doctrine," a "principal," and a "system" in which the forgiveness of all sins is proclaimed as a general truth and "an intellectual assent to that idea is held to be of itself sufficient to secure the remission of sins."[5] Bonhoeffer rightly asserted that this is nothing more than the "justification of sin without the justification of the sinner."[6] He argued that such grace is not grace at all; it is simply unbelievers letting themselves off the hook.[7] His context was different from ours, but his diagnosis is applicable to the church today.

So what is the well-meaning pastor to do in order to combat this problem and biblically shepherd his flock? The answer is simple, but the road he will face in his efforts to move his church toward this biblical teaching is daunting. To begin with, pastors and churches must return to the biblical teaching of salvation and assurance as laid out in 1 John. To do this, it must come from the pulpit. No doubt, it must be done with much grace, for many pastors are teaching in churches where a faulty view of the nature of saving faith and assurance has been taught for years. So the best way to do this may be to teach through this entire epistle so that one's congregation can see that this is not simply the pastor's own view of assurance; it comes straight from the pages of the Bible. Of course our teaching must be balanced here since assurance is grounded in the finished work of Christ and supported by one's lifestyle. Here the wisdom of the Scriptures is on display, for if we overemphasize the finished work of Christ to the neglect of the vital support found in one's lifestyle, we fall into "cheap grace" never intended by John. On the other hand, if we overemphasize the lifestyle of the believer to the neglect of the finished work

[4] D. Bonhoeffer, *The Cost of Discipleship*, trans. R. H. Fuller and I. Booth (New York: Simon & Schuster, 1995), 43–44.

[5] Ibid., 43.

[6] Ibid.

[7] Ibid., 44–45.

of Christ, we fall into a works-based righteousness, which was also never intended by John. The writer of this letter demands that we live and preach within this tension.

Along with preaching through the book of 1 John, it is important that we counsel people before they make a profession. This must include warning seekers to count the cost of discipleship while explaining that the genuine believer is committed to Jesus Christ, obeys His commands, loves the brethren, and endures to the end. All too often, our people do not know how they are to live because they are not reading their Bibles and they are not hearing it from the leadership. Such things, therefore, must be brought to light as you interact with individuals seeking a relationship with Christ.

Finally, the pastor must be willing to engage in lovingly confronting the numerous church members who are indifferent to sin and show no interest in or even have a strong dislike for other brothers and sisters in Christ. Again, this is a delicate situation and must be handled with grace and humility. Nevertheless, if John's teaching is correct (and of course we know it is), then we must have a category for the fact that some of these folks are not believers, so the most unloving thing we could ever do is to say nothing, since John asserts that a day of judgment is coming (4:17).

Spurious Faith

Therefore, as we shepherd our people according to the teachings of John, we must have a biblical category for spurious faith. We have already seen that throughout John's letter there are people who make spiritual claims, but their life demonstrates that such claims are false. This is confirmed in the rest of the New Testament as well, where individuals are portrayed as having some kind of connection to the church, but through their lack of bearing fruit, they ultimately demonstrate that they were never really Christians to begin with.[8] In 1 John 2:19, John contends that those "who went out from us did so because they were never really of us."[9] Perhaps then it is best to evaluate a person's spiritual condition phenomenologically as opposed to

[8] See for example Matt 7:21–23; 13:18–23; John 8:30–31; Heb 3:14–19.

[9] Cp. 2 John 9.

ontologically.[10] In other words, we should evaluate more according to what we see as far as outward fruit than what is going on in a person's very being. Thus, in our years of life, we will see many who make a profession of faith and look like a believer for a time. Nevertheless, if they fail to abide in Christ, they demonstrate that their faith was spurious. Again, however, this runs completely contrary to the teaching in some of our churches today. Many pastors insist that if someone simply utters the words of the "sinners prayer," it doesn't matter how they live.[11] One wonders how they might have responded to the people John calls "antichrists," who no doubt did some sort of initiation rite that could be analogous to a sinner's prayer. According to John's teaching, we cannot assume that simply because somebody walked the aisle of a church and prayed a prayer they have been born of God when their lifestyle does not support it.

Application Is Not Monolithic

The application of John's teaching of assurance of salvation is not monolithic. The pastor simply cannot have one universal answer for all who come to him. Instead, he must view himself as a physician of souls and be willing to seek to diagnose the nature of the person's struggle in order to know what type of "spiritual medication" an individual needs. To do this, however, he must be willing to get to know his people well and interact with them by gently asking probing questions and examining their lives. Consider the following case studies. Each is a real-world situation and each must be handled somewhat differently using the teachings of this letter.[12]

First, consider a man who has been attending your church for several years. When he first came to the church, he told the person who

[10] So D. A. Carson, *The Farewell Discourse and Final Prayer of Jesus: An Exposition of John 14–17* (Grand Rapids: Baker, 1980), 97.

[11] Take for example C. Stanley, the well-known Southern Baptist preacher, who says, "The Bible clearly teaches that God's love for His people is of such a magnitude that even those who walk away from the faith have not the slightest chance of slipping from His hand" (C. Stanley, *Eternal Security: Can You Be Sure?* [Nashville: Thomas Nelson, 1990], 74).

[12] Throughout this section, I will speak of pastoral application. This is not to say that a layman cannot apply such teachings in their dealings with friends and loved ones who are struggling with assurance. While this section is aimed at pastors, it is certainly applicable to all who interact with people wrestling with the assurance of their salvation.

interviewed him that he made a profession of faith when he was 10. However, as you and your staff have come to know him, it has become clear that there is virtually no evidence that he is a believer. When you press him regarding his indifference to living a holy life and query him regarding his salvation, he responds, "I have already done that. I've prayed the sinner's prayer, and once you've prayed this, you can never lose your salvation." Then he looks at you and emphatically tells you, "The Bible clearly teaches that Jesus died for all my sins and I believe that. Moreover, the Bible teaches once saved always saved."

So the question is, How are we to apply John's teaching to this man? It seems evident that he has overemphasized the atoning sacrifice of Christ and has completely disregarded John's teaching on the necessity of a changed life. Therefore, the pastor might take him to some of John's tests of faith and gently ask, "How do you reconcile your life with these verses?" Explain to him that John insists that all who have been born of God fundamentally obey the commands. This man is apparently deceived and needs to be confronted with this truth. While you run the risk of offending him, it would be gracious of you to tell him that there is virtually no biblical evidence that he is believer and to encourage him to consider the gospel and genuinely place his faith in Christ.

The second case to consider is a stay-at-home mom in your congregation. You personally led her to the Lord, and you have witnessed wonderful fruit over the course of several years. One day, however, she calls you on the phone and tells you that she has been struggling with her assurance of late. As you gently probe, it becomes evident that her struggle is not an issue of unconfessed sin or a lack of desire to live for the Lord. Instead, she begins to cry and informs you that she is struggling because she sometimes gets frustrated with her two young boys, she does not read her Bible as much as she did before having children, and she simply does not think her life is holy enough. As you continue to ask questions, you realize that she spends a lot of time in self-examination, which has led her to see that even the good things she does are tainted with sin.

Here it is important to remember that John tells us that he wrote the letter of 1 John to "those who believe in the name of the Son of

God (i.e., believers) so that they might know they have eternal life" (5:13). In other words, he wrote to those he considered genuine believers in order to strengthen their assurance, which makes clear that true believers can struggle with their assurance from time to time.[13] This dear woman is so focused on the support of her assurance that she needs to be pointed back to its foundation. The pastor must encourage her to look to the cross. She needs to be reminded that we live between the already and the not yet (2:8), and as a result, we will still sin. When believers do sin, they must look to Jesus and trust that His work on the cross is sufficient.

The third person we want to look at is a young man in your church who is bold in his assertion that he loves God. He rarely misses corporate worship, and yet he is always the first to leave when the service is over. In fact, this young man always has an excuse for not engaging in fellowship opportunities, and when you talk to him, he makes clear that he does not want to spend time with people, and even more to the point, there are other believers in the church that he simply does not like.

So here is the third person with yet another pastoral application. The pastor needs to sit down with this young man and focus on John's teaching on loving the brethren. He needs to be shown such passages as 4:20, where John asserts, "If someone says, 'I love God,' and hates his brother, he is a liar; for the one who does not love his brother whom he has seen, is not able to love God whom he has not seen." Now it is certainly possible that this young man is a believer and has simply never been confronted with such passages, and when he is, he will repent and begin the process of engaging and loving the brethren. It is also possible, however, that this man is not a believer, as would be made evident by a complete rejection of such

[13] I pointed out in chap.1 that one of the verses cited by the Westminster Confession of Faith in support of their statement that assurance is not of the essence of faith is 1 John 5:13, since John says that he has written to those who believe but nevertheless appear to be in need of assurance. This, however, does necessitate the belief that assurance is "not of the essence of faith," since, as the confession cites elsewhere, "faith is different in degrees, weak or strong" (*WCF*, XVI, 3) and someone who might be struggling with a weak faith might also be struggling with assurance, for the confession also says that "true believers may have the assurance of their salvation divers ways shaken, diminished, and intermitted" (*WCF*, XX, 4).

a teaching and an insistence that he can love God without loving those who are born of God.[14]

The fourth person is a woman who came to an evangelistic Bible study at your church where she came to understand her sin and encountered Jesus in a way that appeared to be real and life changing. She was thrilled to learn that she could have fellowship with a perfectly holy God because Jesus' death on the cross cleansed her of all of her sins. Now, however, several months have gone by, and she is struggling with assurance. She is living for God and has experienced some genuine fruit in her life, but she is confronted by the fact that she still sins and wonders whether she was really saved.

Certainly this story happens time and again in all of our churches. Such a person needs to be reminded of John's teaching on assurance. To begin with, she needs to be pointed back to the cross. She needs to be reminded that even though she is a child of God, she will still sin and needs to confess her sins and trust that Jesus' work on the cross propitiated the wrath of God for all of her sins. Moreover, even though she still sins, she needs to be pointed back to her life, which must serve as vital corroborating evidence. If there were no evidence at all, the pastor would need to be careful not to jump in too soon and offer assurance when he might be dealing with a seeker who simply has not come to faith yet. This, however, does not seem to be the case here, so the pastor needs to point her back to the way God is working in her life. She needs to be reminded that while she is far from perfect, the Holy Spirit is at work in her and she has been growing in holiness, even if slowly, ever since her salvation.

Finally, there is a traveling businessman whom you met on an airplane. He sees that you are reading your Bible and begins to tell you that he has been a believer for more than 20 years. He has been married for about that same period of time and has raised his three boys in the church. This man tells you that even though he does a fair bit

[14] John's insistence on the love of the brethren also cuts at the heart of the common assertion that one can worship God without having to go to church. A person making such a claim should be confronted with John's numerous tests of love and asked to reconcile his view with John's teaching. John is clear: if a person really loves God, he will want to be around God's children so he can fellowship with them and serve them. Such opportunities happen most frequently and most naturally in the context of the local church.

of traveling, he always looks forward to getting home in order to see his family and attend his home church, where he serves as a deacon. As the discussion progresses, however, he informs you that he has been struggling with his assurance over the course of the last three months. As you ask some questions to try to ascertain why he is struggling, eventually he confesses that over this same period of time, he has been having an affair with a coworker whom he regularly finds himself traveling with on business trips. Now he is questioning how a child of God can behave in such a way.

One's response to this man would be similar to that of the first case study above. The difference however, is that you think there is a possibility that this man might well be a believer who has fallen into sin. Here you explain to him that John teaches that the children of God cannot ultimately live in sin. You exhort him to repent, knowing that the sacrifice of Jesus is sufficient to cleanse such sins. Nevertheless, the caring pastor also reminds him that if he refuses to repent and persists in this lifestyle of sin, his struggle with assurance could well be God's kindness in showing him that he was never a believer to begin with.

Summary

It is important that we understand that in the five different case studies above, there were five different pastoral applications. Each response came straight from the pages of 1 John, and yet each was applied differently. This is because the assurance of our salvation is not monolithic. We simply cannot have one pat answer that we try to apply to every situation. People struggle with assurance for a number of reasons, and John's teaching is sufficiently flexible to deal with all of them. Sometimes we might focus more on the atoning sacrifice of Christ while at other times we take them to the numerous tests of life. For each different struggle, though, the answer always comes straight from the pages of Scripture.

Conclusion

This book has argued that John views the believer's assurance of eternal life, which is grounded in the atoning sacrifice of Christ, as compatible with his or her ongoing need to persevere in righteous living. In fact, John has taught that these two ideas are inextricably tied together in that the believers' confidence that they are children of God due to the work of Christ is set forth as a key impetus to their perseverance (3:1–3; 4:7–11; 5:18–21) and their perseverance in righteous living actually serves to bolster their assurance (e.g., 2:3–5; 3:14,19,24; 4:13). This teaching is circular but certainly not fallacious. Rightly understood, the believer's confidence in the work of Christ does not serve as a deterrent to righteousness but actually incites believers to strive to live a holy life (see 3:1–3; 4:7–10; 5:18–21). Nevertheless, John makes clear that there will be sin along the way (1:7,9; 2:1; 5:16–17), and the believer must confess such sin and trust that the work of Christ is sufficient to atone for all unrighteousness. This is why perseverance in righteousness can never be viewed as the ground of the believer's assurance. Therefore, as noted at the outset of this study, assurance of eternal life as taught in the first letter of John is fundamentally grounded in the work of Christ and supported in a vital yet subsidiary way by the lifestyle of the believer.

Appendix
WHO KEEPS WHOM?

Introduction

In 1 John 5:18, John tells his readers, "We know that everyone who has been born of God does not sin, but the One who is born of God keeps him, and the evil one does not touch him." The question that interpreters must answer here is, "Who keeps whom?" In chapter 3 I said that this passage speaks of Jesus keeping believers from sin and the evil one. This reading, however, is debated, and the dispute turns on a textual variant. Therefore, it is important to examine this textual variant in some detail in order to support the above understanding of assurance in this text.

First John 5:13 explains that John has written this letter to assure his readers of eternal life. Nevertheless, it is also evident that the writer is found exhorting his readers to persevere in the faith and avoid the false teachings of the secessionists (2:15,24,26; 3:3–10; 5:21). The textual dispute in this text is a question of whether John was seeking to assure his readers of divine preservation or exhort them to keep themselves from sin and the snares of the Devil. Here I will lay out each of the primary variant readings in order to examine the external evidence.[1] This will be followed by an assessment of the internal evidence, which will include both the transcriptional and intrinsic probabilities.

[1] I use the terminology *primary* to indicate my understanding that there are possibly other readings that I have not come across. It should be noted that B. Aland, K. Aland, G. Mink, and K. Wachtel (eds., *Novum Testamentum Graecum: Editio Critica Maior, The First Letter of John* [Stuttgart: Deutsche Bibelgesellschaft, 2003], 362–63) note that several other important manuscripts are either damaged or have lacunae here and are therefore unreadable for this text. These include P9, P74, C, 048, 0245, 0296, 104, L60, L156, L590.

Possible Readings

1. Reading: ἀλλ᾽ ἐγεννήθη· ὁ δὲ γεννηθεὶς ἐκ τοῦ θεοῦ τηρεῖ ἑαυτὸν
   Support: 33
2. Reading: ἀλλ᾽ ὁ γεγεννημένος ἐκ τοῦ θεοῦ τηρεῖ ἑαυτὸν
   Support: 1874, Or
3. Reading: ἀλλ᾽ ἡ γεννησις ἐκ τοῦ θεοῦ τηρεῖ αὐτόν
   Support: 1127, 1505, 1852, 2138, latt, (syh), bo
4. Reading: ἀλλ᾽ ὁ γεννηθεὶς ἐκ τοῦ θεοῦ τηρεῖ ἑαυτὸν
   Support: ℵ, Ac, K, L, P, Ψ, 1739, 𝔐, Did, PsOec
5. Reading: ἀλλ᾽ ὁ γεννηθεὶς ἐκ τοῦ θεοῦ τηρεῖ αὐτόν
   Support: A*, B, 43, 105, 180, 330, 614, 1875, 2412, L:VT, *pc*

External Evidence

After studying each of the variant readings for this verse, it is evident that readings 1 through 3 should probably be eliminated on external grounds unless there are compelling reasons internally for keeping them. This is due to the fact that the external evidence for these three readings is weak. To begin with, we see that reading 1 has the support of only one manuscript, which should probably be viewed as a scribal attempt to make sense of a difficult passage. Moreover, while readings 2 and 3 have a few more supporting manuscripts, neither has a single "first order" witness behind it.[2] So the external evidence appears to point beyond the first three readings to the fourth and fifth options listed above.

Readings 4 and 5 differ only in the direct object. Hence, the textual issue is that of who keeps whom from sin and the snares of the evil one? Is it the believer who keeps himself (4), or is it Jesus (ὁ γεννηθεὶς

[2] This terminology comes from the introduction to *Nestle* 27th, 51*: "Two orders of consistently cited witnesses are distinguished on the basis of their quality and the way they are cited. The *first order of consistently cited witnesses* includes papyri and the uncials which are independent of the Byzantine Koine text type, and a small number of minuscules which preserve an early form of the text. The *second order of consistently cited witnesses* includes the more important uncials of the Koine text type, and a group of minuscules which are of special interest for the history of the text although they are related to the Byzantine Koine text type."

ἐκ τοῦ θεοῦ) who keeps the believer (5)? The external evidence does not provide a clear answer. First, each reading has at least one early uncial manuscript behind it (reading 4 – א [4th c.]; reading 5 – B [4th c.], A [5th c.]). Second, each reading has both a first and a second order witness standing behind it. Third, each appears to have a variety of "text types" behind it.[3] Finally, while it is true that reading 4 has the numerical advantage due to the support of the Majority Text, text critics generally agree that texts must be weighed and not simply counted.[4] As a result, one must proceed to the internal evidence in order best to decipher which of these two readings should be viewed as original.

Transcriptional Probabilities

Since the external evidence is not decisive for either reading, one must turn to the internal evidence and begin with the transcriptional probabilities. There is only one principle for deciphering transcriptional probabilities that is germane to this issue since the external evidence has enabled us to narrow the readings down to numbers 4 and 5, which differ only in one word.[5] This principle states that the more difficult reading is to be preferred. While this is somewhat ambiguous and is often cited for both sides of an issue, it does prove to be beneficial for this particular text problem.

It is possible to make a case that reading 4 is the more difficult reading. One might assume that a scribe was aware that John used the perfect every time he spoke of a believer with the verb γεννάω. Since the perfect was not used here, the scribe might have wondered what

[3] Reading 4 has both Alexandrian (א, P, Ψ, 1739) and Byzantine (K, L, 𝔐) text types supporting it while reading 5 has Alexandrian (A, B), Western (614), and Byzantine (the rest of the minuscules listed appear to be Byzantine). The broader geographic distribution of reading 5 tips the scales slightly in its favor.

[4] Against Law, *The Tests of Life*, 408, who appears to view the vast number of manuscripts as evidence in strong favor of ἑαυτὸν, since as he says, the ground for choosing αὐτόν "is so narrow."

[5] While the principle that the shorter reading is to be preferred does not help us in deciphering between readings 4 and 5, it does offer some confirmation on our previous findings above in that reading 1 should be discarded. This is the only one of the five readings where we find anything more than a simple change of words. Therefore, this first principle provides little help for the present text problem except that we add confirmation to our earlier decision to discard reading 1, which was weak externally.

John was doing with the change in tense and concluded that he was speaking of Jesus. This scribe might have pondered why Jesus was said to keep Himself from sin and the snares of the evil one, and he therefore changed the reflexive ἑαυτὸν to αὐτόν. Hence, text would be altered to say that it is actually Jesus who keeps believers from apostasy.

Perhaps, on the other hand, the correction found in codex Alexandrinus elucidates which of the readings the scribes found more difficult.[6] In this manuscript the original reading was αὐτόν and a later corrector changed it to ἑαυτὸν. One could therefore argue that the reading with αὐτόν, (reading 5) is more difficult as a result of the scribal reticence to speak of Jesus as "born of God." In this line of argumentation, the scribe (like several modern scholars) preferred to read the aorist γεννηθεὶς as a reference to the believer and therefore changed the direct object to make more sense out of the reading.[7] In so doing, he simplified the difficulty referring to Jesus as "born of God" or saying that the believer "keeps" another believer (or whoever else the αὐτόν was referring) by making it read that the believer keeps himself. To be sure, a decision between these two readings on transcriptional probabilities alone is difficult. While the correction of codex Alexandrinus tips the scales in favor of reading 5, one must proceed to the intrinsic probabilities in order to arrive at a more certain conclusion.

Intrinsic Probabilities

Due to the lack of decisiveness after examining both the external evidence and transcriptional probabilities, it is important to turn to the intrinsic probabilities for this textual question. An appeal will be made to John's context, vocabulary, and style in an attempt to determine the most plausible original reading. The key issues include whether John would have used γεννηθεὶς as a reference to Christ, whether self-preservation or divine preservation better fits the context, and whether John would have used a reflexive pronoun after the verb τηρέω. Each section will

[6] So also Painter, *1, 2, and 3 John*, 320.

[7] See B. M. Metzger, *A Textual Commentary on the Greek New Testament*, 2nd ed. (Stuttgart: Biblia-Druck, 1998), 650.

begin with the arguments of those who view ἑαυτὸν as original[8] followed by a response that favors the originality of αὐτόν.[9]

Γεννηθεὶς: A reference for Christ?

It has been argued that one would not expect to find Jesus introduced here as "the one born of God" (ὁ γεννηθεὶς ἐκ τοῦ θεοῦ) since the phrase "the one born of God" (ὁ γεγεννημένος ἐκ τοῦ θεοῦ) was already used of the believer just one clause earlier. If John were referring to Christ, he would have been more likely to refer to Him as the Christ or the Son of God instead of "the one born of God."[10] Moreover, the verb γεννάω is not typically used in any tense to describe Jesus' origin from God in other Johannine writings. The only place where it is used of Jesus' birth is John 18:37,[11] so it is "highly dubious" to believe that John would say that Jesus was born of God. Thus, ὁ γεννηθεὶς ἐκ τοῦ θεοῦ should be viewed as the believer and the reflexive ἑαυτὸν as original.[12]

Against this view, however, is the fact that John uses the aorist γεννηθεὶς as opposed to his typical perfect γεγεννημένος. John uses γεννάω 10 times (2:29; 3:9 [2x]; 4:7; 5:1 [3x], 4,18 [2x]) in this epistle. In every instance where he is speaking of a believer, he

[8] Some favoring ἑαυτὸν include Brown, *Epistles of John*, 622; Law, *Tests of Life*, 408–9; Houlden, *Johnannine Epistles*, 133, *vid.*; R. S. Candlish, *The First Epistle of John* (Grand Rapids: Zondervan, 1869), 531–32.

[9] Some favoring αὐτόν as original include Brooke, *Johannine Epistles*, 148–50; C. C. Black, *The First, Second, and Third Letters of John: Introduction, Commentary, and Reflections*, in vol. 12 of *The New Interpreters Bible* (Nashville: Abingdon, 1998), 446; Haas, *A Handbook on the Letters of John*, 151; Culpepper, *1 John, 2 John, 3 John*, 113; Strecker, *The Johannine Letters*, 208–9; Kruse, *Letters of John*, 195; Westcott, *Epistles of St. John*, 194; Marshall, *The Epistles of John*, 252; Plummer, *The Epistles of John*, P125; Dodd, *The Johannine Epistles*, 138; T. Griffith, "A Non-Polemical Reading of 1 John," *Tyndale Bulletin* 49 (1998): 267; Smalley, *1, 2, 3 John*, 303; Akin, *1, 2, 3 John*, 212; Stott, *The Letters of John*, 194; D. M. Smith, *First, Second, and Third John*, Interpretation (Louisville: John Knox, 1991), 136; D. E. Cook, "Interpretation of 1 John 1–5," *Review and Expositor* 67 (1970): 459; Bruce, *The Epistles of John*, 126.

[10] So Law, *Tests of Faith*, 408–9; Schnackenburg, *Johannine Epistles*, 280–81; Bultmann, *Johannine Epistles*, 303.

[11] It is also noted that γεννάω is not used by Paul as a reference to Jesus either. The only other place where it is used is in the Gospels referring to His conception (Matt 1:16,20; 2:1,4; Luke 1:35).

[12] Brown, *Epistles of John*, 620–21. So also Law, *Tests of Life*, 409; Schnackenburg, *Johannine Epistles*, 254.

uses the perfect tense (2:29; 3:9 [2x]; 4:7; 5:1 [2x]; 5:4; 5:18).[13] It is therefore difficult to explain the change from the perfect to the aorist if John were speaking of a believer keeping himself.[14] Moreover, while it is affirmed that John does not typically speak of Jesus with the verb γεννάω, the fact that he places this word on Jesus' own lips in John 18:37 regarding His birth demonstrates the plausibility that he might again employ it here.

Self-Preservation or Preservation by Christ?

Another argument in favor of the originality of the reflexive ἑαυτὸν is that the idea of protecting oneself against the evil one, who is mentioned in the next clause, is analogous to the affirmation John gives in 2:13–14. There, John says that the young men have overcome the evil one. Hence, the young men are protecting themselves from the evil one at 2:13–14 and the believer who protects himself in 5:18.[15]

While it is agreed that there is precedent for the believer guarding himself both in John's epistles (2:13–14; 5:21) and in the New Testament as a whole (1 Tim 5:22; Jas 1:27; Jude 21), the idea of divine preservation is clear as well. In John's Gospel, Jesus says that He had "kept" safe all of those God had given Him with the lone exception of Judas, who was the son of perdition (17:12). Moreover, He prays not that the Father would take them out of the world but that He would "keep" them from the evil one (John 17:11–15; cp. Rev 3:10; 1 Pet 1:5; Jude 24).[16]

Another argument against the idea of self-preservation here is the redundancy and awkwardness of the second instance if "the one born of God" refers to the believer. If John were still speaking of the believer

[13] Law, *Tests of Life*, 409, argues that interpretations based on a Johannine distinction between the perfect and aorist are unconvincing. This is because John is willing to change verb tense in a way that is "arbitrary" at times (4:9–10) (Law, *Tests of Life*, 409; cp. Brown, *Epistles of John*, 620–21). This notwithstanding, given the fact that John uses the perfect in every instance where he is referring to the believer in this epistle with the verb γεννάω, the burden of proof remains on those who would wish to explain away the change in tense.

[14] So also Brooke, *Johannine Epistles*, 303; Smalley, *1, 2, 3 John*, 303; Culpepper, *1 John*, 113; Akin, *1, 2, 3 John*, 212; Bultmann, *Johannine Epistles*, 88; Strecker, *Johannine Letters*, 208; Plummer, *Epistles of St. John*, 125.

[15] Brown, *Epistles of John*, 621.

[16] So also Smalley, *1, 2, 3 John*, 303; Akin, *1, 2, 3 John*, 212.

in the second clause, there would be no need for him to include the subject again since he had cited it just six words earlier. Instead, one might have expected something like, "We know that everyone born of God does not sin, but he keeps himself and the evil one does not touch him."[17]

Would John Have Used the Reflexive Εαυτὸν After Τηρέω?

Finally, it is argued that throughout the New Testament believers are exhorted to "keep themselves" (1 Tim 5:22; Jas 1:27; Jude 21). Additionally, Law asserts that in 1 John 3:3 believers are told to "purify themselves," which he sees as "virtually identical" to keeping oneself.[18]

The problem with this view, however, is even though John uses the word τηρέω 25 times in his Gospel and epistles, he never uses a reflexive pronoun as its direct object. In fact, of the 70 times the word is used in the NT, it is only used five times with a reflexive pronoun and in each of these instances, there is further explanation as to what the believer is keeping himself from (see 1 Cor 7:37; 2 Cor 11:9; 1 Tim 5:22; Jas 1:27; Jude 21; cp. 1 John 5:21).[19]

Additional Support for Αὐτόν from the Flow of Thought

Finally, John's flow of thought in verses 18–20 seems to be in favor of the One "born of God" being a reference to Jesus since "the one born of God" is juxtaposed with "the evil one." Jesus is the more likely counterpart to the evil one. John has previously argued that his readers have overcome the false teachers because the One who is in them is greater than the one who is in the world (4:4). This passage also appears to be referring to the idea of divine preservation (cp. 3:9). The reason they are able to overcome is because Jesus/the Holy

[17] Against this, Brown, *Epistles of John*, 621, asserts that "repetition in a slightly variant form . . . is certainly not unJohannine."

[18] Law, *Tests of Life*, 409.

[19] So Smalley, *1, 2, 3 John*, 293; Metzger, *Textual Commentary*, 650; Schnackenburg, *Johannine Epistles*, 280; Bultmann, *Johannine Epistles*, 88; Brooke, *Johannine Epistles*, 149; Strecker, *Johannine Letters*, 208.

Spirit[20] is in them. Likewise, in 5:18, it is precisely because Jesus is the One protecting believers that there is such certainty that the evil one cannot touch them.[21]

Conclusion

Throughout this epistle, John holds in tension the idea that the believer must persevere in his faith and that he can find assurance that he is in fact saved. A case has been made here that 1 John 5:18 bolsters the assurance side of these two compatible ideas by way of arguing for reading 5, which says that it is Jesus who keeps believers from a lifestyle of sin and the snares of the evil one. Externally, this reading had a slight edge over reading 4 in that it had a larger geographic distribution. Moreover, while far from decisive, we said that reading 5 seemed to be the more difficult of the two readings. Finally, the most compelling arguments in favor of reading 5 as the original reading were seen in the examination of the intrinsic probabilities. Here this reading best fits John's context, style, and language.

[20] As is often the case in this letter, it is difficult to decipher which person of the Trinity John is making reference to here.

[21] So also Culpepper, *1 John,* 113; Westcott, *The Epistles of St. John,* 194. Two additional supports for the originality of αὐτόν are worthy of note. First, Smalley (*1, 2, 3 John,* 303) has said that the use of the same verb for both the Christian and Jesus might have been for stylistic purposes in order to "emphasize the identity of God's Son with his disciples (cp. 4:17), whereas the variation of tense mentioned marks an ultimate difference in the two sonships" (so also Westcott, *Epistles of St. John,* 194; Haas, *Translator's Handbook on the Letters of John,* 128). Second, Plummer (*Epistles of St. John,* 125) has said that it might also be "some confirmation" that this is the correct view (or at least the view espoused by the majority of the early church) since the Nicene Creed reads "begotten of the Father" (τὸν ἐκ τοῦ Πατρὸς γεννηθέντα), which is of course the same word used in the phrase in question here.

Bibliography

Commentaries

Akin, Daniel L. *1, 2, 3, John*, The New American Commentary, vol. 38. Nashville: Broadman & Holman, 2001.

Alexander, Neil. *The Epistles of John*. Torch Bible Commentaries. New York: Macmillan, 1962.

Barclay, William. *The Letters of John and Jude*. Rev. ed. Philadelphia: Westminster, 1976.

Bauer, Walter. *Die katholischen Briefe des Neuen Testaments*. Tübingen: J.C.B. Mohr (Paul Siebeck), 1910.

Beasley-Murray, George R. *John*. Word Biblical Commentary, vol. 36. Waco: Word Books, 1987.

Black, Clifton C. *The First, Second, and Third Letters of John: Introduction, Commentary, and Reflections*. In vol. 12 of The New Interpreters Bible. Nashville: Abingdon Press, 1998.

Block, Daniel I. *The Book of Ezekiel*, vol. 1. The New International Commentary on the Old Testament. Grand Rapids: Eerdmans, 1997.

Bonnard, Pierre. *Les Épitres johanniques*. Commentaire du Nouveau Testament. Geneva: Labor et Fides, 1983.

Bonsirven, Joseph S. J. *Epitres de Saint Jean*. Verbum Salutis, vol. 9. Paris: Beauchesne, 1936.

Bray, Gerald. *Ancient Christian Commentary on Scripture: James, 1–2 Peter, 1–3 John, Jude*. Downers Grove, IL: InterVarsity, 2000.

Brooke, A. E. *A Critical and Exegetical Commentary on the Johannine Epistles*. The International Critical Commentary. Edinburgh: T. & T. Clark, 1912, 1976.

Brown, Raymond E. *The Epistles of John: Translated with Introduction, Notes, and Commentary*. The Anchor Bible, vol. 30. New York: Doubleday, 1982.

Bruce, F. F. *The Epistles of John: Introduction, Exposition, and Notes*. Grand Rapids: Eerdmans, 1970, 1979.

Brueggemann, Walter. *A Commentary on Jeremiah: Exile and Homecoming*. Grand Rapids: Eerdmans, 1998.

Büchsel, Friedrich. *Die Johannesbriefe*. Theologischer Handkommentar zum Neuen Testament. Leipzig: Deichert, 1933.

Bultmann, Rudolf. *The Johannine Epistles*. Translated by R. Philip O'Hara, Lane C. McGaughy, and Robert W. Funk. Hermenia. Philadelphia: Fortress, 1973.

Burdick, Donald W. *The Letters of John the Apostle*. Chicago: Moody Bible Institute, 1985.

Burge, Gary M. *The Letters of John*. The NIV Application Commentary. Grand Rapids: Zondervan, 1996.

Calvin, John. *The First Epistle of John*. Translated by John Owen. Vol. 22 of *Calvin's Commentaries*, ed. David W. Torrance and Thomas F. Torrance. Edinburgh: Oliver and Boyd, 1960. Reprint, Grand Rapids: Baker Books, 1999.

Candlish, Robert S. *The First Epistle of John*. Grand Rapids: Zondervan Publishing House, 1869.

Carroll, Robert P. *The Book of Jeremiah: A Commentary*. Philadelphia: The Westminster Press, 1986.

Carson, D. A. *The Gospel According to John*. The Pillar New Testament Commentary. Grand Rapids: Eerdmans, 1991.

Chaine, Joseph. *Les épîtres Catholiques*. Paris: Gabalda, 1939.

Culpepper, R. Alan. *1 John, 2 John, 3 John*. Knox Preaching Guides. Atlanta: John Knox, 1985.

_________. *The Gospel and Letters of John*. Interpreting Biblical Texts. Nashville: Abingdon, 1998.

Culy, Martin M. *I, II, III John: A Handbook on the Greek Text*. Waco: Baylor University Press, 2004.

Dana, H. E. *The Epistles and Apocalypse of John*. Dallas: Baptist Book Store, 1937.

de Dietrich, S. *Les letters Johanniques: Bref commentaire pour groupes d' Etudes*. Geneva: Labor et Fides, 1964.

Dodd, C. H. *The Johannine Epistles*. The Moffat New Testament Commentary. New York: Harper & Brothers, 1946.

Eaches, Owen P. *1, 2, and 3 John, Jude, and Revelation: A Popular Commentary upon a Critical Basis*. Philadelphia: American Baptist Publication Society, 1910.

Gingrich, Raymond E. *Fellowship with the Word of Life: Studies in 1,2,3 John*. Winona Lake, IN: BMH Books, 1977.

Godet, Frederic. *Commentary on the Gospel of John*. Reprint, Grand Rapids: Kregel, 1979.

Goodman, George. *The Epistle of Eternal Life*. London: Pickering and Inglis, 1936.

Gore, Charles. *The Epistles of St. John*. London: John Murray, 1920.

Grayston, Kenneth. *The Johannine Epistles*. New Century Bible Commentary. Grand Rapids: Eerdmans, 1984.

Haas, C., M. de Jonge, and J. L. Swellengrebel. *A Translator's Handbook on the Letters of John*. UBS Handbook Series. New York: United Bible Societies, 1972.

Hauck, F. *Die briefe des Jakobus, Petrus, Judas, und Johannes*. Göttingen: Vandenhoeck & Ruprecht, 1958.

Haupt, Erich. *The First Epistle of St. John: A Contribution to Biblical Theology*. Translated by W. B. Pope. Clark's Foreign Theological Library, n.s., vol. 64. Edinburgh: T. & T. Clark, 1879.

Hobbs, Herschel H. *The Epistles of John*. Nashville: Thomas Nelson Publishers, 1983.

Hodges, Zane. *The Epistles of John: Walking in the Light of God's Love*. Irving, TX: Grace Evangelical Society, 1999.

_________. *1, 2, 3, John*. In *The Bible Knowledge Commentary: New Testament*. Edited by John F. Walvoord and Roy B. Zuck. Wheaton: Victor Books, 1983.

Holladay, William L. *Jeremiah 2: A Commentary on the Book of the Prophet Jeremiah Chapters 26–52*. Hermenia. Minneapolis: Fortress, 1989.

Houlden, J. L. *A Commentary on the Johannine Epistles*. Black's New Testament Commentaries. 2nd ed. London: A & C Black Publishers, 1994.

Ironside, H. A. *Addresses on the Epistles of John*. New York: Loizeaux Brothers, 1931.

Keener, Craig S. *The Gospel of John: A Commentary*. Vol. 2. Peabody, MA: Hendrickson, 2003.

Keil, C. F., and F. Delitzsch. *Ezekiel*. Translated by James Martin. In vol. 9 of *Commentary on the Old Testament*. Grand Rapids: Eerdmans, 1982.

Kelly, William. *An Exposition of the Epistles of John the Apostle*. London: T. Weston, 1905.

Keown, Gerald, L., Pamela J. Scalise, and Thomas G. Smothers. *Jeremiah 26–52*. Word Biblical Commentary, vol. 27. Dallas: Word Books, 1995.

Kistemaker, Simon J. *James and I–III John*. New Testament Commentary. Grand Rapids: Baker Book House, 1986.

Klauck, Hans-Josef. *Der erste Johannesbrief*. Evangelisch—Katholischer Kommentar Zum Neuen Testament, vol. 23.1. Zürich: Benziger; Neukirchen-Vluyn: Neukirchener Verlag, 1991.

__________. *Der zweite und dritte Johannesbrief*. Evangelisch—Katholischer Kommentar Zum Neuen Testament, vol. 23.2. Zürich: Benziger; Neukirchen-Vluyn: Neukirchener Verlag, 1992.

Kohler, Marc. *Le coeur et les mains: Commentaire de la premiére épître de Jean*. Neuchatel: Delachaux & Niestlé, 1962.

Köstenberger, Andreas J. *John*. Baker Exegetical Commentary on the New Testament. Grand Rapids: Baker Academic, 2004.

Kruse, Colin G. *The Letters of John*. The Pillar New Testament Commentary. Grand Rapids: Eerdmans, 2000.

Kysar, Robert. *I, II, III John*. Augsburg Commentary on the New Testament. Minneapolis: Augsburg, 1986.

Loisy, Alfred F. *Les Epîtres dites de Jean*. In *Le Quatrième Evangile*. 2nd ed. Paris: Émile Nourry, 1921.

Lundbom, Jack R. *Jeremiah 21–36: A New Translation with Introduction and Commentary*. The Anchor Bible, vol. 21B. New York: Doubleday, 2004.

Malatesta, Edward. *The Epistles of St. John: Greek Text and English Translation Schematically Arranged*. Rome: Pontifical Gregorian University, 1973.

Marshall, I. Howard. *The Epistles of John*. The New International Commentary on the New Testament. Grand Rapids: Eerdmans, 1978.

Mitchell, A. F. *Hebrews and the General Epistles*. The Westminster New Testament. New York: Revell, 1911.

Mollat, Donatien, and F. M. Braun. *L'Évangile er les Épîtres de saint Jean*. 2nd ed. Paris: Éditions du Cerf, 1960.

Morris, Leon. *The Gospel According to John*. The New International Commentary on the New Testament. Rev. ed. Grand Rapids: Eerdmans, 1995.

Painter, John. *1, 2, and 3 John*. Sacra Pagina, vol. 18. Collegeville, MN: The Liturgical Press, 2002.

Perkins, Pheme. *The Johannine Epistles*. New Testament Message. Wilmington, DE: Michael Glazier, 1979.

Plummer, Alfred. *The Epistles of John*. Pineapple Commentaries. Cambridge: Cambridge University Press, 1886. Reprint, Grand Rapids: Baker, 1980.

Rennes, Jean. *La première épître de Jean*. Geneva: Éditions Labor et Fides, 1968.

Roberts, J. W. *The Letters of John*. Abilene, TX: Abilene Christian University Press, 1984.

Ross, Alexander. *The Epistles of James and John*. Grand Rapids: Eerdmans, 1954.

Schlatter, Adolf. *Die Briefe und die Offenbarung des Johannes*. Stuttgart: Calwer Verlag, 1950.

Schnackenburg, Rudolf. *The Johannine Epistles: Introduction and Commentary*. Translated by Reginald and Ilse Fuller. New York: Crossroad, 1992.

Schrage, Wolfgang, and Horst R. Balz *Die "Katholischen" Briefe: die Briefe des Jakobus, Petrus, Johannes und Judas*. Göttingen: Vandenhoeck & Ruprecht, 1973.

Smalley, Stephen S. *1, 2, 3, John*. Word Biblical Commentary, vol. 51. Waco: Word Books, 1984.

Smith, D. Moody. *First, Second, and Third John*. Interpretation. Louisville: John Knox Press, 1991.

Strecker, Georg. *The Johannine Letters: A Commentary on 1, 2, and 3 John*. Translated by Linda M. Maloney. Hermenia. Minneapolis: Fortress, 1996.

Stott, John R. W. *The Letters of John: An Introduction and Commentary*. Tyndale New Testament Commentaries. Rev. ed. Grand Rapids: Eerdmans, 1964; reprint, 2000.

Thompson, J. A. *The Book of Jeremiah*. The New International Commentary on the Old Testament. Grand Rapids: Eerdmans, 1980.

Thompson, Marianne M. *1–3 John*. The IVP New Testament Commentary Series. Downers Grove, IL: InterVarsity, 1992.

Ward, Ronald A. *The Epistles of John and Jude: A Study Manual*. Grand Rapids: Baker, 1965.

Weiss, Bernhard. *Kritisch exegetisches Handbuch über die drei Briefe des Apostel Johannes*. Kritisch-exegetischer Kommentar über das Neue Testament 14. 6th ed. Göttingen: Vandenhoeck and Ruprecht, 1899.

Wengst, Klaus. *Der erste, zweite und dritte Brief des Johannes*. Ökumenischer Taschenbuchkommentar zum Neuen Testament, vol. 16. Gütersloh: Gütersloher Verlagshaus Gerd Mohn, 1978.

Westcott, Brooke F. *The Epistles of St. John: The Greek Text with Notes and Essays*. Grand Rapids: Eerdmans, 1955.

Williams, R. R. *The Letters of John and James*. Cambridge: Cambridge University Press, 1965.

Windisch, Hans. *Die katholischen Briefe*. Handbuch zum Neuen Testament, vol. 15. Tübingen: J. C. B. Mohr, 1951.

Whitacre, Rodney A. *John*. The IVP New Testament Commentary Series. Downers Grove, IL: InterVarsity, 1999.

Books

Aquinas, Thomas. *Summa Theologica*, vol. 2. Edited by Robert M. Hutchins. Great Books of the Western World, vol. 20. Chicago: William Benton, 1952.

Arminius, Jacobus. *The Writings of James Arminius: Translated from the Latin in Three Volumes*. Translated by James Nichols and W. R. Bagnall. Grand Rapids: Baker, 1956.

Bangs, Carl. *Arminius: A Study in the Dutch Reformation*. Grand Rapids: Francis Asbury, 1985.

Bauer, Walter. *Orthodoxy and Heresy in Earliest Christianity*. Philadelphia: Fortress, 1971.

Beeke, Joel R. *Assurance of Faith: Calvin, English Puritanism, and the Dutch Second Reformation*. New York: Peter Lang, 1991.

Bell, Charles M. *Calvin and Scottish Theology: The Doctrine of Assurance*. Edinburgh: Handsel, 1985.

Berkhof, Louis. *The Assurance of Faith*. Grand Rapids: Smitter Book Co., 1928.

Berkouwer, G. C. *Faith and Perseverance*. Translated by Robert D. Knudsen. Grand Rapids: Eerdmans, 1958.

Black, David A. *New Testament Textual Criticism: A Concise Guide*. Grand Rapids: Baker, 1994.

Blass, F., and A. Debrunner. *A Greek Grammar of the New Testament and Other Early Christian Literature*. Translated and revised by Robert W. Funk. Chicago: University of Chicago Press, 1961.

Boecker, Hans J. *Law and the Administration of Justice in the Old Testament and Ancient East*. Translated by Jeremy Mosier. London: SPCK, 1980.

Bogart, John. *Orthodox and Heretical Perfectionism in the Johannine Community as Evident in the First Epistle of John*. Society of Biblical Literature Dissertation Series 33. Missoula, MT: Scholars, 1977.

Bonhoeffer, Dietrich. *The Cost of Discipleship*. Translated by R. H. Fuller and Irmgard Booth. New York: Simon & Schuster, 1995.

Bonnard, Pierre. *Anamnesis: Recherches sur le Nouveau Testament*. Lausanne: Revue de Théologie et de Philosophie, 1980.

Borig, Rainer. *Der Wahre Weinstock: Untersuchungen zu Jo 15, 1–10*. München: Kösel, 1967.

Brown, Raymond E. *The Community of the Beloved Disciple: The Life, Loves, and Hates of an Individual Church in the New Testament Times*. New York: Paulist, 1979.

__________. *An Introduction to the Gospel of John*. The Anchor Bible Reference Library. Edited by Francis J. Maloney. New York: Doubleday, 2003.

Burge, Gary M. *The Anointed Community: The Holy Spirit in the Johannine Tradition*. Grand Rapids: Eerdmans, 1987.

Callahan, Allen D. *A Love Supreme: A History of Johannine Tradition*. Minneapolis: Fortress, 2005.

Calvin, John. *Institutes of Christian Religion*. 2 vols. Edited by John T. McNeill. Translated by Ford Lewis Battles. Library of Christian Classics, vols. 20–21. Philadelphia: Westminster, 1960.

Carson, D. A. *The Difficult Doctrine of the Love of God*. Wheaton: Crossway, 2000.

_________. *Divine Sovereignty and Human Responsibility: Biblical Perspectives in Tension*. Eugene: Wipf and Stock Publishers, 1994, 2002.

_________. *Exegetical Fallacies*. 2nd ed. Grand Rapids: Baker, 2001.

_________. *The Farewell Discourse and Final Prayer of Jesus: An Exposition of John 14–17*. Grand Rapids: Baker, 1980.

_________, and Douglas J. Moo. *An Introduction to the New Testament*. Rev. ed. Grand Rapids: Zondervan, 2005

Clifford, Alan C. *Atonement and Justification: English Evangelical Theology 1640–1790, An Evaluation*. Oxford: Clarendon, 1990.

Cook, Robert W. *The Theology of John*. Chicago: Moody, 1979.

Cullmann, Oscar. *Early Christian Worship*. Studies in Biblical Theology 10. Translated by A. Stewart Todd and James B. Torrance. Chicago: H. Regnery, 1953.

Cunningham, William. *Historical Theology: A Review of the Principal Doctrinal Discussions in the Christian Church Since the Apostolic Age*. 2 vols. Edinburgh: Clark, 1863. Reprint, London: Banner of Truth Trust, 1960.

_________. *The Reformers and the Theology of the Reformation*. Edinburgh: Clark, 1862. Reprint, London: Banner of Truth Trust, 1967.

Deissmann, Adolf. *Light from the Ancient East: The New Testament Illustrated by Recently Discovered Texts of the Graeco-Roman World*. Translated by Lionel R. M. Strachan. New York: George H. Doran, 1927.

de la Potterie, Ignace. *La vérité dans Saint Jean*. 2 vols. Analecta Biblica 73–74. Rome: Biblical Institute, 1977.

Dulles, Avery. *The Assurance of Things Hoped For: A Theology of Christian Faith*. Oxford: Oxford University Press, 1994.

Eaton, Michael. *No Condemnation: A Theology of Assurance*. Downers Grove, IL: InterVarsity, 1995.

Edwards, Ruth B. *The Johannine Epistles*. New Testament Study Guides. Sheffield: Sheffield Academic Press, 1996.

Ellis, E. Earle. *The World of St. John: The Gospel and Epistles*. Bible Guides 14. Edited by William Barclay and F. F. Bruce. New York: Abingdon, 1965.

Ely, Mary R. *Knowledge of God in Johannine Thought*. New York: Macmillan Company, 1925.

Epp, Theodore H. *Studies in the General Epistles of John*. Lincoln, NE: Back to the Bible Broadcast, 1957.

Fanning, Buist M. *Verbal Aspect in New Testament Greek*. Oxford: Clarendon, 1990.

Findlay, George G. *Fellowship in the Life Eternal*. Grand Rapids: Eerdmans, 1955.

Gesenius, W. *Gesenius' Hebrew Grammar*. Edited by E. Kautzsch and A. E. Cowley. 2nd ed. Oxford: Clarendon, 1910.

Greenlee, Harold J. *Introduction to New Testament Textual Criticism*. Rev. ed. Peabody, MA: Hendrickson Publishers, 1995.

__________. *Scribes, Scrolls, and Scripture: A Student's Guide to New Testament Textual Criticism*. Grand Rapids: Eerdmans, 1985.

Griffith, Terry. *Keep Yourselves from Idols: A New Look at 1 John*. Journal for the Study of the New Testament Supplement Series 233. Sheffield: Sheffield Academic Press, 2002.

Guthrie, Donald. *New Testament Introduction*. Downers Grove, IL: InterVarsity, 1990.

Hays, D. A. *John and His Writings*. New York: Methodist Book Concern, 1917.

Hill, David. *Greek Words and Hebrew Meanings: Studies in the Semantics of Soteriological Terms*. Cambridge: Cambridge University Press, 1967.

Hodges, Zane. *Absolutely Free! A Biblical Reply to Lordship Salvation*. Grand Rapids: Zondervan, 1989.

__________. *The Gospel Under Siege: A Study on Faith and Works*. 2nd ed. Dallas: Rendencion Viva, 1991.

Holmgren, Fredrick C. *The Old Testament and the Significance of Jesus*. Grand Rapids: Eerdmans, 1999.

Horton, Michael. *Christ the Lord: The Reformation and Lordship Salvation*. Grand Rapids: Baker, 1992.

Ironside, H. A. *Full Assurance*. New York: Loizeaux Brothers, 1937.

Joüon, Paul. *A Grammar of Biblical Hebrew*. Translated and revised by T. Muraoka. Rome: Editrice Pontificio Istituto Biblico, 2003.

Kendall, R. T. *Calvin and English Calvinism to 1649*. Oxford: Oxford University Press, 1979.

_________. *Once Saved Always Saved.* Chicago: Moody Press, 1983.

Kenney, Garrett C. *The Relationship of Christology to Ethics in the First Epistle of John.* New York: University Press of America, 2000.

King, Guy H. *The Fellowship.* London: Marshall, Morgan, and Scott, 1954.

Latourette, Kenneth S. *Christianity Through the Ages.* New York: Harper & Row, 1965.

Law, Robert. *The Tests of Life: A Study of the First Epistle of St. John.* 3rd ed. Edinburgh: T. & T. Clark, 1914. Reprint Grand Rapids: Baker, 1968.

Lieu, Judith M. *The Second and Third Epistles of John: History and Background.* Edinburgh: T. & T. Clark, 1986.

_________. *The Theology of the Johannine Epistles.* Cambridge: Cambridge University Press, 1991.

Lohfink, Norbert. *The Covenant Never Revoked.* Translated by John J. Scullion. New York: Paulist, 1991.

Luther, Martin. *Luther's Works.* Edited by Jaroslav Pelikan (vols. 1–30) and Helmut T. Lehmann (vols. 31–55). Philadelphia: Muhlenberg; St. Louis: Concordia, 1955–86.

Malatesta, Edward S. J. *Interiority and Covenant: A Study of* εἶναι ἐν *and* μένειν ἐν *in the First Letter of Saint John.* Analecta Biblica 69. Rome: Biblical Institute, 1978.

Marshall, I. Howard. *Kept by the Power of God: A Study of Perseverance and Falling Away.* Minneapolis: Bethany Fellowship, 1974.

McGaughy, Lane C. *A Descriptive Analysis of* Ειναι *as a Linking Verb in New Testament Greek.* Society of Biblical Literature Dissertation Series 6. Missoula, MT: Society of Biblical Literature, 1972.

McGiffert, Arthur. *A History of Christian Thought.* Vol. 2. New York: Scribner's, 1954.

Metzger, Bruce M. *The Text of the New Testament: Its Transmission, Corruption, and Restoration.* 3rd ed. New York: Oxford University Press, 1992.

_________. *A Textual Commentary on the Greek New Testament.* 2nd ed. Stuttgart: Biblia-Druck, 1998.

Mitchell, John G. *An Everlasting Love*. Portland, OR: Multnomah, 1982.

Morris, Leon. *The Apostolic Preaching of the Cross*. 3rd ed. London: Tyndale, 1965.

Nauck, Wolfgang. *Die Tradition und der Charakter des ersten Johanesbriefs*, Wissenschaftliche Untersuchungen zum Neuen Testament 3. Tübingen: Mohr Siebeck, 1957.

O'Neill, J. C. *The Puzzle of 1 John: A New Examination of Origins*. London: SPCK, 1966.

Painter, John. *John: Witness and Theologian*. London: SPCK, 1975.

Pancaro, Severino. *The Law in the Fourth Gospel: The Torah and the Gospel, Moses and Jesus, Judaism and Christianity According to John*. Supplements to Novum Testamentum. Leiden: E. J. Brill, 1975.

Pelikan, Jaroslav. *Reformation of Church and Dogma (1300–1700)*. Chicago: University of Chicago Press, 1984.

Pentecost, J. Dwight. *The Joy of Fellowship*. Grand Rapids: Zondervan, 1977.

Pfürtner, Stephen H. *Luther and Aquinas, a Conversation: Our Salvation, Its Certainty and Peril*. Translated by Edward Quinn. London: Darton, Longman, & Todd, 1964.

Piper, John. *Brothers, We Are Not Professionals: A Plea to Pastors for Radical Ministry*. Nashville: Broadman & Holman, 2002.

Porter, Stanley E. *Idioms of the Greek New Testament*. 2nd ed. Sheffield: Sheffield Academic Press, 2004.

_________. *Verbal Aspect in the Greek of the New Testament, with Reference to Tense and Mood*. New York: Peter Lang, 1989.

_________, and Craig A. Evans, eds. *The Johannine Writings*. The Biblical Seminar 32. Sheffield: Sheffield Academic Press, 1995.

Pryor, John W. *John: Evangelist of the Covenant People. The Narrative and Themes of the Fourth Gospel*. Downers Grove, IL: InterVarsity Press, 1992.

Reitzenstein, Richard. *Die hellenistischen Mysterienreligionen*. Leipzig and Berlin: B.G. Teubner, 1927.

_________. *Die Vorgeschichte der christlichen Taufe*. Leipzig and Berlin: B.G. Teubner, 1929.

Rendtorff, Rolf. *Canon and Theology*. Minneapolis: Fortress, 1993.

Robertson, A. T. *A Grammar of the Greek New Testament: In Light of Historical Research*. Nashville: Broadman, 1934.

Robinson, James M. *The Nag Hammadi Library*. Rev. ed. San Francisco: Harper, 1990.

Schaff, Philip. *History of the Christian Church*. New York: Charles Scribner's Sons, 1910; reprint, Grand Rapids: Eerdmans, 1995.

________. *A Select Library of the Nicene and Post-Nicene Fathers of the Christian Church*. New York: Christian Literature, 1887–94. Reprint, Grand Rapids: Eerdmans, 1975.

Schreiner, Thomas R. *The Law and Its Fulfillment: A Pauline Theology of the Law*. Grand Rapids: Baker, 1993.

________, and Ardel B. Canaday. *The Race Set Before Us: A Biblical Theology of Perseverance and Assurance*. Downers Grove, IL: InterVarsity, 2001.

Seeberg, Reinhold. *Text-book of the History of Doctrines*. Translated by Charles Hay. Grand Rapids: Baker, 1966.

Shank, Robert. *Life in the Son: A Study of the Doctrine of Perseverance*. 2nd ed. Springfield, MO: Westcott, 1976.

Silva, Moisés. *Biblical Words and Their Meaning: An Introduction to Lexical Semantics*. Grand Rapids: Zondervan, 1983.

Smalley, Stephen S. *John: Evangelist and Interpreter*. New Testament Profiles. 2nd ed. Downers Grove, IL: InterVarsity Press, 1998.

Stanley, Charles. *Eternal Security: Can You Be Sure?* Nashville: Thomas Nelson, 1990.

Stülmacher, Peter. *How to Do Biblical Theology*. Princeton Theological Monographs 38. Translated by J. M. Whitlock. Allison Park, PA: Pickwick, 1995.

Troeltsch, Ernst. *The Social Teaching of the Christian Churches*. 2 vols. Translated by Olive Wyon. Chicago: University of Chicago Press, 1981.

Vellanickal, Matthew. *The Divine Sonship of Christians in the Johannine Writings*. Analecta Biblica 72. Rome: Biblical Institute Press, 1977.

von Wahlde, Urban C. *The Johannine Commandments: 1 John and the Struggle for the Johannine Tradition*. Theological Inquiries: Studies in Contemporary Biblical and Theological Problems. Edited by Lawrence Boadt. New York: Paulist, 1990.

Wallace, Daniel B. *Greek Grammar Beyond the Basics: An Exegetical Syntax of the New Testament*. Grand Rapids: Zondervan, 1996.

Waltke, Bruce K., and M. O'Connor. *An Introduction to Biblical Hebrew Syntax*. Winona Lake, IN: Eisenbrauns, 1990.

Wengst, Klaus. *Häresie und Orthodoxie im Spiegel des ersten Johannesbriefs*. Gütersloh: Gütersloher Verlagshaus G. Mohn, 1976.

Whale, John S. *The Protestant Tradition: An Essay in Interpretation*. Cambridge: Cambridge University Press, 1955.

Whitacre, Rodney A. *Johannine Polemic: The Role of Tradition and Theology*. Society of Biblical Literature Dissertation Series 67. Chico, CA: Scholars Press, 1982.

Woll, Bruce D. *Johannine Christianity in Conflict: Authority, Rank, and Succession in the First Farewell Discourse*. Society of Biblical Literature Dissertation Series 60. Chico, CA: Scholars, 1981.

Yamauchi, Edwin M. *Pre-Christian Gnosticism: A Survey of the Proposed Evidences*. Grand Rapids: Eerdmans, 1973.

Yates, Arthur S. *The Doctrine of Assurance with Special Reference to John Wesley*. London: Epworth, 1952.

Articles and Essays

Bass, Christopher D. "A Johannine Perspective of the Human Responsibility to Persevere in the Faith Through the Use of Μένω and Other Related Motifs." *Westminster Theological Journal* 69 (2007): 305–25.

Baylis, Charles P. "The Meaning of Walking 'In the Darkness' (1 John 1:6)." *Bibliotheca Sacra* 149 (1992): 214–22.

Beale, G. K. "Positive Answer to the Question: Did Jesus and His Followers Preach the Right Doctrine from the Wrong Texts? An Examination of the Presuppositions of Jesus' and the Apostles' Exegetical Methods." In *Right Doctrine from the Wrong Texts: Essays on the Use of the Old Testament in the New*, ed. G. K. Beale. Grand Rapids: Baker, 1994.

Beeke, Joel R. "Does Assurance Belong to the Essence of Faith?: Calvin and the Calvinists." *The Masters Seminary Journal* 5, no. 1 (1994): 43–71.

Behm, Johannes. "Παράκλητος." In *Theological Dictionary of the New Testament*, ed. Gerhard Kittle, trans. Geoffrey W. Bromiley. Grand Rapids: Eerdmans, 1965, 1999.

Black, David A. "An Overlooked Stylistic Argument in Favor of *panta* in 1 John 2:20." *Filologia Neotestamentaria* 5 (1992): 205–8.

Bock, Darrell F. "A Review of *The Gospel According to Jesus*." *Bibliotheca Sacra* 141 (1989): 21–40.

Boismard, Marie. E. "La connaissance dans l'alliance nouvelle d'après la première letter de Saint Jean." *Revue Biblique* 56 (1949): 365–91.

Borchert, Gerald L. "Light." In *New Dictionary of Biblical Theology: Exploring Unity and Diversity of Scripture*, ed. T. Desmond Alexander, Brian S. Rosner, D. A. Carson, and Graeme Goldsworthy. Downers Grove, IL: InterVarsity Press, 2000.

Boyer, James L. "A Classification of Imperatives: A Statistical Study." *Grace Theological Journal* 8 (1987): 35–54.

_________. "Relative Clauses in the Greek New Testament: A Statistical Study." *Grace Theological Journal* 9 (1988): 233–56.

_________. "Third (and Fourth) Class Conditions." *Grace Theological Journal* 3 (1982): 163–75.

Breck, John. "The Function of *PAS* in 1 John 2:20." *St. Vladimir's Theological Quarterly* 35 (1991): 187–206.

Brooks, Oscar. S. "The Johannine Eucharist: Another Interpretation." *Journal of Biblical Literature* 82 (1963): 293–300.

Bultmann, Rudolf. "Γινώσκω." In *Theological Dictionary of the New Testament*, ed. Gerhard Kittle, trans. Geoffrey W. Bromiley. Grand Rapids: Eerdmans, 1965, 1999.

Burge, Gary M. "John, Letters of." In *Dictionary of the Later New Testament and Its Developments*, eds. Ralph P. Martin and Peter H. Davids. Downers Grove, IL: InterVarsity Press, 1997.

Carl, K. J. "The Idea of 'Knowing' in the Johannine Literature." *Bangalore Theological Forum* 25 (1993): 53–75.

Carson, D. A. "The Johannine Letters." In *New Dictionary of Biblical Theology: Exploring Unity and Diversity of Scripture*, ed. T. Desmond Alexander, Brian S. Rosner, D. A. Carson, and Graeme Goldsworthy. Downers Grove, IL: InterVarsity, 2000.

_________. "Johannine Perspectives on the Doctrine of Assurance." In *Explorations: Justification and Christian Assurance*, ed. R. J. Gibson. Adelaide, South Australia: Openbook, 1996.

_________. "John and the Johannine Epistles." In *It Is Written: Scripture Citing Scripture: Essays in Honour of Barnabas Lindars*, ed. D. A. Carson and H. G. M. Williamson. New York: Cambridge University Press, 1988.

_________. "The Purpose of the Fourth Gospel: John 20:30–31 Reconsidered." *Journal of Biblical Literature* 108 (1987): 639–51.

_________. "Reflections on Assurance." In *Still Sovereign: Contemporary Perspectives on Election, Foreknowledge, and Grace*, ed. Thomas R. Schreiner and Bruce A. Ware. Grand Rapids: Baker Books, 2000.

_________. "Reflections on Salvation and Justification in the New Testament." *Journal of the Evangelical Theological Society* 40 (1997): 581–608.

_________. "The Three Witnesses and the Eschatology of 1 John." In *To Tell the Mystery: Essays on New Testament Eschatology in Honor of Robert H. Gundry*, Journal for the Study of the New Testament Supplement Series 100, ed. T. E. Schmidt and M. Silva. Sheffield: Sheffield Academic Press, 1994.

Clavier, Henri. "Notes sur un mot-clef du Johannisme et de la soteriologie biblique: *hilasmos*." *Novum Testamentum* 10 (1968): 287–304.

Coetzee, J. C. "The Holy Spirit in 1 John." *Neotestamentica* 13 (1979): 43–67.

Colwell, E.C. "A Definite Rule for the Use of the Article in the Greek NT." *Journal of Biblical Literature* 52 (1933): 12–21.

Conzelmann, Hans. "φῶς." In *Theological Dictionary of the New Testament*, ed. Gerhard Kittle, trans. Geoffrey W. Bromiley. Grand Rapids: Eerdmans, 1965, 1999.

_________. "Was von Anfang war." In *Theologie als Schriftauslegung*. München: Kaiser,1974.

Cook, Donald E. "Interpretation of 1 John 1–5." *Review and Expositor* 67 (1970): 445–59.

Court, J. M. "Blessed Assurance?" *Journal of Theological Studies* 33 (1982): 508–17.

de Boer, Martinus C. "The Death of Jesus Christ and His Coming in the Flesh (1 John 4:2)." *Novum Testamentum* (1991): 326–46.

_________. "Jesus the Baptizer: 1 John 5:5–8 and the Gospel of John." *Journal of Biblical Literature* (1988): 87–106.

de Jonge, Marinus. "The Use of the Word ΧΡΙΣΤΟΣ in the Johannine Epistles." In *Studies in John, Presented to Professor Dr. J. N. Sevenster*. Leiden: Brill, 1970.

de la Potterie, Ignace. "Anointing of the Christian by Faith." In *The Christian Lives by the Spirit*, ed. Ignace de la Potterie and Stanislaus Lyonnet. New York: Alba House, 1971.

_________. "La Connaissance de Dieu dans le dualisme eschatologique d'apres I Jn, 2:12–14." In *Au service de la parole de Dieu*. Gembloux: J. Duculot, 1969.

_________. "'Sin Is Iniquity' (I Jn 3, 4)." In *The Christian Lives by the Spirit*, ed. Ignace de la Potterie and Stanislaus Lyonnet. New York: Alba House, 1971.

_________. "The Truth in Saint John." In *The Interpretation of John*, ed. John Ashton. Philadelphia: Fortress, 1986.

Delling, Gerhard. "ἀρχή." In *Theological Dictionary of the New Testament*, ed. Gerhard Kittle, trans. Geoffrey W. Bromiley. Grand Rapids: Eerdmans, 1999.

Derickson, Gary W. "What Is the Message of 1 John?" *Bibliotheca Sacra* 150 (1993): 89–105.

Derrett, J. Duncan. "Mt. 23,8–10 a Midrash on Is 54,13 and Jer 31,31–34." *Biblica* 62 (1981): 372–86.

Dodd, C. H. "HILASKESTHAI, Its Cognates, Derivatives, and Synonyms, in the Septuagint." *Journal of Theological Studies* 32 (1931): 82–95.

Dryden, J. de Waal. "The Sense of ΣΠΕΡΜΑ in 1 JOHN 3:9: In Light of Lexical Evidence." *Filologia Neotestamentaria* 11 (1999): 85–100.

du Preez, J. "'Sperma autou' in 1 John 3:9." *Neotestamentica* 9 (1975): 105–10.

du Toit, B. A. "The Role and Meaning of Statements of 'Certainty' in the Structural Composition of 1 John." *Neotestamentica* 13 (1979): 84–100.

Ehrman, Bart E. "1 John 4:3 and the Orthodox Corruption of Scripture." *Zeitschrift für die neutestamentliche Wissenschaft und die Kunde der älteren Kirche* 79 (1988): 221–43.

Foxgrover, David. "'Temporary Faith' and the Certainty of Salvation." *Calvin Theological Journal* 15 (1980): 220–32.

Grayston, Kenneth. "'Logos' in 1 John 1." *Expository Times* 86 (75): 279.

_________. "The Meaning of *Parakletos*." *Journal for the Study of the New Testament* 13 (1981): 67–82.

Grech, Prosper. "Fede e sacramenti in Giov 19,34 e 1 Giov 5,6–12." In *Fede e sacramenti negli Scritti giovannei*, ed. Puis-Ramn Tragon. Rome: Abbazia S Paulo, 1985.

Griffith, Terry. "A Non-Polemical Reading of 1 John." *Tyndale Bulletin* 49 (1998): 253–76.

Grundmann, Walter. "Χριστός." In *Theological Dictionary of the New Testament*, ed. Gerhard Kittle, trans. Geoffrey W. Bromiley. Grand Rapids: Eerdmans, 1999.

Han, Hans-Christoph. "Φῶς." In *The New International Dictionary of New Testament Theology*, ed. Colin Brown. Grand Rapids: Zondervan, 1978.

Hansford, Keir L. "The Underlying Poetic Structure of 1 John." *Journal of Translation and Textlinguistics* 5 (1992): 126–74.

Häring, Theodor. "Gedankengang und Grundgedanke des ersten Johannesbriefs." In *Theologische Abhandlungen Carl von Weizsäcker zu seinem siebzigsten Geburtstage*, ed. Adolf Harnack. Freiburg: J.C.B. Mohr, 1892.

Hauck, Friedrich. "Κοινωνία." In *Theological Dictionary of the New Testament*, ed. Gerhard Kittle, trans. Geoffrey W. Bromiley. Grand Rapids: Eerdmans, 1999.

_________. "Μένω." In *Theological Dictionary of the New Testament*, ed. Gerhard Kittle, trans. Geoffrey W. Bromiley. Grand Rapids: Eerdmans, 1999.

Hawkes, R. M. "The Logic of Assurance in English Puritan Theology." *Westminster Theological Journal* 52 (1990): 247–61.

Heibert, D. Edmond. "An Exposition of 1 John. Pt. 1, An Exposition of 2:18–28." *Bibliotheca Sacra* 146 (1989): 76–93.

_________. "An Exposition of 1 John. Pt. 9, An Exposition of 1 John 5:1–12." *Bibliotheca Sacra* 147 (1990): 216–30.

Hills, Julian. "'Little Children, Keep Yourselves from Idols': 1 John 5:21 Reconsidered." *Catholic Biblical Quarterly* 51 (1989): 285–310.

Hodges, Zane C. "We Believe in: Assurance." *Journal of the Grace Evangelical Society* 3, no. 2 (1990): 9.

Howard, W. F. "The Common Authorship of the Johannine Gospel and Epistles." *Journal of Theological Studies* 48 (1947): 12–25.

Hunt, Steven A. "Light and Darkness." In *The Dictionary of the Latter New Testament and Its Development*, ed. Ralph P. Martin and Peter H. Davids. Downers Grove, IL: InterVarsity, 1997.

Inman, Kerry. "Distinctive Johannine Vocabulary and the Interpretation of 1 John 3:9." *Westminster Theological Journal* 40 (1977–78): 136–44.

Jackson, Howard M. "Ancient Self-Referential Conventions and Their Implications for the Authorship and Integrity of the Gospel of John." *Journal of Theological Studies* 50 (1999): 1–34.

Johnson, D. H. "Assurance." In *The Dictionary of the Latter New Testament and Its Development*, ed. Ralph P. Martin and Peter H. Davids. Downers Grove, IL: InterVarsity, 1997.

Kaiser, Walter C. "The Old Promise and the New Covenant: Jeremiah 31:31–34." *Journal of the Evangelical Theological Society* 25 (1972): 11–24.

__________. "Paul, Women, and the Church." *Worldwide Challenge* 3 (1976): 9–12.

Kendall, R. T. "Living the Christian Life in the Teaching of William Perkins and His Followers." In *Living the Christian Life*. London: The Westminster Conference, 1974.

__________. "The Puritan Modification of Calvin's Theology." In *John Calvin*, ed. W. Stanford Reid. Grand Rapids: Zondervan, 1982.

Kennedy, H. A. A. "The Covenant Conception in the First Epistle of John." *Expository Times* 28 (1916–17): 23–26.

Kines, William L. "Abiding." In *Dictionary of Jesus and the Gospels*, ed. Joel B. Green, Scott Mcknight, and I. Howard Marshall. Downers Grove, IL: InterVarsity Press, 1992.

Klauck, Hans-Josef. "Bekenntnis zu Jesus und Zeugnis Gotts: Die christologische Linienführung im Ersten Johannesbrief." In *Anfänge der Christologie. Festschrift für Ferdinand Hahn zum 65. Geburtstag*, ed. Cilliers Breytenbach and Henning Paulsen. Göttingen: Vandenhoeck & Ruprecht, 1991.

_________. "Internal Opponents: The Treatment of the Secessionists in the First Epistle of John." *Concilium* 200 (1988): 55–65.

Kotzé, P. P. A. "The Meaning of 1 John 3:9 with Reference to 1 John 1:8 and 10." *Neotestamentica* 13 (1979): 68–83.

Kubo, Sakae. "I John 3:9: Absolute or Habitual." *Andrews University Seminary Studies* 7 (1969): 47–56.

Kügler, Joachim. "'Wenn das Herz uns auch verurteilt . . .': Ägyptische Anthropologie in 1 Joh 3,19–21?" *Biblische Notizen* 66 (1993): 10–14.

Lane, A. N. S. "Calvin's Doctrine of Assurance." *Vox Evangelica* 11 (1979): 32–54.

Laney, Carl J. "Abiding Is Believing: The Analogy of the Vine in John 15:1–6." *Bibliotheca Sacra* 146 (1989): 55–66.

Letham, Robert. "Assurance." In *New Dictionary of Theology*, ed. Sinclair B. Ferguson. Leicester: InterVarsity, 1988.

_________. "Faith and Assurance in Early Calvinism: A Model of Continuity and Diversity." In *Later Calvinism: International Perspectives*, ed. W. Fred Graham. Kirksville, MO: Sixteenth Century Journal Publishers, 1994.

Lieu, Judith. "'Authority to Become Children of God': A Study of 1 John." *Novum Testamentum* 23 (1981): 210–28.

_________. "What Was from the Beginning: Scripture and Tradition in the Johannine Epistles." *New Testament Studies* 39 (1993): 458–77.

Louw, J. P. "Verbal Aspect in the First Letter of John." *Neotestimentica* 9 (1975): 98–104.

Lovelace, Richard E. "Evangelicalism: Recovering a Tradition of Spiritual Depth." *The Reformed Journal* 40 (1990): 20–25.

Lyonnet, Stanislaus. "The Notion of Sin in the Johannine Writings." In *Sin, Redemption, and Sacrifice: A Biblical and Patristic Study*, ed. Stanislaus Lyonnet and Léopold Sabourin. Rome: Biblical Institute Press, 1970.

Malatesta, Edward. "Covenant and Indwelling." *The Way* 17 (1977): 23–32.

_________. "*Ten agapen hen hechei ho theos en hemin:* A Note on 1 John 4:16a." In *The New Testament Age: Essays in Honor of Bo Reicke*, ed. William C. Weinrich, vol. 2. Macon, GA: Mercer University Press, 1984.

Manns, Frédéric. "'Le péché, c'est Bélial' 1 Jn: 3,4 à la lumière du Judaïsme." *Revue des sciences religieuses* 62 (1988): 1–9.

Marshall, I. Howard. "The Problem of Apostasy in New Testament Theology." In *Jesus the Saviour: Studies in New Testament Theology*. London: SPCK, 1990.

Michl, Johann. "Der Geist als Garant des rechten Glaubens." In *Vom Wort des Lebens: Festschrift für Max Meinertz*, ed. Nikolaus Adler. Münster: Aschendorffsche Verlagsbuchhandlung, 1951.

Mills, Donald W. "The Eschatology of 1 John." In *Looking into the Future: Evangelical Studies in Eschatology*, ed. David W. Baker. Grand Rapids: Baker Academic, 2001.

________. "The Holy Spirit in 1 John." *Detroit Baptist Seminary Journal* 4 (1999): 35–50.

Minear, Paul S. "The Idea of Incarnation in First John." *Interpretation* 24 (1970): 291–302.

Munzer, K. "Μένω." In *New International Dictionary of New Testament Theology*, ed. Colin Brown. Grand Rapids: Zondervan, 1986.

Nicole, Roger R. "C. H. Dodd and the Doctrine of Propitiation." *Westminster Theological Journal* (17): 117–57.

Noack, Bent. "On I John II.12–14." *New Testament Studies* 6 (1960): 236–41.

Noll, Mark. "John Wesley and the Doctrine of Assurance." *Bibliotheca Sacra* 132 (1975): 161–77.

Padilla, René C. "A Reflection on 1 John 3:16–18." *Transformation* 6 (1989): 15–18.

Painter, John. "The 'Opponents' in 1 John." *New Testament Studies* 32 (1986): 48–71.

Perkins, Pheme. "*Koinonia* in 1 John 1:3–7: The Social Context of Division in the Johannine Letters." *Catholic Biblical Quarterly* 45 (1983): 631–41.

Poythress, Vern S. "Testing for Johannine Authorship by Examining the Use of Conjunctions." *Westminster Theological Journal* 46 (1984): 350–69.

Pryor, John W. "Covenant and Community in John's Gospel." *Reformed Theological Review* 47 (1988): 44–51.

Reynolds, S. M. "The Sin unto Death and Prayers for the Dead." *Reformation Review* 20 (1973): 130–39.

Robinson, J. A. T. "The Destination and Purpose of the Johannine Epistles." *New Testament Studies* 7 (1960): 56–65.

Schmid, Josef. "Bund." In *Lexicon Für Theologie und Kirche*, vol. 2, ed. Michael Buchberger. Freiburg: Verlag Herder, 1958.

Scholer, David M. "1 John 4:7–21." *Review and Expositor* 87 (1990): 309–14.

_________. "Gnosis, Gnosticism." In *Dictionary of the Later New Testament and Its Developments*, ed. Ralph P. Martin and Peter H. Davids. Downers Grove, IL: InterVarsity, 1997.

_________. "Sins Within and Sins Without: An Interpretation of 1 John 5:16–17." In *Current Issues in Biblical and Patristic Interpretation: Studies in Honor of Merrill C. Tenney Presented by His Former Students*, ed. Gerald F. Hawthorne. Grand Rapids: Eerdmans, 1975.

Schreiner, Thomas R. "Perseverance and Assurance: A Survey and a Proposal." *The Southern Baptist Journal of Theology* 2 (1998): 32–63.

Smalley, Stephen S. "What About 1 John?" In *Studia Biblica 1978*. Journal for the Study of New Testament Supplement Series 3. Edited by E. A. Livingston. Sheffield: JSOT Press, 1980.

Stählin, G. "σκάνδαλον." In *Theological Dictionary of the New Testament*, ed. Gerhard Kittle, trans. Geoffrey W. Bromiley. Grand Rapids: Eerdmans, 1999.

Strecker, Georg. "Der religionsgeschichtlichen Hintergrund von 1 Joh 2,18.22; 4,3 und 2 Joh 7." In *Text and Testimony: Essays on New Testament and Apocryphal Literature in Honour of A. F. Klijn*, ed. T. Baarda, A. Hilhorst, G. P. Luttikhuizen, and A. S. van der Woulde. Kampen: J. H. Kok, 1988.

Sugit, J. N. "I John 5:21: ΤΕΚΝΙΑ, ΦΥΛΑΞΑΤΕ ΕΑΥΤΑ ΑΠΟ ΤΩΝ ΕΙΔΩΛΩΝ." *Journal of Theological Studies* 36 (1985): 386–90.

Swadling, Harry C. "Sin and Sinlessness in I John." *Scottish Journal of Theology* 35 (1982): 205–11.

Synge, F. C. "1 John 3,2." *Journal of Theological Studies* 3 (1952): 79.

Tan, Randall K. J. "Should We Pray for Straying Brethren? John's Confidence in 1 John 5:16–17." *Journal of the Evangelical Theological Society* 45 (2002), 599–609.

Thompson, Marianne M. "Intercession in the Johannine Community: 1 John 5:16 in the Context of the Gospel and Epistles of John." In *Worship, Theology and Ministry in the Early Church: Essays in Honor of Ralph P. Martin*. Journal for the Study of New Testament Supplement Series 87. Edited by Michael J. Wilkins and Terence Paige. Sheffield: Sheffield Academic Press, 1992.

Thornton, T. C. G. "Propitiation or Expiation?" *Expository Times* 80 (1968): 53–55.

Tollefson, K. D. "Certainty Within the Fellowship: Dialectical Discourse in 1 John." *Biblical Theology Bulletin* 29 (1999): 79–89.

Venetz, Herman-Josef. "'Durch Wasser und Blut gekommen:' Exegetishce Überlegungen zu 1 Joh 5,6." In *Die Mitte des Neuen Testaments: Einheit und vielfalt neutestamentlicher Theologie. Festschrift für Eduard Schweizer zum siebsigsten Geburtstag*, ed. Ulrich Luz and Hans Weder. Göttingen: Vandenhoeck & Ruprecht, 1983.

Verhoef, Pieter A. "חָדַשׁ." In *New International Dictionary of Old Testament Theology and Exegesis*, ed. Willem A. VanGemeren. Grand Rapids: Zondervan, 1997.

Walvoord, John F. "The Doctrine of Assurance in Contemporary Theology." *Bibliotheca Sacra* 116 (1959): 195–204.

Ward, Tim. "Sin 'Not unto Death' and Sin 'Unto Death' in 1 John 5:16." *Churchman* 109 (1995): 226–37.

Watson, Duane F. "An Epideictic Strategy for Increasing Adherence to Community Values: 1 John 1:1–2:29." In *Proceedings: Eastern Great Lakes and Midwest Biblical Societies* 11 (1991).

________. "1 John 2.12–14 as *Distributio, Conduplicatio,* and *Expolitio*: A Rhetorical Understanding." *Journal for the Study of the New Testament* 35 (1989): 97–110.

Weir, J. Emmette. "The Identity of the Logos in the First Epistle of John." *Expository Times* 86 (1975):118–20.

Wendt, H. H. "Der 'Anfang' am Beginne des I. Johannesbriefes." *Zeitschrift für die Neutestamentliche Wissenschaft* 21 (1922): 38–42.

Wilson, W. G. "An Examination of the Linguistic Evidence Adduced Against the Unity of Authorship of the First Epistle of John and the Fourth Gospel." *Journal of the Evangelical Theological Society* 49 (1948): 147–56.

Witherington, Ben, III. "The Waters of Birth: John 3.5 and 1 John 5.6–8." *New Testament Studies* 35 (1989): 155–60.

Yamauchi, Edwin M. "Gnosticism." In *Dictionary of New Testament Backgrounds*, ed. Craig A. Evans and Stanley E. Porter. Downers Grove, IL: InterVarsity, 2000.

Zens, John. "The Doctrine of Assurance: A History and an Application." *Baptist Reformation Review* 5 (Summer 1976): 34–64.

Theses and Dissertations

Atchison, Thomas F. "Towards a Theology of Christian Assurance from 1 John with Reference to Jonathan Edwards." Ph.D. diss., Trinity Evangelical Divinity School, 2004.

Blankley, Ronald A. "The Contribution of First John to the Doctrine of Perseverance." Th.M. thesis, Dallas Theological Seminary.

Christie, G. B. "An Interpretive Study of 1 John 1:9." Th.M. thesis, Dallas Theological Seminary, 1975.

Curtis, Edward M. "The Purpose of 1 John." Th.D. diss., Dallas Theological Seminary, 1986.

Derickson, Gary W. "An Evaluation of Expository Options of 1 John." Th.D. diss., Dallas Theological Seminary, 1993.

Dyck, Ronald J. "The Doctrine of the New Birth in the Theology of John." Th.M. thesis, Dallas Theological Seminary, 1981.

Johnson, D. K. "Johannine Abiding: Perseverance in the Faith." Th.M. thesis, Dallas Theological Seminary, 1975.

Kim, Jintae. "The Concept of Atonement in 1 John: A Redevelopment of the Second Temple Concept of Atonement." Ph.D. diss., Westminster Theological Seminary, 2003.

Kim, Seung L. "John Wesley's Doctrine of the Witness of the Spirit, or, the Assurance of Salvation." Ph.D. diss., The Southern Baptist Theological Seminary, 1932.

Letham, Robert. "The Relationship Between Saving Faith and Assurance of Salvation." Th.M. thesis, Westminster Theological Seminary, 1976.

_________. "Saving Faith and Assurance in Reformed Theology: Zwingli to the Synod of Dort." 2 vols. Ph.D. diss., University of Aberdeen, 1979.

Sun, Poling J. "Menein in the Johannine Traditions: An Integrated Approach to the Motif of Abiding in the Fourth Gospel, I and II John." Ph.D. diss., The Southern Baptist Theological Seminary, 1993.

Wetzler, Wellington. "The Doctrine of Assurance in 1 John." Th.M. thesis, Dallas Theological Seminary, 1956.

Wright, Shawn D. "The Pastoral Use of the Doctrine of God's Sovereignty in the Theology of Theodore Beza." Ph.D. diss., The Southern Baptist Theological Seminary, 2001.

AUTHOR INDEX

SUBJECT INDEX

SCRIPTURE INDEX*

*Entries in bold indicate extended discussion of passage.

QUMRAN

APOCRYPHA

PSEUDEPIGRAPHA